GETTING
TO ZERO

Canada Confronts Global Warming

GETTING TO ZERO

Canada Confronts Global Warming

TONY CLARKE

James Lorimer & Company Ltd., Publishers
Toronto

James Lorimer & Company Ltd., Publishers acknowledges funding sup-port from the Ontario Arts Council (OAC), an agency of the Government of Ontario. We acknowledge the support of the Canada Council for the Arts, which last year invested $153 million to bring the arts to Canadians throughout the country. This project has been made possible in part by the Government of Canada and with the support of the Ontario Media Develop-ment Corporation.

Cover design: Tyler Cleroux
Cover images: Shutterstock

Library and Archives Canada Cataloguing in Publication

Clarke, Tony, author

      Getting to zero : Canada confronts global warming / Tony Clarke

Includes bibliographical references and index.
Issued in print and electronic formats.
ISBN 978-1-4594-1079-4 (softcover).--ISBN 978-1-4594-1089-3 (EPUB)

      1. Global warming--Canada--Prevention--Citizen participation. 2. Global warming--Prevention--Government policy--Canada. 3. Greenhouse gas mitigation--Government policy--Canada. 4. Corporations--Environmental aspects--Canada. 5. Environmental policy--Canada. 6. Canada--Environmental conditions. I. Title.

QC981.8 G56 C59 2017   363.738'7460971   C2017-903832-X
                                                C2017-903833-8

James Lorimer & Company Ltd., Publishers
117 Peter Street, Suite 304
Toronto, ON, Canada
M5V 0M3
www.lorimer.ca

Printed and bound in Canada.

**To John Dillon, an Eco-Warrior
in his own right for our Times**

*John was a very active member of the Green Economy Network
steering committee where he represented KAIROS, a leading faith-based
coalition for social justice in Canada. Originally, John was a largely
self-taught economist who focused much of his work on developing
alternative approaches for building a more just, sustainable
and participatory economy.*

*Through more than four decades, he researched and developed papers
on major public policy issues for the GATT-Fly project, the Ecumenical
Coalition for Economic Justice and KAIROS. In doing so, his starting
point was always the people most directly affected — the unemployed,
the working poor, exploited workers, small farmers, Indigenous peoples
etc. Engaging with these and other sub-sectors of our economy and
society was, therefore, a vital part of his work as an economist.*

*Before his sudden untimely death in May 2017, he had begun doing
considerable research and writing on Indigenous Wisdom in terms
of the guidance it could provide in transitioning to a more just and
sustainable economic future. For these and related reasons, John was
an important source of inspiration for the Green Economy Network's
initiatives, especially the common platform on Making the Shift to a
Green Economy.*

CONTENTS

List of Figures

List of Tables

Preface

When I finished my book tour for *Tar Sands Showdown* in November 2008, I felt as though I had a big empty pit in the bottom of my stomach. There was something missing. It was not enough to research into, take action on and write about the threats and dangers of continuing to build an economy and society mainly on the dubious foundation of extracting, producing and consuming bitumen and other fossil fuels, — especially given the increasing number of reports from scientists about the growing pace and scope at which the planet is heating in this age of climate change. After all, scientists had shown conclusively that the main cause of global warming is the burning of fossil fuels which release greenhouse gas emissions that, in turn, trap heat in the atmosphere, thereby increasing the temperature of the planet. While there was some talk back then about taking this opportunity to make "a great transition" from an older but dirtier industrial economy and society dependent on fossil fuel energy sources to a newer, cleaner and more ecological economy and society, there was little or nothing in the way of a clear program and plan of action to get us there.

About the same time, I read *The Great Work* by Thomas Berry, the eminent eco-cultural historian who, by then had achieved a distinctive stature as one often introduced or referred to as a human "spokesperson for the Earth." One of Berry's main themes was his constant reminder that we are living in a unique and defining historical moment of transition between an old industrial age of the past and a new ecological age of the future. Here, Berry often raised the question of whether or not humans, as a species, would rise to the occasion and make this transition happen as deeply and seamlessly as needed or whether they would obstruct the process altogether. Throughout much of his life, Berry conveyed this challenge in terms of messages of hope, appealing to peoples' basic values and instincts. In his writings, public talks and actions, Berry invited people to join together in a common journey to make this "great transition" happen. In doing so, however, he also warned that making this transition happen was imperative if humanity, the planet and all living species are to survive the twenty-first century. Even so, there were still lingering questions about how previous periods of "transition" had "left people behind," including displaced workers, Indigenous peoples and impoverished communities.

And now, let us flash forward another 10 years to 2018 and the purpose of this publication, *Getting to Zero*. In essence, it is a series of reflections on why and how Canada needs to confront the global warming and climate change challenge by making this historic transition in our economy and society. In 2009, after consultations with various Indigenous communities, environmental organizations, labour unions and other public-interest organizations, the Green Economy Network was formed. Its basic aim was to develop a program and plan of action for reducing and eventually eliminating the main structural causes of greenhouse gas emissions in the Canadian economy and to chart the transition to a new, more just and sustainable economy and society. After conducting various research initiatives, the Green Economy Network steering committee targeted three sectors of the Canadian economy that were collectively responsible for up to 81 percent of Canada's greenhouse gas emissions — energy, transportation and construction. A common platform was put together that includes a plan of action, which we call "eco-pathways" on how Canada could reach net-zero greenhouse gas emissions over the next two to three decades. If fully applied and repeated in five-year cycles, the Green Economy Network platform could also create well over a million new decent-paying jobs by the end of each decade.

To make this transition happen, however, requires major and strategic transformations in the key sectors of the Canadian economy that generate the bulk of the Greenhouse gas emissions in this country. This is what we call here the "Big Shift" simply because it demands a "real change" in the way we fuel our economy and society; move people and freight over short, medium and long distances; plus more efficiently heat and cool our homes and buildings. In turn, this Big Shift can be broken down into three basic shifts in our economy and society — the "energy shift" from the extraction, production and consumption of fossil fuels to increasing development of and reliance on clean, renewable sources of energy (i.e., solar, wind, geothermal, tidal and small scale hydro) along with a new nationwide energy grid; the "transportation shift" of taking more combustion engine cars and trucks off the roads and encouraging greater use of and reliance on public transit within cities, higher-speed rail between cities in urban corridors, as well as the shift to electric vehicles; and the "building shift," through retrofitting homes and workplaces to significantly reduce energy use for heating and cooling and thereby reduce energy waste and costs. To move in this direction will require nothing short of targeted public investments, new industries and new job creation, plus corresponding measurable greenhouse gas emission reductions, plus creative national, regional and local co-ordination.

In short, *Getting to Zero* attempts to set the stage for such a transition by proposing a possible program and plan of action to get us moving and get us there.

Acknowledgements

To date, many people deserve to be recognized for their contribution to this book, but here are a few:

- A special shout-out to Marny Girard, former research co-ordinator of the Green Economy Network, for her ongoing enthusiasm and encouragement plus expert fact-checking and commentary;
- Many thanks to Sara D'Agostino who co-ordinated the preparation of the manuscript for publication, and to Robert Chodos and his team for their creative editing;
- Appreciation to publishers Carrie Gleason and Jim Lorimer for not giving up on me or the project, despite delays and rewrites due to sudden, fast-moving parts and game changing events;
- Gratitude for the corresponding work of people in the Canadian environment movement such as Catherine Abreu at CAN/Rac, Tzeporah Berman from Tar Sands Solutions, Clayton Thomas Mueller at 350.Org, Keith Stewart from Greenpeace and many more;

- A vote of thanks to people in the Canadian labour movement who have supported the work of the Green Economy Network, including Hassan Yussuff, Donald Lafleur, Angella McEwan, Andrea Peart, Matt Firth, Carolyn Egan, Howie West and more;
- Appreciation for valuable insights and advice from international players in the global climate justice movement, including Bill McKibben, Pablo Solon and Sean Sweeney;
- And, finally, as always, deep gratitude to my immediate family — Carol, our two children Tanya and Chris, their partners Mike and Melanie, plus grandchildren Silo, Keiran, and Lola — for their enduring support and patience. Who knows, maybe one of these grandkids will someday become an "eco-warrior"?

Introduction

In 2016, all across Canada, millions of people were glued to their television sets and watched in horror and disbelief as raging wildfires swept down and blanketed the town of Fort McMurray, Alberta. During those early days of May, some 90,000 people were evacuated and more than 1,600 buildings and structures were destroyed, as 850 square kilometres were embroiled in flames. The evacuation was carried out in an orderly fashion, with convoys of trucks and cars moving southward along the highways bumper to bumper. It took some 250 firefighters plus 12 firefighting helicopters to finally bring the blaze under control. Miraculously, there were no fatalities.

Fort McMurray was and is the epicentre of and commercial headquarters for the massive array of tar sands operations — the largest of its kind in the world. Just north of Fort McMurray, thousands of workers who toil in the tar sands energy industry, extracting and upgrading bitumen for crude oil production and export, are housed in work camps. In the aftermath of the inferno that struck Fort McMurray, multiple explanations were debated. Yet during this period, little or no attention was given to the realities of climate change as a major cause, let alone the distinctive role played by Big Oil companies and the tar sands industry itself.

In retrospect, there should be little doubt that this industry, the single largest generator of greenhouse gas emissions in Canada, was a major factor in creating the conditions that led to the burning of Fort McMurray. The tar sands industry is expected to pump between 72 and 100 million tonnes of greenhouse gases into the atmosphere annually by 2020. These gases end up trapping the sun's heat closer to the surface of Earth, accelerating the heating of the planet and especially affecting ecologically sensitive regions, such as northern Canada. The tar sands industry is not only the largest generator of these emissions in our economy, but the fastest-growing one as well.

Another reason the wildfires came to burn so closely to the town of Fort McMurray, overtaking several neighbourhoods and turning much of the town into an inferno, is that the surrounding forests and turf were bone dry. Simply put, the natural groundwater systems had been steadily drained in recent years, largely by the tar sands industry through the in situ method of extracting bitumen from beneath the sedimentary rock basin, which requires huge amounts of fresh water. To be sure, record warm temperatures, reduced precipitation, a vanishingly small snowpack and increasing drought conditions — all symptoms of climate change — were also contributing factors. But the driving force behind these factors was arguably the industry's expanding use of its water-guzzling extractive technology.

Moreover, warned Canadian scientist Brian J. Stocks, the worst is still to come. "We're at a crossroads," he said in an interview with the *New York Times* following the Fort McMurray tragedy. "We anticipate more fires and more intense fires, in the future."[1] Stocks went on to highlight "a dangerous feedback loop" in the making involving the boreal forests that border the Arctic Circle. On the one hand, the boreal forests serve as one of the planet's major carbon sinks, absorbing a significant portion of the carbon dioxide spewed into the atmosphere by the burning of fossil fuels. On the other hand, with the boreal forests seriously threatened by wildfires every summer, there is the corresponding danger that their destruction will result in a reverse scenario, in which significant portions of the carbon locked in the forests will be released in the form of carbon dioxide into the atmosphere. This will greatly intensify the melting of the Arctic ice pack and, consequently, the further heating and burning of the planet.

Meanwhile, Canada can no longer ignore, gloss over or cover up the deeper and broader implications of its climate destiny. As the largest industrial project of its kind on the planet, the mega–tar sands development in the Athabasca region of Alberta has major geopolitical ramifications. The boreal forest encircles the northern hemisphere of the planet. Along with the United States, Russia and Scandinavian countries, Canada has a key role in protecting the boreal forest and ensuring that it remains nature's great storehouse for carbon on the planet.

Tar sands production releases millions of tonnes of greenhouse gas emissions, not only carbon dioxide but also methane and others (largely through burning natural gas to power its upgrading operations), which, in turn, causes the trapping of heat in the northern atmosphere. In consequence, the tundra in the Northwest Territories rapidly melts and releases methane, which is 85 times more potent than carbon dioxide over a 20-year period. This accelerated melting of the Arctic ice paves the way for the opening of the Northwest Passage, which will both speed up the global economy's shipping trade and spark large-scale oil exploration and production in one of the most ecologically fragile regions on the planet. Indeed, the Fort McMurray inferno provides a window into the threats and dangers of the looming climate crisis in Canada. Despite political rhetoric to the contrary, Canada has been more of a climate laggard than a climate leader when it comes to reducing greenhouse gases responsible for runaway climate change. Since the early 1990s, when serious international negotiations on climate change were initiated, Canada's annual greenhouse gas emissions have steadily risen from around 600 million tonnes to well over 700, reaching a high of 745 million tonnes in 2007.[2] As a result, in 2018 Canada was ranked among the 10 biggest greenhouse gas polluters in the world and fourth among the 35 counties classified as having "developed" economies. In a report released in December 2017, the Organisation for Economic Co-operation and Development (OECD) concluded that "without a drastic decrease in the emissions intensity of the oil sands industry," Canada's climate mitigation targets are in jeopardy.[3]

To be sure, the Trudeau Liberal government has done more than its Conservative predecessor in raising public awareness about climate change and the need for government action in this country. In so doing, it has adopted and applied a formula that links the economy and the environment together in a common enterprise. The problem, however, is that it's the wrong formula. The Trudeau government's objective is still to make, if not compel, the environment to serve the economy's priorities, namely the ongoing production and consumption of fossil fuels. Herein lies the fundamental contradiction. One cannot "grow the economy" — at least an economy based on the prevailing industrial model and the combustion engine — and, at the same time, substantially reduce greenhouse gas emissions. For example, a country cannot replace coal with natural gas to fire up its electrical generators and claim it is substantially reducing greenhouse gas emissions. Natural gas is also a fossil fuel that traps heat in the atmosphere, albeit with less intensity than the burning of coal.

Although the solution does involve finding the right relationship between the economy and the environment, the time has come for the economy to be transformed to better serve the priorities of the environment, not the reverse. When it comes to mitigating against runaway climate change, this means reducing greenhouse gas emissions to net zero. Thus, the tar sands industry must rethink its priorities for production and consumption of crude oil based on the extraction of bitumen for export. Take, for example, the climate test developed by the former National Energy Board for assessing whether or not pipeline projects would be approved for the delivery of bitumen-based crude to markets. Such a test must be comprehensive, covering greenhouse gas emissions from upstream as well as downstream operations. It must also be equally applied to all proposed pipeline construction projects rather than being more rigorously applied to TransCanada's Energy

East pipeline project through Ontario, Quebec and the Maritime provinces than to Kinder Morgan's Trans Mountain pipeline through British Columbia to the Pacific coast.

At the same time, transforming the economy to function with greater harmony in relation to the environment ultimately requires making a determined shift in the source, production and use of clean, renewable energy alternatives. Around the world, some countries are committed to making the transition from fossil fuels to 100 percent renewable energy to power their economies by mid-century, if not before. These countries include Germany, Norway, Sweden, Denmark and Chile, all of which have passed national legislation to this effect. For its part, Canada has considerable potential for renewable energy development — solar, wind, geothermal and tidal power — which, along with hydroelectric power, could be used to provide the energy needed for a national electrical grid. Yet the federal government has made comparatively little investment in developing this infrastructure. Instead, governments of almost all political stripes appear content with continuing the status quo by shoring up and strengthening the fossil fuel industry in this country. This includes adding new fossil fuel production, such as liquefied natural gas for export to Asian countries.

To date, it's fair to say that governments and industries alike have failed to measure up to the challenges of runaway climate change. Although the Trudeau government and some provincial governments have developed and implemented several public policy frames and regulatory measures, such as the carbon tax, to tackle climate change through reductions in greenhouse gas emissions, there is still more confusion than clarity, not to mention seeds of opposition. So far, some of the more creative initiatives have been coming out of municipal governments, often prompted by local, progressively minded citizen and community groups, as well as organizations such as the Federation of Canadian Municipalities. Government and industry clearly have important roles to play, but when they fail to act progressively and effectively, then other concerned citizens and community groups must step into the breach and provide the climate leadership needed.

Once again, the climate clock is ticking away. Yet Canada still has no coherent and credible plan of action in place to take on the structural causes of greenhouse gas emissions and provide inspiration to ignite citizen and community-based grassroots action on these issues. Hopefully, this book will shed some light on the depth of the challenges that lie ahead and thereby contribute to building momentum for bolder actions urgently needed to transform our economy in order to effectively confront and overcome the challenges of runaway climate change.

CHAPTER 1
Burning Planet

On June 23, 1988, an accomplished and respected scientist took the witness stand at a U.S. congressional hearing in Washington, D.C. His name was Dr. James Hansen, and he was a climate scientist and director of NASA's Goddard Institute for Space Studies in New York. His main intention that day was to sound the alarm about the growing problems of global warming and climate change caused by the release of heat-trapping greenhouse gas emissions into the atmosphere. His dramatic testimony served to put the challenge of climate change squarely on the global agenda and subsequently helped to make global warming a major priority for the United Nations Earth Summit in Rio de Janeiro in 1992 and follow-up negotiations leading to the Kyoto Protocol in 1997.

Twenty years after delivering his path-breaking testimony, Hansen returned to Congress, where he sounded a further alarm about the climate change crisis, based on the latest evidence. The planet, he admonished, had reached a state of emergency. Citing the melting of the Arctic, he warned that Earth's climate was coming dangerously close to its tipping point. Once past its tipping point, he cautioned, there is little or no chance that the trend can be reversed. In his 2008 statement, he called on governments to adopt a carbon tax as an incentive for slowing down the greenhouse gas emissions caused by burning fossil fuels. Hansen also went so far as to declare that the CEOs of energy corporations be tried in court for crimes against humanity and nature.[1]

Every year since 2008, Hansen has continued his mission of declaring a planetary emergency on climate change. He has also maintained his influence and leadership role within the scientific community. For climate change deniers in both government and corporations, Hansen has become a major target. Even so, he has continued to speak out about the planetary emergency generated by the climate crisis and has also participated in public protests on these issues, even being arrested for doing so. Of course, Hansen has by no means been alone in issuing warnings about impending climate crises. Other climate scientists, Indigenous peoples and environmental activists alike have continuously spoken out and taken initiatives in calling for bold actions on climate issues. Hansen and his fellow scientists do not necessarily have all the answers.

People directly affected by climate change — people in small island states and communities faced with the threat of being wiped out by rising sea levels, people experiencing extreme weather patterns resulting in widespread flooding, wildfires, tornadoes, hurricanes, droughts and tsunamis — have also been organizing, speaking out and demanding action.[2] In other words, grassroots resistance and actions have been emerging around the world, in both the global South and the global North. This increasing sense of a planetary emergency culminated in the Paris climate summit, known as Conference of the Parties 21, in December 2015.

Yet despite growing public awareness, unrest and resistance to the realities and challenges of climate change, there has been limited political momentum in response. To be sure, the growing recognition of the global climate crisis prompted the United Nations to establish an international process of annual conferences for national governments to negotiate and co-ordinate a global plan of action. At the Rio Earth Summit in 1992, the *United Nations Framework Convention on Climate Change* was adopted, officially coming into being in 1994. Under the framework convention, the Conference of the Parties was formed out of the 197 countries that signed on to the Rio agreement; the Inter-governmental Panel on Climate Change, largely composed of the world's leading climate scientists, was set up and annual conferences of government officials representing the Conference of the Parties were organized. But for the most part, governments and policy-makers participating in the twenty or so annual events leading up to the Paris climate summit mainly dithered rather than exercising the bold leadership needed in response to this global crisis.

Meanwhile, the depth and scope of the climate change challenge have become increasingly evident. On the one hand, climate change is a dynamic force of *nature,* which is heating the planet through a mix of extreme weather patterns that are occurring more frequently, at a faster pace and with greater intensity throughout the world. On the other hand, climate change is also a dynamic force of *history* insofar as its prime causes, as scientists have shown, are human made. It occurs primarily as a result of the production processes of industrialized economies and societies that continuously spew greenhouse gases such as carbon dioxide and faster-acting methane into the atmosphere, trapping the rays of the sun closer to Earth's surface. This dual dynamic characterizes the threat to and challenge faced by all living species on Earth, including humans. The climate change generating this emergency is not only global and systemic, but also out of control.

As various scientists have emphasized, the planet is currently going through its sixth period of mass extinction. Somewhere between 150 and 200 species on the planet are becoming extinct every day. Indeed, the pace of extinction is 1,000 times the natural extinction rate. In terms of both speed and intensity, it may well be comparable to, or even exceed, what happened during the Permian mass extinction, or what is often called the "Great Dying," some 250 million years ago.[3] A more recent example occurred some 55 million years ago when Earth's temperature spiked 5 degrees Celsius over a 13-year period, wiping out most living species. The big difference, of course, is that our current period of mass extinction, called the Anthropocene era, is primarily human caused and is happening at a much faster pace.

The Global Challenge

In 2016, record-high temperatures allowed people in Canada to see and feel the onslaught of global warming on a month-by-month basis. Canada was not alone. Ominous signs of a burning planet appeared then and continue to do so almost everywhere through the

- spread of droughts and famine in regions of Africa and Asia,
- wildfires destroying northern regions like Russia's boreal forests,
- multiple tornadoes that rip through villages and cities in the United States,
- tsunamis that threaten to drown villages and towns,
- rapid melting of the planet's polar ice caps in the Arctic and Antarctic,
- drying up of rivers, streams and lakes in many areas where precipitation has diminished,
- melting of glaciers on a once-and-for-all basis, resulting in flash floods and the loss of annual spring runoffs into riverbeds,
- increased power and scope of hurricanes and electrical storms that destroy everything lying in their path and
- vulnerability of coastal regions and small island states to suddenly being swept into the ocean by rising sea levels.

Climate change emerged out of the Industrial Revolution and is now responsible for the heating and burning of the planet. Climate change is largely caused by the release of greenhouse gases — notably carbon dioxide and methane — into the atmosphere. Both gases have an insulating effect on the atmosphere. As they build up, they trap more and more heat, thereby raising the planet's temperature. The release of carbon dioxide is mainly caused by burning fossil fuels — coal, oil and gas — whereas the release of methane generally comes from farms, coal mines and landfill sites, along with burning natural gas. Since trees have been one of nature's carbon sinks, the widespread clear-cutting of forests has also been a major source of greenhouse gas emissions and therefore an ongoing cause of climate change.

Scientists studying ice cores from the Antarctic have concluded that the levels of carbon dioxide and methane in the atmosphere in 2018 were higher than at any other time in the past 800,000 years.[4] Of the two greenhouse gases, carbon dioxide has so far been the prime focus of attention (the climate impact of methane and others is generally measured in terms of equivalent carbon dioxide). In 2008, the concentration of carbon dioxide in the atmosphere was 380 parts per million — a huge jump from the 280 parts per million measured 400 years earlier. By 2012, scientists were warning that the concentration of carbon dioxide in the atmosphere was about to pass 400 parts per million, which it did four years later and permanently in 2016.[5] According to a study by Bill Hare and Malte Meinshausen for the Potsdam Institute for Climate Impact Research, a two-thirds probability of holding global temperatures at 2 degrees Celsius above preindustrial levels this century would require stabilizing concentrations of greenhouse gases in the atmosphere at or below the equivalent of 440 parts of carbon dioxide per million.[6]

Meanwhile, predictions of temperature rise in the twenty-first century by climate research bodies have been fluctuating wildly. Just before the global climate conference in Copenhagen in 2009, the United Nations Environment Programme released a report predicting a 3.5-degree Celsius temperature increase by 2100. A year and a half later, the United Nations Environment Programme revised its predictions, forecasting a 5-degree Celsius increase by 2050. The more conservative-leaning International Energy Agency, in its 2012 *World Energy Outlook* report, predicted that the planet was moving to a 2-degree Celsius temperature increase by as early as 2017 and would reach a 3.5-degree Celsius increase by 2035.[7] Given the 2015 voluntary pledges for greenhouse gas emission reductions by countries (i.e., intended nationally determined contributions), the *United Nations Framework Convention on Climate Change*'s synthesis report then predicted a global temperature rise of between 2.7 and 3.9 degrees Celsius this century.[8]

If the world is going to get back on track for keeping the temperature rise to 2 degrees Celsius (let alone the 1.5-degree Celsius target adopted at the Paris summit), then significant progress must be made by 2020 toward effectively closing the emissions gap.[9] On the basis of annual voluntary pledges made by each country, the United Nations Environment Programme tries to assess how much progress has been made in reducing emissions. After years of studies, conferences and negotiations, governments have only managed to reduce in total 3 gigatons of greenhouse gas emissions per year from the business-as-usual scenario.[10] If the world does not manage to close the emissions gap by 2020, the opportunity to catch up and prevent the burning of the planet by stopping runaway climate change may well have been lost.

According to the United Nations Environment Programme's *Emissions Gap Report* in 2014, for example, global greenhouse gas emissions need to be reduced to 44 gigatons per year by 2020 just to remain on target for meeting the 2-degree Celsius threshold.[11] Yet, as Pablo Solon, currently director of the Solon Foundation and former Bolivian ambassador to the UN, pointed out, given the voluntary pledges that governments made at the UN climate summits in Copenhagen (2009) and Cancun (2010), global emissions will be around 56 gigatons, which amounts to a gap of more than 12 gigatons per year.[12] Moreover, to keep pace with the 2-degree scenario, annual emissions must be reduced to 35 gigatons by 2030, yet annual emissions are forecast to increase to as high as 60 gigatons by 2030 given the voluntary pledges made by governments prior to the Paris climate summit.[13]

In short, the burning of the planet and correlated mass species extinction poses a monumental challenge. To more fully grasp the global challenge of responding to this emergency in a way that portrays the gravity and urgency of this moment, we need to take a closer look at what was and what was not accomplished at the Paris climate summit.

Paris Showdown

During the months leading up to the Paris summit, Bill McKibben and his new and expanding U.S.-based environmental organization, 350.org, launched a campaign challenging people to "do the math" on climate change. In November 2012, he hit the road for a tour across the United States.

Keeping to below the 2-degree limit, McKibben calculated, meant that only 565 more gigatons of carbon dioxide could be emitted into the atmosphere for the rest of the century. He warned that anything beyond this amount risks catastrophe for life on this planet. The problem was that the major energy corporations currently have fossil fuels in their reserves, which if extracted and combusted, would result in the emission of 2,795 gigatons of carbon dioxide — five times the safe amount. "The fossil fuel companies are planning to burn it all," McKibben warned his audiences, "unless we rise up to stop them."[14]

McKibben's math is largely based on what's known as the "carbon budget," produced by the Global Carbon Project.[15] The term refers to the amount of carbon that can be released into the atmosphere in the form of carbon dioxide without disrupting our chances of keeping global warming to less than 2 degrees Celsius above preindustrial levels during this century. According to the research done so far, over two thirds of this carbon budget has already been expended, mostly since the Industrial Revolution. Pierre Friedlingstein's team of Exeter University scientists calculated that if greenhouse gas emissions continue at their 2014 levels, the planet's entire carbon budget will be used up in less than 30 years.[16]

Meanwhile, the Intergovernmental Panel on Climate Change used the Global Carbon Project to develop a comprehensive set of calculations. In its carbon countdown, the panel calculated how many years are left in the global carbon budget at current rates of fossil fuel consumption to achieve different levels of warming — 3 or 2 or 1.5 degrees Celsius. If, for example, the desired goal is a 66 percent chance of remaining below 2 degrees Celsius this century, then there are fewer than 21 years left. If, however, the world wants a 66 percent chance of stabilizing temperature rise at 1.5 degrees Celsius — which was the aspirational goal of the Paris Agreement — then there are fewer than six years left in the carbon budget.

The Paris Agreement is not a legally binding document, and the commitments made by governments to meet specified emission targets are voluntary. There are, as yet, no enforcement mechanisms to ensure that the emission reduction targets will be realized.[17] Until the gigaton gap is systematically addressed through a legally binding international treaty with built-in enforcement mechanisms, the prospects for progressively moving toward the goal of limiting the planet's temperature rise to below the 2-degree Celsius (let alone 1.5-degree) danger level remain dim. Such a process will require a disciplined strategic approach to emission reductions based on a global carbon budget and carbon countdown.

The Paris Agreement also contains several other roadblocks that could have major implications for making real progress. Here are some examples.

First, although the Paris commitment to move from a 2- to a 1.5-degree Celsius scenario was positive and ambitious, it is effectively meaningless unless it is backed up by a co-ordinated regime of targets and strategies for the systemic reduction of greenhouse gas emissions. To be sure, the Paris summit adopted a five-year cycle for countries not only to make new pledges but also to review and revise them on an ongoing basis through a firm and cyclical science-based process. Although this new regime could potentially make the pledge process more disciplined, it lacks built-in incentives to encourage countries to stimulate a ratcheting-up of their targets for emission reductions, including clear commitments for faster and stronger measures to achieve those targets. Moreover, the pledges remain voluntary, which means that countries can still make lofty pledges without an effective plan of action, including the resources needed to carry them out, along with penalties for non-compliance. Unless the targets and pledges made are subject to a legally binding regime and timetable, there is no assurance that the actions being taken will collectively be sufficient to keep within the bounds of the global carbon budget and thereby stem the tide of runaway climate change.

Second, the Paris deal gave at least two major sectors of the global economy, the airline travel and international shipping industries, a free pass when it comes to greenhouse gas emissions. In effect, this means that not only will countries not have to account for greenhouse gas emissions from either international shipping or airline travel in the intended nationally determined contributions that they submit, but also the annual emissions from these two industries will be exempted because they are international in scope. International shipping produces 2.4 percent of global greenhouse gas emissions, the same percentage as all of Germany. Total aviation travel yields about 2 percent of global emissions, with an estimated 65 percent of that accounted for by international flights. Emissions from these two sectors are expected to rise dramatically by 2050. Estimates warn that aviation and shipping could account for as much as one third of global emissions by 2050 as demand for consumer goods through international trade grows along with air travel and as emissions from other sectors, such as energy, are curbed.[18]

Third, rather than calling for urgent and substantial cuts in greenhouse gas emissions between 2018 and 2030, the Paris negotiators "kicked the can down the road" to a post-2050 period when the world may be able to rely on new technologies to "suck the carbon pollution it produces back out of the atmosphere in the longer term," according to British climate scientist Kevin Anderson.[19] One of the new technologies advanced at the Paris summit is called biomass energy carbon capture and storage. The strategy, Anderson explained, calls for "apportioning huge swaths of the planet's landmass (an area one to three times that of India) to the growing of bioenergy crops (from big trees to tall grasses) which absorb carbon dioxide through photosynthesis as they grow." When these crops are harvested, said Anderson, they are then processed, shipped around the world and combusted in thermal power stations. The carbon dioxide is then stripped from the waste gases, compressed in a liquid form and pumped (often over long distances) through pipelines to be stored in underground geological formations such as exhausted petroleum reservoirs or saline aquifers. This technology has neither been adequately tested nor proven. What is most disturbing, said Anderson, is that most of the 2015 voluntary emission cuts submitted by countries, plus the 2- and now 1.5-degree Celsius goals, have been "premised on the massive uptake of [biomass energy carbon capture and storage]" post-2050. The whole strategy, he warned, "risks being total fantasy."[20]

Fourth, the failure of the Paris negotiations to adopt urgent commitments and mechanisms for dramatic reductions in greenhouse gas emissions between now and 2030 and the strategy of "kicking the can down the road" until after 2050, when the biomass energy carbon capture and storage technology "may" have been tested and proven, have provoked some scientists to call for a priority to be put on geoengineering solutions now. In a joint letter, 11 highly respected, well-placed climate scientists warned that the Paris Agreement is "dangerously inadequate" and exposed some of the "deadly flaws" lying behind the "veneer of success." They wrote, "The time for wishful thinking and blind optimism that has characterized the debate on climate change is over. The time for hard facts and decisions is now . . . Our backs are against the wall and we must now start the process of preparing for geoengineering," including carbon sequestration through restored rainforests and seeding of oceans or solar radiation management through artificially whitening clouds. While acknowledging that there are "high political and environmental risks," that "its chances of success are small" and that the "risks of implementation are great," the letter urged that this strategy be undertaken now, "not as an alternative to making the carbon cuts that are urgently needed" but rather as a challenge to "the narrative of wishful thinking that has infested the climate change talks for the past twenty-one years."[21]

Finally, the Paris process did not make any real progress on stable financing, which is critically important, especially for global South countries. Growth in greenhouse gas emissions will increasingly come from the global South (notably China and India), and a high-speed transition to renewable energy will be crucial in those countries and in the industrialized North. According to the International Energy Agency, the global energy transitions required will cost around $2 trillion per year (both public and private) for several decades. To effectively pursue a 2-degree Celsius pathway, it is estimated that public investments of between $166 and $266 billion per year will be required for mitigation in developing countries alone.[22] Yet, reported Oxfam, only about $15 billion per year is being raised for the public financing of international mitigation assistance through the UN's Green Climate Fund.[23]

The basic problem is that the emission reductions pledged by the participating 197 countries of the world, especially the big industrial polluters, do not begin to measure up to the challenges required to meet the goal of a 2-degree scenario, much less a 1.5-degree scenario. Perhaps nobody was more acutely aware of this setback than Christiana Figueres, the UN's climate chief, who had worked tirelessly to cultivate a sense of urgency and call to action among government diplomats, business executives and community-based organizations leading up to the Paris summit. Going into the Paris summit, Figueres had already done the math and concluded that the latest commitments of member countries to reduce their greenhouse gas emissions were certainly "not enough." In fact, as noted earlier, the official synthesis report of the *United Nations Framework Convention on Climate Change*, which had analyzed the intended nationally determined contributions, had also concluded that they were going in the wrong direction. Instead of ensuring that the temperature rise remained at or below the dangerous 2-degree threshold, the result of current intended contributions would be a rise in global temperature of somewhere between 2.7 and 3.9 degrees Celsius this century.[24]

Threat Multipliers

As a planetary emergency, however, runaway climate change also has a multiplier effect. As a 2012 report by the British think tank Chatham House put it, climate change is a potent "threat multiplier." Here the realities of climate change can be viewed in at least two ways. First, the chemistry of climate change involves a mix of greenhouse gases that can suddenly accelerate the pace of heat trapping in the atmosphere, which would speed up the burning process and its corresponding threats to life. Second, the scope and reach of climate change and its impacts threaten the basics of life on this planet, including land, soil, food, water, oceans, forests, minerals and sources of energy, especially when combined with the increasing scarcity of natural resources. By taking a closer look at the speed and scope of climate change, we can develop a deeper understanding of the emergency at hand.

According to the Intergovernmental Panel on Climate Change, a variety of greenhouse gases have heat-trapping capacities when released into the atmosphere. Besides carbon dioxide and methane, these include nitrous oxide, perfluorocarbons, hydrofluorocarbons, sulphur hexafluoride and nitrogen trifluoride. To date, the most attention by far has been focused on carbon dioxide. More recently, however, scientists have become increasingly concerned about the role of methane in climate change chemistry. Their studies now show us that although it produces only half as much carbon as coal when burned, if methane itself is directly released as a gas into the atmosphere, it traps the heat much more efficiently than carbon dioxide.

In effect, methane is both an extremely potent and an extremely fast-acting greenhouse gas. But unlike carbon dioxide, which lasts for centuries once released into the atmosphere, a methane molecule will only last a few decades. According to the outdated chemistry applied by the Environmental Protection Agency (EPA) in the United States, methane was assigned a heating value of 28 to 36 times that of carbon dioxide over a 100-year time frame. Now scientists such as Robert Howarth and Anthony Graffea of Cornell University have concluded that a more accurate estimate would be that releases of methane into the atmosphere will be between 86 and 105 times more potent than carbon dioxide over the next decade or two in terms of trapping heat in the atmosphere.[25] As climate activist McKibben put it, this is "global warming's new terrifying chemistry." Moreover, the Arctic permafrost, both onshore and offshore, is one of the planet's prime storehouses for methane and carbon dioxide. If the Arctic's onshore and offshore permafrost melts, vast quantities of both methane and carbon dioxide will be released into the atmosphere.

These and related warnings by scientists were reported in Dahr Jamail's 2013 stirring article, "The Coming 'Instant Planetary Emergency,'" published in the *Nation* in December 2013.[26] During the summers of 2010 and 2011, scientists found active and growing methane vents in the Arctic Ocean that measured up to 150 kilometres. One scientist on a research ship described it as "bubbling seawater" that looked like "a vast pool of seltzer." Also, over the course of one year, observed the NASA scientists, methane vents grew from 30 centimetres wide to one kilometre wide — a 3,333-fold increase. Methane hydrates, frequently described as "methane gas surrounded by ice," also permeate the Arctic Ocean floor. In the March 2010 edition of *Science*, a report estimated that there were between 1,000 and 10,000 gigatons of carbon in the offshore seabed.[27] If the permafrost beneath the Arctic Ocean continues to thaw, the release into the atmosphere of even a portion of this carbon in the form of methane and carbon dioxide would certainly be catastrophic, greatly accelerating the heating of the planet.

In July 2013, the journal *Nature* published a report indicating that a 50-gigaton "burp" was "highly possible at any time" as a result of the rapid melting of the Arctic permafrost beneath the East Siberian Sea.[28] If this were to happen, scientists estimate that it would amount to a release equivalent to at least 1,000 gigatons of carbon dioxide. Comparatively speaking, the planet would suddenly encounter a cumulative release of greenhouse gases into the atmosphere that is well over three times the amount of carbon dioxide emitted by humans since the beginning of the Industrial Revolution.

The critical problem emerging from these revelations in the Arctic is the reality of runaway climate change. Its damaging impact is due not only to the quantity of greenhouse gases being emitted but also to the speed at which these developments are taking place. "The Arctic is warming faster than anywhere else on the planet," warned James Hansen. "Between 1979 and 2012," said oceanographer Wielslaw Maslowski, "we have a decline of 13 percent per decade in the sea ice, accelerating from 6 percent between 1979 and 2000. If this trend continues, we will not have sea ice by the end of this decade."[29]

At the same time, the scope and reach of climate change now penetrate most of the building blocks of life on this planet. Take, for example, the twin crises of soil erosion and ocean sickness. Good soil conditions are essential for growing crops and feeding people. To add 2.5 centimetres of topsoil involves a 500-year process. Each year, the planet loses 23 billion tons of soil. Put another way, over the past 20 years, the planet has lost the equivalent of all the soil that now covers the agricultural lands of both India and France. Spurred on by climate change, this soil erosion is turning arable lands into deserts. It is now estimated that 65 percent of once arable lands have been lost, and a further 15 percent of the planet's land surface is turning into desert.[30]

Meanwhile, the oceans, where 90 percent of all living beings on this planet reside, are sick and dying. Oceans absorb at least one third of all carbon dioxide emissions and 80 percent of all the heat generated by climate change and the burning of fossil fuels.[31] Over a third of the oceans' coral reefs have been destroyed, and half of the remaining ones are in danger. The plankton of the oceans, which are a key source of nutrients for marine life as well as the primary lungs of the planet (providing 50 percent of Earth's oxygen), are now endangered by changing ocean chemistry.[32]

In turn, the combined effect of soil erosion and ocean sickness generates yet another threat multiplier: harvest and food shocks. As the Chatham House report put it, "Increased frequency and severity of extreme weather events, such as droughts, heat waves and floods, will also result in much larger and more frequent local harvest shocks around the world." These shocks "will affect global food prices whenever key centres of agricultural production area are hit — further amplifying global food price volatility." Thus, for example, when a brutal heat wave struck Russia in the summer of 2010, the global price of wheat, and therefore bread as a staple of life, turned sharply upwards, reaching unprecedented levels in North Africa and the Middle East.

Soil moisture needed for agriculture depends on access to groundwater systems. Climate change is contributing to the depletion of fresh water from groundwater systems. When the surface temperature of Earth rises, water evaporates more rapidly from the soil, resulting in less water being stored in groundwater systems. At the same time, water in lakes and rivers also evaporates more quickly in warmer temperatures, and when snowpacks melt earlier than normal, they tend to evaporate rather than flow into streams and rivers that feed lakes. If warmer temperatures mean that lakes do not freeze over in the winter, then more water goes into the atmosphere and less is saved in groundwater systems.[33] Moreover, warned the Chatham House report, one of the main climate-driven threats is diminished precipitation available for rain-fed agriculture. "By 2020, yields from rain-fed agriculture could be reduced by up to 50% in some areas."

It may be argued that more rapid evaporation is good news for Earth's hydrologic cycle — the natural cyclical process whereby fresh water falls to Earth in the form of precipitation, seeps into the ground and then evaporates again into the atmosphere, where it then accumulates and eventually falls again. Yet there is substantial evidence that the hydrologic cycle itself has suffered serious damage. According to studies carried out by Michael Kravčik and his team of water scientists in Slovakia, the natural flow of the hydrologic cycle has been damaged by the processes of urbanization and industrialization (such as industrial agriculture and manufacturing) to the point where the amount of fresh water that is available on the planet is rapidly depleting. If this trend continues, by 2025 the world's land mass will have lost an estimated 45 trillion cubic metres of renewable fresh water, amounting to about one quarter of the volume of water in Earth's entire hydrologic cycle.[34]

Indeed, an increasingly waterless planet is fast becoming a major threat multiplier of climate change. According to the forecasts of some scientists, significant portions of the Amazon basin in South America, which has been the home of rainforests and a source of biodiversity for much of the planet, will become a desert by 2050. In Africa, climate change has also become one of the prime motivating factors behind land grabs taking place throughout the continent, especially of arable land to grow food with access to sources of fresh water. According to Anuradha Mittal of the Oakland Institute, "almost 75 percent of the land deals over the last decade have taken place in Africa." Not only are investors from North America engaged in this African land grabbing, but it is also being carried out by governments and investors from European countries, where there is an increasing lack of arable land to grow sufficient food to feed their populations. More recently, investor priority has been put on African land grabs for the production and export of agrofuel crops to Europe, which robs local farmers and communities of their domestic food supplies and livelihood while threatening the biodiversity of the land through monoculture.

Finally, by adding to this list the rapid and massive destruction of Earth's forests, we get a glimpse of the scope and magnitude of climate change as a threat multiplier and the corresponding emergency facing the planet. After all, forests are not only the most biologically rich ecosystems on land but also nature's most effective carbon sink. Since 1950, however, the planet has lost more than half of all the forests that existed at that time. Although some reforestation has taken place, tree farms are generally no match for the highly diverse and dense old-growth forests they have replaced.[35] In effect, the widespread deforestation that has occurred around the world over a period of less than 75 years has had a dramatic impact on the planet's carbon budget. Not only is humanity in a race against time to close the gigaton gap in global greenhouse gas emissions, but this must also be done at a critical moment when the planet's natural capacity to capture, absorb and store these emissions has been substantially destroyed.

Unheeded Warnings

When asked what he thought the prospects were for negotiating an effective global climate treaty at the Paris summit, the executive secretary of the last global treaty-making attempt, Conference of the Parties 15 in Copenhagen in 2009, had this to say: "There is nothing that can be agreed in 2015 that would be consistent with the two degrees. The only way that a 2015 agreement can achieve a two-degree goal is to shut down the whole global economy."[36]

Yvo de Boer's comment is not to be taken lightly. By naming the "whole global economy," he publicly identified the core of the crisis and the challenge as few officials have done before or since. Yet he was not alone in expressing this viewpoint. In recent years, a small but growing number of scientists, increasingly aware of just how globalized the economy has become, were reaching similar conclusions. Take, for example, Kevin Anderson and his colleague Alice Bows, a climate change mitigation expert, both from the Tyndall Centre for Climate Change Research in the United Kingdom. Together they have built a case that, in effect, demonstrates that Earth's climate is now on a collision course with the operations of the global economy.[37]

Indeed, Anderson's public presentations in recent years have become increasingly urgent and alarmist. Through PowerPoint presentations, Anderson has highlighted themes such as "Climate Change: Going Beyond Dangerous" and "Brutal Numbers and Tenuous Hope," emphasizing that much time has been lost in recent decades as a result of political procrastination and inadequate climate policy–making. Hence, emissions have continued to rapidly increase and expand, greatly diminishing the chances of staying within the 2-degree Celsius threshold, let alone the 1.5-degree target. If there is to be a 50-50 chance of limiting global temperatures to the 2-degree target, then wealthy, industrialized countries will have to start reducing their emissions by 8 to 10 percent per year now.[38]

Yet all the signs indicate that these warnings are not being heeded in the corridors of power. After the Paris summit, it was largely "business as usual" for both political and economic elites. What was consistent following the Paris Agreement was a return to the relentless call for "expanding economic growth" and "expanding the global economy." Plans such as opening the Northwest Passage through the ecologically fragile Arctic for the purpose of greatly accelerating and expanding global trade with China continue apace, as if nothing really happened in Paris. Indeed, in and of itself, this message is completely inconsistent with the 2-degree goal, much less a 1.5-degree threshold.

Meanwhile, in a 2016 report entitled *The Sky's Limit: Why the Paris Climate Goals Require a Managed Decline in Fossil Fuel Production*, Oil Change International compared the world's fossil fuel reserves to various scenarios of the global carbon budget.[39] If this planet is to stand a 66 percent chance of staying within the 2-degree Celsius threshold this century, then 68 percent of the world's fossil fuel must be declared "unburnable." Or, if the planet is to have a 50 percent chance of limiting global temperature increases to 1.5 degrees Celsius this century (the Paris goal), then 85 percent of fossil fuel reserves worldwide must be declared "unburnable." Climate science is telling us that the global targets for emission reduction cannot be achieved without ensuring that between 68 and 85 percent of global fossil fuels (coal, oil, gas) remain in the ground. See figure 1.1.

Figure 1.1 Global Fossil Fuel Reserves Compared to Carbon Budgets

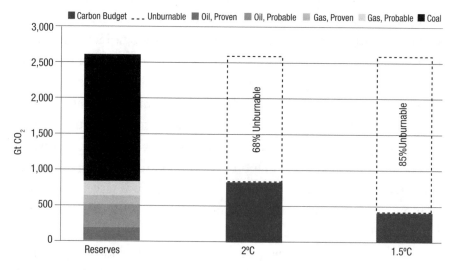

Source: Rystead Energy, World Energy Council, Intergovernmental Panel on Climate Change

In effect, this requires not only a major energy transition from fossil fuels to renewable energy sources by 2050, but also corresponding transformations in both the global economy at large and domestic economies. Failure to heed this fundamental warning is to continue down the road toward planetary disaster.

All of this serves to magnify both the urgency and the scope of the challenge facing Canada in the aftermath of the Paris Agreement. According to one of Environment Canada's latest *National Inventory Reports*, for example, Canada's economy spewed 704 million tonnes of greenhouse gas emissions into the atmosphere in 2016.[40] Since then, it's been estimated that 572 million tonnes, or 81 percent of all Canada's emissions, were and remain associated with the energy sector, either in the form of combustion of natural gas to produce crude oil and other fossil fuels, in the burning of fossil fuels for the transport of people and freight by cars and trucks or in the fugitive release of greenhouse gas emissions through leaks into the atmosphere. Although its total emissions are relatively low in comparison with most other industrialized economies, Canada's heavy reliance on the fossil fuel energy sector for our economy plus the industry's strategic location in ecologically sensitive regions such as the boreal forest and the Arctic considerably magnify this country's role in and impact on the future of the planet. The greenhouse gas emissions of Canada's global warming machine, the tar sands industry, amounted to 72 million tonnes in 2014. By 2020, however, greenhouse gas emissions from the tar sands are expected to rise to 102 million tonnes — a whopping 41 percent increase in just over five years. Moreover, if plans for the new liquefied natural gas plant on the west coast of British Columbia go ahead, another 21 million tonnes of greenhouse gas emissions will be added annually.[41] As Naomi Klein put it:

> *The bottom line is what matters here: our economic system and our planetary system are now at war. Or, more accurately, our economy is at war with many forms of life on earth, including human life. What the climate needs to avoid collapse is contraction in humanity's use of resources; what our economic model demands to avoid collapse is unfettered expansion. Only one of these sets of rules can be changed, and it's not the laws of nature.[42]*

CHAPTER 2
Global Economy

Economic Globalization

To grasp the correlation between climate change and the global economy, we need to recall and unpack some pivotal moments during the last three decades of the twentieth century. In 1972, in Stockholm, the first UN Conference on the Human Environment brought together representatives from government, corporations and civil society. The declaration coming out of the Stockholm summit was focused on the theme of "sustainable development," which to some observers was an oxymoron.

After all, the Club of Rome was generating considerable public discussion about these issues through its research into *limits* to growth, already circulating at international conferences and published as a book in 1972.[1] Yet there appeared to be very little questioning at the Stockholm conference about whether the prevailing models of economic development, based on expanding economic growth, were themselves the source of environmental damage and destruction. On the contrary, the operating assumption was that the economic model of "development" was essentially compatible with the goal of "sustainability." Subsequent events soon demonstrated the opposite.

Other tensions were developing on the economic front. Some countries in the global South appealed to the UN to create a new international economic order. The new order, which the UN General Assembly endorsed in 1974, was primarily designed to overcome the disparities in wealth and power between "developed" economies in the global North and "underdeveloped" economies in the South.

Meanwhile, in 1973, the Trilateral Commission was formed, composed of CEOs from the world's largest transnational corporations, along with presidents and prime ministers plus senior government and some media officials. Their objectives included reinstatement of big business's role in economic and social policy–making within nation-states, along with restructuring the global economy. The first objective involved the dismantling of the Keynesian model of government and the social welfare state, which had been installed to varying degrees in many of the northern industrialized countries. The second objective involved developing and implementing strategies designed to change the policies of international institutions governing global finance, trade and investment.

Throughout the 1980s, these environmental and economic processes more or less moved along separate tracks. During this period, however, the economic track gained considerable momentum. Once the new international economic order faded from view, the Trilateral Commission's agenda gained a foothold and began to pave the way for restructuring the global economy, including

- establishing big business coalitions in leading industrialized countries;
- promoting the sovereign rights of corporations to operate in any country;
- reducing trade and non-trade barriers to the free flow of capital;
- removing restrictions on foreign investment;
- weakening the public sector and
- advancing structural adjustment programs that compelled

developing countries to adopt these and related policy measures.[2]

The collapse of the Berlin Wall in 1989 symbolized the end of the bipolar global economy (the coexistence of capitalism and communism) built up since World War II. In other words, capitalism had triumphed over communism as the dominant economic model for "development."

By the early 1990s, the Trilateral Commission's agenda had been largely encapsulated in what became known as the Washington Consensus for restructuring the global economy. In a "new world order" governed by nation-states rooted in capitalist economies, there was general agreement among economic and political elites that transnational corporations could move capital and their operations anywhere in the world to produce their products, create new markets and expand global trade in goods and services, unfettered by either government intervention or regulation. The platform also included

- privatization of public enterprises and services,
- deregulation of national economies,
- free trade regimes and
- a corresponding body of rules to ensure that these changes were entrenched.

This was the strategy known as "neoliberalism," which has increasingly gained momentum over the last four decades.[3] Its ultimate achievement has been to restore capitalism as the dominant economic model both nationally and globally.

During the 1990s, even as economic and environmental negotiating processes continued on their separate paths, the clash between climate change and the remaking of the global economy began to surface. The macro-strategy that was initially launched at the 1992 Earth Summit in Rio de Janeiro opened the door for commercializing and privatizing nature's periodic table. With official sanction given to patenting a variety of nature's products, the stage was set for 23.8 percent of the periodic table to be bought and sold in national and international markets. Twenty years later, at the 2012 Rio Earth Summit, the remaining 76.2 percent of nature's products in the periodic table would be subject to an elaborate process of commodification, privatization and financialization. In other words, nature's products and the periodic table itself were in the process of becoming fully integrated within the processes of economic globalization.

Coincidentally, the stage was also set during the 1990s for international negotiations by governments on the reduction of greenhouse gas emissions causing climate change. In 1997, the Kyoto Protocol was concluded with a corresponding process for participating governments to negotiate nation-state commitments to reducing emissions below 1990 levels. However, unlike bilateral and global negotiations of trade and investment treaties that took place during the same period, the country commitments under the protocol were voluntary and non-binding. Moreover, no enforcement mechanisms were put in place to ensure that countries met their commitment quotas. Even more problematic was the absence of major industrial polluters such as the United States and China from the protocol, which would ultimately render it ineffective from a global standpoint.

The New Trade Regimes

Meanwhile, progress of a different sort was being made on the economic track with the completion in 1994 of negotiations to establish the first comprehensive, binding free trade regime between Canada, Mexico and the United States — the North American Free Trade Agreement (NAFTA). A year later, the World Trade Organization (WTO) was inaugurated, replacing the former General Agreement on Tariffs and Trade with a more comprehensive set of binding and enforceable trade rules governed by a much more centralized authority.[4] NAFTA was thereafter recognized as the model free trade regime for most bilateral and regional free trade deals to be negotiated elsewhere in the world.

However, these new trade regimes did nothing to strengthen nation-state commitments to substantially reduce greenhouse gas emissions. On the contrary, these commitments effectively functioned as an institutional check on mitigating climate change, all the while championing the rights of energy-producing nation-states to export and import fossil fuels that spew billions of tons of greenhouse gas emissions into the atmosphere, with little or no reference to the collateral ecological damage being done to the planet.

Although governments fail to provide adequate financing for the transition to renewable energy, they continue to subsidize the fossil fuel industry through the public purse. Direct fossil fuel industry subsidies in 2012 alone, for example, amounted to an estimated $775 billion and may have gone as high as $1 trillion in other years.[5] Moreover, according to a study done for the International Monetary Fund (IMF), if you include the "environmental damage associated with energy consumption" in calculations about fossil fuel subsidies, then the annual figure for government subsidies to energy industries balloons to $5.3 trillion — equivalent to $10 million a minute.[6] The prominent British economist Nicholas Stern called this subsidization of the fossil fuel industry "the greatest market failure the world has ever seen."[7] Ending these fossil fuel subsidies, it's been estimated, would alone reduce global carbon emissions by 20 percent.[8]

Governments around the world are using trillions of dollars in public finance every year to subsidize the fossil fuel industry, thereby propping up an energy system that must be dismantled if any real progress is to be made in enabling all countries, especially those in the global South, to implement effective mitigation strategies and a high-speed transition to clean, renewable energy. Although the Paris Agreement did include provisions for reviewing and recommending improvements in public financing for both mitigation and adaptation by 2017, it appears that no real plan of action exists, as yet, for dismantling the fossil fuel subsidy juggernaut.

For that to change, wealthy industrialized states will have no choice but to confront the growth-based logic that underlies our economic system. In other words, nothing effective can be done to curb and reverse the powerful processes of climate change without taking on and overhauling the engine that has been the driving force behind greenhouse gas emissions: the global economy plus its dominant transnational corporate players and institutions.

So what, then, is the relationship between climate change and the global economy? Just how, when and where did this relationship develop? Has the process of economic globalization over the past 40 or more years hastened the release of greenhouse gases and the burning of the planet? If so, is the climate of the planet on a collision course with the expansion of the global economy?

As Naomi Klein reminded us, it is worth keeping in mind that climate change is not just another issue, like health care, unemployment or affordable housing, that requires public debate about policy changes. It's a phenomenon that permeates these and many other issues. Indeed, climate change is nothing less than a dynamic force of both nature and history and, as such, has a life of its own. These days, adds Klein, this dynamic force has "a powerful message spoken in the language of fires, floods, drought, and extinction — telling us we need an entirely new economic model and a new way of sharing on this planet. Telling us we need to evolve" as a species.[9]

Trade Trumps Climate

On a global level, the WTO claims to be committed to "environmental protection" and "sustainable development." According to Article XX of the old General Agreement on Tariffs and Trade regime that was grandfathered into the WTO in 1994, any country can be exempted from the WTO rules to bring in policy measures "necessary to protect human, animal or plant life or health" (Article XX–b) or measures "relating to the conservation of exhaustible natural resources" (Article XX–g). At first glance, these provisions may sound "environmentally friendly," but they are conditioned by a big caveat in the article's preamble (or "chapeau"), which, in effect, puts the onus on countries initiating environmental protection measures to prove that their actions will not cause "arbitrary or unjustifiable discrimination" or pose as a "disguised restriction on international trade."

In other words, global trade rules guaranteeing the free flow of capital, goods and services trump environmental protection priorities. Thus, measures designed by governments to prevent climate change can be challenged and struck down for being a "disguised restriction on international trade." Indeed, as a result of economic globalization, under the overarching "most favoured nation" and "national treatment" clauses of the WTO regime, transnational corporations based in member countries now effectively have "sovereign rights" over laws in the countries in which they operate. Moreover, these same rules, designed to ensure that governments' environmental regulations do not supersede global trade rules, were incorporated into the charter of the *United Nations Framework Convention on Climate Change* that was adopted at the Rio de Janeiro Earth Summit in 1992 (Article 3.5).

From this point onward, the agendas for slowing climate change on the one hand and growing the global economy on the other were increasingly on a collision course, with the global economy and corporate driven globalization process clearly maintaining the upper hand. The terms of negotiation around the Kyoto Protocol and its mechanisms became increasingly subject to the dictates of market fundamentalism and market logic. Any collective mechanisms to reduce greenhouse gas emissions or make the transition from fossil fuels to renewable energy had to be developed in accordance with the demands and rules of global institutions such as the WTO, designed to further market-based economies through corporate globalization. Furthermore, the Kyoto Protocol itself was hampered by being a non-binding treaty based on voluntary commitments, along with the fact that the big polluters, such as the United States and China, were not parties to the agreement. Lacking sufficient enforcement mechanisms, the Kyoto process soon unravelled as the principal international instrument for slowing and reversing the heating of the planet.

At the same time, greenhouse gas emissions continued to increase by more than 60 percent, primarily through expansion of the global economy and the process of corporate globalization; during most of the first decade of the new millennium, the annual rate of increase hovered around 3.4 percent.[10] Quite simply, promoting export-oriented production in developing countries, shipping mass production over long distances and importing wasteful products into developed countries are a recipe for intensifying the heating of the planet. The rapid growth in emissions during the first decade of the twenty-first century was only briefly interrupted in 2009 as a result of the worldwide financial crisis. By the next year, the rate of increase had again soared to 5.9 percent.[11]

The new global trade rules have served to greatly increase worldwide greenhouse gas emissions on multiple fronts. Industrial agriculture and industrial transportation offer two informative case studies:

- The creation of a global supermarket in recent decades, whereby food crops are grown in the global South and then shipped to consumers in the global North, has been a major source of escalating emissions. Estimates suggested that today's globalized food system is responsible for generating between 19 and 29 percent of the world's greenhouse gas emissions.[12]
- Over the past 20 years, the traffic flow of container ships transporting agricultural and industrial products being exported from producing countries to consuming countries has expanded almost 400 percent.[13] The net effect of this ever-increasing cross-border trade in goods and corresponding worldwide transportation by container ships is that shipping emissions are expected to at least double, if not triple, by 2050, further undermining efforts to bring runaway climate change under control by mid-century.

Worse still, the emissions accounting procedure for greenhouse gases does not provide a comprehensive picture. As Klein pointed out, the so-called emerging economies such as China and India are going through their own industrialization process, manufacturing a broad range of products mostly for export back to North America and Europe, but the consumer demand side of the equation is usually missing when it comes to calculating related greenhouse gas emissions. According to one study, 48 percent of China's increase in emissions between 2002 and 2008 was due to foreign trade — producing products for export mostly to meet consumer demands generated in other industrialized countries.[14] The accounting procedure adopted by the *United Nations Framework Convention on Climate Change*, however, only assigns responsibility for greenhouse gas emissions generated within a country's own borders. The emissions generated, for example, through production of a flat-screen TV in China for export to Canada, are attributed to China's ledger only, even though the consumer demand resides in Canada. Responsibility for the emissions generated by the container ship transporting the TV set from China to Canada is not attributed to either country.

Furthermore, the global economy's new trade and investment rules are being used increasingly to block countries from changing their economies to reduce greenhouse gas emissions in response to climate change. A case in point is the 2012 WTO action against Canada in which Ontario's *Green Energy Act* was declared in violation of WTO rules.

The *Green Energy Act* was designed to promote the development of renewable energy as a measure for mitigating climate change while also strengthening the local economy by creating new jobs. It allotted the majority of producer power rights to Ontario companies, thereby making it possible for the province to make the transition from coal, oil and gas without completely damaging its local economy. Its "domestic content requirements," which stipulated that 25 percent of all wind projects and 50 percent of all solar projects be produced by workers and industries in the province, ensured that new manufacturing jobs would be created in Ontario as it transitioned to renewable energy sources. The *Act* also guaranteed a preferential 20-year purchase price for electricity from wind and solar generators of companies that had a certain percentage of their costs originating from Ontario.[15]

In its first two years, this program created more than 20,000 jobs in Ontario and was on track to create a total of 50,000. It was accelerating the production of renewable energy while simultaneously reducing both greenhouse gas emissions and unemployment. Although there were concerns about the program's implementation, it was recognized as an innovative step toward tackling climate change. In 2010–11, however, Japan and the European Union, representing the interests of their own transnational corporations, filed cases in the WTO against Ontario's renewable energy incentives program, claiming that it was violating the "national treatment" rule of the WTO. This rule established that transnational corporations shall be treated no less favourably than domestic enterprises when it comes to laws, regulations and requirements affecting products, "their sale, purchase, transportation, distribution or use." In effect, under the WTO rules, you can give more benefits to foreign-based transnational corporations but never less than what you have already given to a domestic enterprise.[16]

When it comes to climate change, this implies that a nation-state (or a subnational government such as Ontario) cannot promote the development of a national industry of solar panels, wind energy or other forms of renewable energy by using national regulations primarily designed to benefit domestic companies or products. If a government wants to give subsidies or preferences to those national companies or products, it must also give the same incentives to transnational corporations. In May 2013, the Dispute Settlement Body of the WTO in its final ruling said that Canada (Ontario) was in violation of WTO rules. One month later, the Ontario minister of energy announced through the Government of Canada that the Ontario government would "comply with the World Trade Organization's ruling on the domestic content provision."[17]

The WTO ruling against Ontario is just one of many cases that have emerged. In the Uttarakhand of India, for instance, more than 1,000 people have died, 3,000 more have disappeared and 100,000 have been evacuated as a result of extreme flooding caused by deforestation and climate change. Yet the U.S. government filed a case on behalf of its own transnational corporations at the WTO in February 2013 challenging India's use of subsidies and "buy local" rules to stimulate its own domestic solar development. The U.S. complaint against India was based on the same logic as the case against Ontario and eventually forced India's government to change its renewable energy program. At the same time, other disputes are arising in the WTO between China, the European Union and the United States in relation to wind power equipment and solar panels. Instead of achieving lower prices for renewable energy, these disputes are aimed at moving in the opposite direction by protecting the markets and profits of transnational corporations.

Denmark has one of the world's most successful and far-reaching renewable energy programs; fully 40 percent of that country's energy comes from renewable sources, mostly wind power.[18] Fortunately for the Danish people, the country embarked on this program in the 1980s, before the new global trade rules were fully developed and implemented. Had Denmark begun its renewable energy program after the mid-1990s, it would no doubt be a major target of global trade and investment challenges as its policies and strategies favoured locally owned co-operatives as the preferred vehicle for producing and delivering renewable energy. The Danish government granted generous subsidies to community-controlled wind-powered projects. Today, this preferential treatment would have been in direct conflict with the WTO's "national treatment" and "most favoured nation" rules.

More recently, a new era of corporate free trade regimes has been launched in which trade rules again trump climate. Take, for example, the Trans-Pacific Partnership (TPP) — recast as the Comprehensive and Progressive Agreement for Trans-Pacific Partnership after the United States withdrew immediately following Donald Trump's inauguration — involving at least 11 countries, stretching from Japan to Chile (including Canada).[19] Even without the United States, the agreement represents 14 percent of world trade. Without even uttering the words *climate change,* the TPP is designed to go well beyond NAFTA by greatly accelerating the exploration, extraction and export of fossil fuels.[20] Moreover, the TPP includes provisions to screen out all environmental (including climate) policies that interfere with, or impinge on, the promotion of trade and investment. As well, fossil fuel corporations will be able to use the investor-state provisions to sue governments directly for climate policies and regulatory measures that curb their operations to mitigate climate change. Indeed, a September 2016 report by the Institute for Agriculture and Trade Policy predicted that "as countries take action to protect the climate, conflicts between trade rules and climate goals will escalate."[21] The report went on to say that trade agreements such as the TPP set broad-reaching rules for the economy for expanding trade in the resource sector, which, in turn, serve to protect fossil fuel corporations and financial firms "from future measures to stabilize the climate."

Corporate Powers

The real driving forces behind economic globalization have been transnational corporations. They have been the principal beneficiaries and the architects of most global trade and investment rules that came into being from the 1990s onward, creating a corporate-driven global economy. The Trilateral Commission of the early 1970s had outlined and implemented a plan of action for restoring and revitalizing the powers of corporations and big business in public policy–making. One of the planks in the commission's program had been the establishment of big business coalitions in key countries to politically advance this corporate agenda. During the 1980s, these big business coalitions were operating in all the major industrialized economies, including Canada, where the coalition was originally known as the Business Council on National Issues and later renamed the Canadian Council of Chief Executives.[22]

By the mid-1990s, transnational corporations had virtually assumed sovereign powers within an increasingly globalized economy, reinforced by the Washington Consensus, bilateral and regional trade and investment rules and global institutions such as the WTO and World Bank. Moreover, the new trade and investment regimes served to codify the rights and powers of corporations, including their rights to sue governments for alleged violations. Had the Multilateral Agreement on Investment (MAI) negotiated through the OECD, which would have enshrined the sovereignty of transnational corporations, not been exposed and stopped by the anti-MAI campaign of civil society groups in 1997–98, the powers of corporations would have become even more entrenched globally.[23]

Studies have shown that the fossil fuel industry — comprising mainly coal, oil and gas companies — is the driving force behind increasing greenhouse gas emissions. A study conducted by the Climate Accountability Institute in Colorado, for example, found that 90 companies produced 63 percent of the cumulative global emissions of industrial carbon dioxide and methane between 1751 and 2010, amounting to about 914 gigatonnes of carbon dioxide emissions. Eighty-three of the 90 were energy companies producing oil, gas and coal; the remaining seven were cement manufacturers. Of the 90, 50 were private investor-owned oil companies such as Chevron, Exxon, BP and Shell and coal producers such as British Coal Co., Peabody Energy and BHP Billiton, whereas the remaining 40 were state-owned corporations.[24]

More recently, the fossil fuel industry, starting with petroleum giant ExxonMobil, became the target of a multistate investigation and litigation in the United States. In late March 2016, 20 state attorneys general launched an unprecedented initiative to investigate and prosecute ExxonMobil and other industry giants for fraud and suppression of findings by climate scientists about fossil fuels and the causes and impacts of global warming. According to the investigation conducted, ExxonMobil and the rest of the industry had known for decades and suppressed evidence about the dangers that their fossil fuel products posed to the environment. Not only did they choose not to share this information with their investors, consumers and the public at large, but they have also been charged with purposely disseminating false information to boost their profit margins. The action of the attorneys general is "a clear demonstration of climate leadership," declared Annie Leonard, executive director of Greenpeace USA. "Big Polluters have done everything in their power to deny climate change . . . it's time for our justice system to take back the climate debate."[25]

Indeed, the charges against ExxonMobil and other fossil fuel giants concerning organized fraud, deception and denial of climate science may well turn out to be, as May Boeve, executive director of 350.Org, put it, "the largest corporate scandal in history."[26] Certainly, this trial has all the makings of a litigation that will be even bigger than the cases brought against the Big Tobacco corporations in the 1990s, when investigations by U.S. state attorneys general dealt a serious blow to that industry. After a battery of lawsuits were launched, the companies were compelled to release a swath of internal documents containing revelations of what they had done to protect their own interests, and they paid high costs for the impacts of their actions on society as a whole. Since everyone is affected by climate change, the multistate litigation against ExxonMobil and the fossil fuel industry is likely to go even further in holding the industry accountable for its decades of public deception.

Fortified by massive government subsidies plus new extractive technologies, the fossil fuel industry has focused its sights on extraction from sources that are both hard to reach and highly environmentally sensitive, including

- hydraulic fracturing for shale oil and gas,
- extracting bitumen from the tar sands,
- deep sea oil drilling in ecologically sensitive coastal areas and the Arctic and
- destroying mountain tops and glaciers to get at hidden deposits of coal and other mineral resources.

As noted earlier, this state-supported fossil fuel system, therefore, is one of the main roadblocks in the way of making the transition to a new economy based on renewable energy. This roadblock is made all the more difficult to overcome by the global economy's trade and investment rules, which protect the fossil fuel industry's dominance.

At their core, global trade and investment rules are designed to enhance the ability of transnational corporations to produce, transport and market their products cheaply. Since the early days of the Industrial Revolution, the rising corporate elite has striven to remove barriers to the free flow of capital so that corporations could roam the planet at will, taking advantage of opportunities to exploit both cheap labour and the environment. If demands for increasing workers' wages intensified or environmental regulations became too restrictive, corporations could pack up and move their operations to countries where the conditions for cheap production were more favourable. The trail that began with the *maquiladoras* in Mexico and Central America spread to the sweatshops of South Korea and other Southeast Asian countries, before going on to China and now increasingly to Bangladesh and elsewhere. In virtually every case, the main motivating factor has been to produce goods more cheaply by exploiting both labour and the environment.

Today, the WTO set of trade and related investment rules constitutes much of the legal architecture of the modern global economy and serves as the driving force behind the process of corporate globalization. Overlying this legal architecture is a maze of bilateral and regional regimes known as WTO-Plus agreements. Besides NAFTA and the TPP, they include the Central American Free Trade Agreement, the Canada-European Union Comprehensive Economic and Trade Agreement, the Trans-Atlantic Free Trade Agreement, the European Partnership Agreements and a host of others. Unlike the WTO, which only permits state-to-state disputes, many of these bilateral and regional regimes include an investor-state mechanism that allows corporations to sue governments directly for alleged violations of the rules.

As a result, there are dozens of cases all over the world of foreign corporations demanding large compensation payments from nation-states using these investor-state mechanisms to either ratchet down national environmental regulations or eliminate them altogether.[27] Under NAFTA, Canada has become the most-sued state for its environmental legislation, including $2.6 billion in corporate challenges against Canadian laws that restrict or ban carcinogenic additives in gasoline, lawn pesticides and fracking.

For many countries, the threat of a corporate suit becomes a "political chill," causing governments to quietly change their domestic laws or programs to appease the demands of a particular transnational corporation rather than risk being sued for heavy compensation. Indeed, some governments have refrained from developing their own climate change laws and policies for fear of being sued by transnational corporations operating in their countries.

Recently, proposals have been made by progressive trade law experts to insert a "carve-out clause," allowing governments to pursue climate change and other environmental policy–making without the threat of multimillion- or billion-dollar suits.[28] So far, these proposals have not been adopted by the *United Nations Framework Convention on Climate Change* through discussions that took place concerning the Paris Agreement or incorporated through renegotiated amendments to existing trade regimes.

Corporate Mega-strategies

Economic and political elites are not prepared to do anything that will challenge corporate dominance or slow down the process of economic globalization — in particular, anything that will challenge the fossil fuel industry as the lifeblood of our high-tech industrial society. At the same time, they can't be seen to be completely ignoring the threat of runaway climate change. So how can they square the circle, appearing to tackle the problem of climate change while leaving their economic interests intact?

The answer has been to advance various mega-schemes and strategies, essentially designed to sidestep facing up to the challenge of taking bold action to reduce humanity's dependence on fossil fuels. To better understand these false solutions, we briefly focus here on three currently proposed mega-strategies.

1. Carbon markets

The first of these is the so-called "green economy agenda" that emerged out of the Rio+20 summit in 2012. Recognizing the multiple crises — climate, economic and social — facing the planet, national governments and transnational corporations took advantage of the political moment to launch a new cycle of capitalist expansion. The official Rio+20 document, *The Future We Want*, outlined the objective of creating a strategy to generate new sources of profit or capital accumulation.[29] To do so, nature would have to be explicitly treated as capital — natural capital — and all that remains in nature would be integrated into the market.

The strategy is based on three pillars:

- **Commodification:** putting a monetary value on both the rest of biomass and biodiversity (e.g., soils, plants, animals) and specific functions of ecosystems (e.g., water filtration, crop pollination, carbon storage, coral reef protection) and then developing a market for each of these elements and functions of nature, thereby providing incentives for making profits and expanding wealth from the production of these goods and services.
- **Privatization:** establishing ownership of nature's goods, functions and environmental services and, in doing so, identifying who is responsible for them — appropriating nature and its functions to serve the interests of capital just as human labour has been appropriated.
- **Financialization:** creating derivative financial markets in this new sector of the economy for capital expansion by issuing and negotiating new bonds in international financial markets, plus setting up the institutional framework required to integrate these parts of nature into financial markets and provide insurance against the risks of such investment, thereby putting the planet's future into the hands of private banks and financial operators — the same forces that drive economic globalization and climate chaos.

In effect, the objective of these three pillars is to commercialize the remaining elements of nature as a means of triggering a new spurt of economic growth for global capitalism. Just as the door was opened at the earth summit 20 years before for the privatization of 23.8 percent of the periodic table by allowing the patenting of a variety of natural products, at Rio+20, the stage was set for commodifying and commercializing the remaining 76.2 percent of nature's elements.

The difference in 2012 was that the focus was no longer on turning natural products (trees) into commodities (wood) but on taking control of natural processes (forests) by rebranding them as "environmental services" to be bought and sold through market mechanisms. As a result, the last and greatest frontier of the "commons" on this planet, nature itself, would be subjected to the same system of derivatives trading and financial speculation that ironically had just finished dealing serious blows to the global economy and the capitalist system itself through the Great Recession of 2008–11.

2. Technofixes

The second mega-strategy concerns technofixes such as geoengineering. For some members of the global economic and political elite, these new technologies, designed to manipulate Earth's natural systems, will provide a quick-fix solution if the pace of climate change continues to accelerate.

Behind the scenes, some governments and corporations have enabled scientists to actively investigate various technological strategies that could be deployed to reduce or delay climate change, thereby providing, at the very least, more time and space to secure an effective agreement to prevent climate chaos. What would be required is a daring, science-based "coalition of the willing" to take unilateral action.[30] Once scientists deliver the "shock" that climate chaos is on the horizon and greenhouse gas emissions won't be arrested in time, then corporations will move in with their technofix therapies for manipulating and altering the stratosphere and ocean surfaces to buy more time.

When it comes to manipulating the climate system, three technofix schemes stand out[31]:

- blasting sulphate particles into the stratosphere to reflect

the sun's rays in such a way as to reduce the heat trapping and burning of the planet,
- using ocean fertilization, whereby iron particles are dumped into oceans to nurture the spread of plankton, which absorb carbon dioxide the way that plants do on land and
- genetically engineering crops on land so that their leaves will reflect more sunlight and absorb more carbon and other greenhouse gas emissions.

Although research is being pursued on all three of these geoengineering schemes, it was the third, in the form of biomass energy carbon capture and storage, that gained traction at the Paris summit. As noted in Chapter 1, this technology has never been tested, proven or verified for its effectiveness, let alone its ecological and social impacts. Yet the shift from a 2-degree to a 1.5-degree target for global temperature rise this century is largely predicated on there being a massive uptake of the technology post-2050, as were the 2015 voluntary reductions in greenhouse gas emissions submitted by nation-states (which still fell considerably below the performance standards needed to achieve the 2-degree, let alone the 1.5-degree, target).

3. Military operations
A third false solution has to do with the expansion of military operations to deal with the potential chaos and random movement of peoples that is likely to erupt as a result of runaway climate change. It is well known that military operations are big contributors to greenhouse gas emissions, especially in countries such as the United States, where the military is the largest institutional consumer of oil and the biggest emitter of carbon dioxide. In recent years, however, the U.S. military has ostensibly begun to take climate change seriously, now requiring the use of alternative fuels and solar-powered generators designed for combat uses plus "more ecologically friendly weapons," such as lead-free bullets and biodegradable explosives.

Although the switch to environmentally sustainable technologies is designed to improve efficiency and effectiveness on the battlefield, military strategists see climate change as providing conditions for a new and expanding role for troops and their operations.[32] Labelling climate change as a "threat multiplier," the U.S. Defense Department views it as a "catalyst for conflict," creating conditions for terrorist activities and other forms of violence. In short, the military is clearly positioning itself to be the best institution capable of intervening in and responding to such multiple threats and crises on a mass scale. To do so, the role and capacity of the military will have to be expanded.

However, the military as an institution is not primed to mitigate crises or prevent them from unfolding. On the contrary, it is primarily designed to respond to crises through defensive and protective measures. A military is inherently nationalistic, and its prime purpose is to defend domestic interests, especially the economic priorities of capital.[33]

We can see this unfolding in the Arctic, where a major military buildup is taking place to protect national economic interests. In addition to more oil drilling, these interests include opening up the Northwest Passage for intercontinental trade, which has been made possible by the ice melt caused by climate change. Opening the Northwest Passage will greatly accelerate global shipping trade between East and West and simultaneously facilitate access to untapped oil and gas reserves.

As a result, the Arctic has rapidly become a focal point for geopolitical tensions and military buildup as neighbouring nation-states scramble to claim land and underwater territorial rights to the region under the *United Nations Convention on the Law of the Sea*. Russia and Canada, for example, have each claimed the region as its own domestic waterways, whereas other countries, including the United States, contend that the Arctic and the Northwest Passage are international waters.

The massive increase in shipping trade between East and West, which the military buildup in the Arctic for the opening of the Northwest Passage is designed to promote, will be a major contributor to runaway climate change. Despite the military makeover to play a leading role in the fight against climate change, the increasing military presence in regions such as the Arctic is part of the problem much more than part of the solution.34

The Trump Effect

The morning after U.S. election night 2016, many people in the United States and in much of the rest of the world, including Canada, woke up in a state of shock and dismay over the stunning victory of Donald J. Trump. Suddenly, the man once dubbed the "voice of anger" had become the world's most powerful leader.

During his first year in office, Trump chose to govern by being "dangerously unpredictable"— a rogue style similar to his behaviour on the campaign trail. The objective was to establish conditions of "instability" and "uncertainty" as operating ground rules while making use of the element of "surprise." Through convening meetings with the CEOs of America's leading corporations, he sought not only to reinforce the realities of "corporate rule," in both domestic and international affairs, but also to take decisive leadership in identifying what he thinks are the economic challenges that need to be resolved through direct action by the "captains of industry." In doing so, he positioned himself to be the "super dealmaker," economically and politically. By extending this rogue style of governance internationally as well as domestically, the Trump administration began, in effect, to turn America more and more into a "rogue empire."

One area where Trump's agenda and style of governance are undoubtedly having a significantly challenging impact is climate change and international efforts to mitigate it before its effects are irreversible. Part of Trump's rogue persona is his stance on climate change. Throughout his campaign for the Republican nomination and then the presidency, he repeatedly declared that climate change was a hoax perpetrated by the Chinese on the rest of the world. One of the cornerstones of his platform was the pledge to revive the coal industry and give coal miners their jobs back, even though international scientists had long since proven that the coal industry is a major cause of greenhouse gas emissions and the burning of the planet.

According to Trump, making America "great" again meant taking the United States out of the Paris climate accord and putting a priority on restoring Big Oil and the fossil fuel industry, including the construction and expansion of pipelines such as the Keystone XL. He vowed to overturn President Obama's Clean Power legislation and overhaul the EPA, especially its work to reduce greenhouse gas emissions, if not scrap it altogether. To ensure that this agenda was carried out, Trump's strategy for making cabinet appointments involved the strategic placement of climate change skeptics or deniers in key posts to oversee economic and environmental policy–making:

- Take, for example, Scott Pruitt. The former attorney general of Oklahoma had been suing the EPA for its action to reduce greenhouse gas emissions; until he resigned in July 2018, he was Trump's EPA director. Quipped one commentator, that was like "putting Darth Vader in charge of the Rebel Alliance."[35]
- For secretary of the interior, Trump chose Montana's Congressional representative Ryan Zinke, who holds the position that climate change may not be a hoax, but it has not been proven by science either. Given that federal lands contain 20 percent of remaining U.S. oil and gas reserves and 40 percent of remaining coal reserves, this cabinet post is of strategic importance to Trump and his "drill, drill, drill" plans.
- Trump's choice of the former governor of Texas, Rick Perry, to be secretary of energy was also strategic for those plans. In his 2012 campaign for the Republican presidential nomination, Perry famously called for the elimination of the Department of Energy. Under the Obama administration, the department had been given major responsibilities for climate mitigation and renewable or low-carbon energy sources.
- Topping this list of climate skeptics appointed to Trump

cabinet posts was Rex Tillerson, the secretary of state, arguably the most powerful cabinet position after the president.
As the former CEO of ExxonMobil, Tillerson was previously
known for having presided over the oil industry cover-up
of increasingly documented evidence from scientists about
climate change over the past four decades. Meanwhile,
Trump's later firing of Tillerson from his cabinet raised
new questions and speculation about what happens now
with the priority to rebuild the fossil fuel industry to "make
America great again."

On June 1, 2017, President Trump announced his administration's
intention to pull out of the Paris climate accord, which President
Obama had co-signed along with close to 200 other national governments in the fall of 2016. Although a formal withdrawal from the Paris
accord could take up to three or four years to implement, a more expe-
ditious exit strategy would be to directly withdraw from membership in
the *United Nations Framework Convention on Climate Change*.[36] Either
way, the departure of the world's second largest emitter of greenhouse
gases from the accord constitutes a major blow to the global struggle
against climate change, just as U.S. withdrawal from the Kyoto Protocol some two decades ago served to substantially weaken the international momentum that was then building.[37] The difference today, of
course, is that the stakes are now considerably higher.

Indeed, Trump's derailment of U.S. federal climate leadership leaves
a gaping hole when it comes to meeting, let alone surpassing, the Paris
climate accord's greenhouse gas emission reduction targets, both
domestic and international. Without Washington in the game, it is very
difficult to see how the United States will meet its target reductions
of 17 percent greenhouse gas emissions below 2005 levels by 2020, let
alone another 26 to 28 percent below 2005 levels by 2025.

And if Washington is not in the game, what will happen to China's
commitments to cap its industrial production by 2030, accelerate the
phase-out of its reliance on coal-burning power plants and make the

transition to hydroelectric, wind, solar and nuclear power? After all, a core component of the Paris accord process was the joint agreement between the United States and China — the world's two largest emitters — to reduce their emissions through targeted reductions by 2030 and beyond. Despite its shortcomings, this was the historic pact that created the conditions for the Paris prophecy. With Washington dropping out, it now remains to be seen what moves, if any, Beijing is willing and able to make to keep the Paris prophecy alive.

Trump's move to take the United States out of the Paris climate accord constitutes a death blow internationally to the Paris process itself. Although the accord remains far from perfect, one of its most valuable ingredients is what has been called its built-in "self-realizing prophecy." For its architects and supporters, explained Laurence Tubiana, the lead negotiator for France, the Paris accord's function is to send "unambiguous signals that the world will shift its economic and social activity toward more climate friendly and sustainable pathways."[38] In other words, the "momentum" generated by the accord will "inspire" the "transformational change" needed by all stakeholders, not only nation-states but also local governments, businesses, investors, non-governmental organizations, community groups and citizens at large.

Trump's removal of the United States from the Paris accord has delivered a crushing blow to this momentum. As Paris-based commentators Edouard Morena and Maxime Combes suggested, "by dropping out of the equation," the United States has turned "the Paris prophecy into a nightmare."[39]

Major Impacts of Economic Globalization on Climate Change

- Country commitments under international and bilateral trade and investment agreements are binding, whereas commitments under international environmental agreements are voluntary and non-binding.
- Global trade rules guaranteeing the free flow of capital,

goods and services trump environmental protection priorities. Although the WTO claims to be committed to "environmental protection" and "sustainable development," countries initiating environmental protection measures need to prove that their actions will not cause "arbitrary or unjustifiable discrimination" or pose a "disguised restriction on international trade."

- All over the world, foreign corporations are demanding large compensation payments from nation-states under investor-state mechanisms in international trade agreements, using these mechanisms to ratchet down national environmental regulations or eliminate them altogether.

- Emissions generated by producing a consumer product for export are attributed to the manufacturing country alone, even though the consumer demand resides in the importing country. Emissions generated by shipping the product or good from one country to another are not attributed to either country.

CHAPTER 3
Extractive Economy

A paradox lies at the heart of the relationship between Canada's political economy and the ecological challenges facing the future of our planet. To understand this paradox, we must explore the extractive heritage that underlies Canada's 150-year-old history as a country, along with the political, economic and environmental consequences that flow from it.

Extractivist Heritage

Canada is endowed with a wealth of natural resources, both renewable and non-renewable. The extractive model of production that emerged in the colonial crucibles of European empires and their expansion to the New World entailed a form of private 'accumulation through exploitation' of these resources. Long before the European occupation, Indigenous peoples (First Nations, Inuit and later Métis) developed economies and cultivated societies based on a fundamentally different understanding of the relationship between people and nature — one in which such natural resources were considered part of the "commons," for public use to promote communal wealth and well-being.[1]

European economic powers, however, viewed Canada as a storehouse of raw materials required for their own industrial development and expansion. Consequently, instead of developing along more diversified lines based on a balanced mix of resource, manufacturing and service sectors, Canada's economy was primarily based on the appropriation, extraction and exploitation of the country's natural resources.

The first wave of occupation in what would become Canada came from the French empire in the seventeenth century, followed by the British empire in the eighteenth and nineteenth centuries. The primary purpose of European settlement in Canada was to provide a resource colony for these powers. Fish and furs were the initial staple products exported to Britain and France, followed by wheat and timber. Then, during the key decades of the Industrial Revolution, substantial deposits of minerals required for steel production were opened up, extracted and transported to Europe. Soon thereafter, U.S. canal systems and railway lines were constructed to transport and deliver these raw materials to seaports for ships to carry them to Europe or trains to take them to diverse parts of the United States. Through this process, a series of staple products became the driving forces that spurred on successive stages of economic development in this country.

During the postwar era of the twentieth century, Canada's imperial linkage as a major resource supplier shifted from Britain to America. The prime raw material exports to the United States included hydroelectric power, timber products, oil and natural gas and a variety of strategic minerals. Enormous investments were made in infrastructure, such as pipelines, power generators and railways, to transport and deliver these resources to U.S. processing industries.

By the turn of this century, Canada had become America's main foreign energy supplier, providing 100 percent of U.S. hydroelectric power imports and 94 percent of natural gas imports and challenging Saudi Arabia's position as lead foreign supplier of oil. As a result of this further reorientation and realignment of the economy, Canada is serving as a resource colony of the United States, now the world's leading imperial power. Moreover, under the "proportional sharing clause" incorporated into the free trade regimes of 1989 and 1994, Canada is legally obligated to continue exporting this energy at the same rate even if public policy decisions are made in this country to cut back on fossil fuel production and consumption.[2] We have come to the point of a reckoning over Canada's ongoing role (and impact) as an extractive economy and society.

Extractivism — Economic Fallout

Harold Innis, one of Canada's best known political economists, studied and wrote extensively on extractive economies and models of resource development, often using Canada as a prime case.[3] More specifically, Innis's work focused on Canada's traditional role as a supplier of raw materials, or what he called "staples," through exports to industrial powers. He labelled these powers the "centres" and the resource suppliers at the "margins" of the global economy. Through Innis's work, a school of thought emerged in the twentieth century that has helped us better understand the strengths and weaknesses, along with the opportunities and risks, involved in an economic model that is primarily based on extracting natural resources and supplying raw materials to industrial powers in the global economy.[4]

In developing this analysis of Canada's economic history, Innis and his followers highlighted what Mel Watkins and others later called the "staples trap."[5] This trap has several characteristics[6]:

- The belief that resource extraction and export must be the cornerstone of economic development in a country that possesses natural resources is widely promoted. Powerful political interests, including government leaders, public policy–makers, corporate leaders in resource and other industries and media personalities play a major role in promoting this belief.
- The economy is designed for export-oriented production and is primarily geared to extracting and exporting raw materials to serve the consumer demands of industrial

powers rather than producing the products or goods required to serve domestic needs.

- Unprocessed or barely processed raw materials that are extracted and transported to more advanced industrialized economies are then transformed into value-added products. These products are then sold back to consumers in resource-supply economies, generally at much higher prices.

- Production and development follow a "boom-and-bust" pattern, often provoked by the volatility of commodity prices on world markets. Sudden and dramatic swings from high to low prices on these markets for the resource products being extracted result in production slowdowns and worker layoffs, which then generates uneven patterns of economic development and income distribution.

- Staple economies are required to make heavy, upfront investments in technology for the extraction of the resource and in infrastructure (e.g., canals, railways, pipelines) for delivery of the raw materials to markets. As a result of these fixed costs, staple- or resource-based economies tend to function in a more rigid and inflexible manner in response to changes in priorities and demands within the global economy.

- Staple economies rely on centralized resource corporations, both domestic and global, which have the capacity to develop the required technology and infrastructure and the organizational and financial wherewithal to deal with major overhead costs. To pay off these costs and reward investors, an extractive economy will put greater priority on rapidly selling more and more of its staple.

- In the medium to long term, the strategy of producing and exporting the staple at an ever-faster rate is both expensive and self-defeating. Not only does rapid export drive down the unit cost of a staple, but also changes in technology and consumer tastes in the markets of industrial powers can suddenly reduce demand.

- Reinforcing their initial beliefs, the political masters of an extractive economy tend to become more rigid in defending and protecting the staple industry. Rather than reducing dependency on production of the staple and diversifying the economy, priority is put on extracting and exporting more of the staple or searching for a substitute. Either way, the staples trap becomes further entrenched.

Figure 3.1 The "Staples Trap" of Extractive Economies

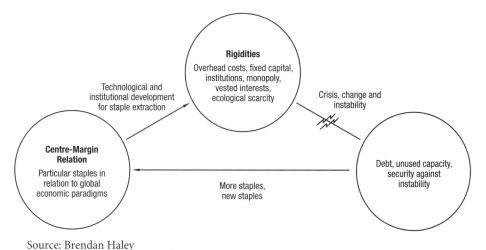

Source: Brendan Haley

Figure 3.1, originally developed by Canadian political economist Brendan Haley, illustrates how the staples trap operates.[7] This brings us back to the essence of an extractive society and culture. Extractivism is essentially a mode of being in relationship with Earth and nature. As Naomi Klein explained, extractivism is a mentality of "taking and taking without giving back":

> *Extractivism is a nonreciprocal, dominance-based*
> *relationship with the earth, one purely of taking. It is the*
> *opposite of stewardship, which involves taking but also*

taking care that regeneration and future life continue.
Extractivism is the mentality of the mountaintop remover
and the old-growth clear-cutter. It is the reduction of
life into objects for the use of others, giving them no
integrity or value of their own — turning living complex
ecosystems into "natural resources," mountains into
"overburden" (as the mining industry terms the forests,
rocks and streams that get in the way of its bulldozers).
It is also the reduction of human beings either into
labour to be brutally extracted, pushed beyond limits, or,
alternatively, into social burden, problems to be locked
out at borders and locked away in prisons or reservations.
In an extractivist economy, the interconnections amongst
these various components of life are ignored; the
consequences of severing them are of no concern.[8]

Indeed, our extractive economy is the centrepiece of the Canadian paradox and the core factor standing in the way of effective action to mitigate against runaway climate change. Reviving the extractive economic model, as former Canadian prime minister Stephen Harper encouraged, not only reactivates the mentality of being a resource colony for imperial powers but also makes our economic future even more vulnerable. Until and unless a determined political commitment is made to transform our economic model — by structurally balancing the major sectors of the economy (i.e., resource, manufacturing, services), diversifying the economy as a whole and making it much more innovative — the key structural deficiencies will remain in place.

Extractivism — Political Fallout

Canadians should also be concerned about the political factors that reinforce Canada's role as an extractive economy. This has to do with the public policy–making apparatus on energy priorities, which has become increasingly dominated over the past half-century or more by the petroleum industry. In an extractive economy, political and economic elites tend to coalesce and co-ordinate their activities to promote, protect and defend the extraction, development and export of its prime staple. Throughout Canada's economic history, various political and economic players have promoted the production of key staples of the times, such as wheat, hydroelectric power or particular minerals. The pattern continues today, when a close collaboration between the petroleum industry and governments, both provincial and federal, supports the production and export of bitumen for crude oil from the tar sands.

In her book *The Paradox of Plenty*, Terry Lynn Karl coined the term *petro-states* to describe this phenomenon.[9] A distinguishing feature of petro-states, she said, is the disproportionate amount of power and influence the petroleum industry exercises over various forms of public policy–making, to the detriment of other sectors of the economy and society. Viewed through this lens, it can be argued that a petro-state model of governance has emerged, in varying ways, both in Alberta, as the main producing province, and federally in Ottawa.

Although the stage was initially set over a century ago through the massive land grab of Indigenous peoples' territory via Treaty 8 in 1899, the seeds of the "petrolization" of governance, as Karl called it, were planted when the Alberta government initiated its Athabasca land-leasing program in 1951, granting oil companies and their investors prospecting and development rights for bitumen at rock bottom fees (initially $1 per acre, later reduced to 25 cents).[10]

As Larry Pratt documented in his seminal work *The Tar Sands*, the two major players that emerged were Suncor, initially the largest producer of bitumen-based oil in the tar sands, and Syncrude, a consortium of U.S. and Canadian oil companies.[11] The Syncrude consortium took the lead in mounting a powerful lobbying campaign, provincially and federally, between 1972 and 1975. Policy issues on the Syncrude agenda included pricing, taxation, environmental regulations, labour legislation and related policies and programs affecting the extraction and export of bitumen. One of the consortium's major victories during this period was to persuade both federal and provincial governments to provide the burgeoning tar sands industry with generous subsidies and to underwrite much of the risk associated with bitumen production. The government received little or nothing in return; more public control over this new industry and its development, for example, was not on the table. The basic ground rules governing the relationship between governments and the petroleum industry had been established, and the petro-state model gradually took shape.[12]

Although Syncrude and Suncor continue to dominate the Canadian tar sands industry, they have long since been joined by other players from the oil patch, including some Canadian-based companies, such as Canadian Natural Resources Ltd. and Petro-Canada, along with pipeline companies such as Enbridge and TransCanada. Most of the new players, however, have been international conglomerates.[13]

The first decade and a half of the twenty-first century has seen several waves of foreign takeovers. The first wave came from large oil conglomerates in the United States, including ExxonMobil, ConocoPhillips and Chevron Texaco, plus smaller oil companies such as Marathon Oil and Occidental Petroleum. The second wave consisted of major European Union oil companies such as Shell Oil and BP based in the United Kingdom, Total SA from France and Statoil from Norway. More recently, a third wave has emerged involving China's state-owned oil companies — Sinopec Corporation, China Investment Corporation and China National Offshore Oil Corporation — which have made significant investments. Other Asian oil companies, such as Malaysia's state-owned PETRONAS, Korea's National Oil Corporation and the Thai oil company PTTEP, have all purchased facilities and operations in the Athabasca tar sands.

Canada's position as a petro-state has taken on a peculiar and unique shape in comparison with others. Not only are the central players in the Canadian model, the major petroleum companies, from the private sector, but they are also largely dominated by foreign-owned corporations. The degree of power exercised by the petroleum companies and the tar sands industry itself in the affairs of the Canadian state becomes more evident when we look at their lobbying machinery and how they use it.[14]

Each of the Big Oil extractive corporations and pipeline companies has its own professional in-house lobbyists. The system itself is largely based on the proverbial "revolving door" that exists between senior government offices and high-level positions in petroleum companies. Through this mechanism, senior personnel in both petroleum companies and the federal government (the Prime Minister's Office and specific departments, such as Natural Resources Canada) exchange positions on a regular basis.[15] In addition to their in-house lobbyists, most of the corporations are clients of prominent lobbying firms on Parliament Hill. Professional lobbying firms with major oil industry corporations among their top clients include the Earnscliffe Strategy Group, Hill+Knowlton Strategies, Global Public Affairs and TACTIX Government Relations and Public Affairs.[16]

Two industry associations, the Canadian Association of Petroleum Producers and the Canadian Energy Pipeline Association, also wield considerable influence and power in Ottawa. Both of these work hand-in-glove with their member companies to promote their agendas. For example, the petroleum association's lobbying campaigns are frequently reinforced by producers in the tar sands such as Suncor and Imperial Oil; the pipeline association's lobbying agenda is further advanced by major pipeline companies such as Enbridge and TransCanada.

Through these lobbying campaigns, the tar sands industry is able to have relatively easy access to cabinet ministers, senior government officials and members of Parliament. This allows them to mount co-ordinated campaigns to directly influence relevant public policy and legislation. Moreover, the Canadian Association of Petroleum Producers has played a leading role in moulding public opinion through relentless television and radio ads heralding the achievements of the tar sands industry, the importance of pipelines to get their product to market and contributions the industry makes toward funding Canada's social programs and public services.

In 2018, however, the Canadian Association of Petroleum Producers took its political advertising to unprecedented levels. According to the Toronto Star's Investigative Unit (plus the National Observer and Global News), the organization targeted thirteen swing ridings in Ontario for a political advertising campaign to further promote federal government action on the construction of the Kinder Morgan Trans Mountain pipeline. Public rallies were organized and letters sent to 24,000 "key decision makers" in these ridings and elsewhere in the country. The campaign occurred between April 8 and May 29, 2018 — the period in which the Trudeau government was deciding what action to take to advance the construction of the Trans Mountain pipeline and the period leading up to the Ontario provincial election. As a result issues and questions of election tampering on the part of the Canadian Association of Petroleum Producers were raised.

As well, the petroleum industry exerts considerable power and influence over government regulatory bodies, notably the National Energy Board. Until recently, the board has been essentially mandated to review the economic and technical feasibility of building proposed energy infrastructure projects such as pipelines and make recommendations to the federal government, in the "national interest." The board has not been mandated to factor in, let alone focus on, what impacts such energy projects will have on Canada's obligations and commitments for reducing greenhouse gas emissions and fossil fuel use or impacts on Indigenous peoples and their communities.

The National Energy Board's 2016 *Canada's Energy Future* report offers ample evidence. As Greenpeace analyst Keith Stewart pointed out, the board's report on Canada's energy future was heavily biased toward the oil industry. Its underlying assumption was that "over the long term, energy production will find markets and infrastructure will be built as needed."[17] It ignored government measures to reduce the demand for fossil fuels, such as the federal carbon tax. Instead, the report "assumes that world demand for oil increases endlessly," despite other forecasts of demand peaking by the beginning of the 2020s as a result of climate policies and strategies being developed by governments following the Paris accord. "Tar sands production will somehow grow by 72 percent" in this country, the board stated.[18] Not surprisingly, the board has become a target of resistance for citizen groups engaged in various regional pipeline and climate struggles across the country.[19]

Finally, this petro-state machinery is reinforced by trade regimes such as NAFTA and its successors. As mentioned above, under the so-called proportional sharing rule, Canada is compelled to provide the United States with a continuous supply of energy (primarily raw bitumen or heavy crude oil, natural gas and hydroelectric power) through exports. Under Article 315, it is compulsory for Canada, even in an emergency, to continue its energy exports to the United States in the same proportion of its total supply as the average of the previous three years. Article 605 reinforces Article 315 by ensuring that petroleum companies continue to export raw bitumen rather than refining the bitumen into value-added products before proceeding to export.[20]

NAFTA's Chapter 11 adds another enforcement mechanism, an investor-state procedure granting corporations the right to sue the governments of member countries for alleged violations of the NAFTA rules and other related measures that undermine the profitability of their foreign-owned operations.[21] Under NAFTA's dispute settlement mechanism, suits by corporations against governments are adjudicated by NAFTA tribunals appointed by the three member governments; the NAFTA rules take precedence over the domestic laws of the country being sued.

Harper's "Energy Superpower"

Canada's economy was not always destined to remain a resource colony for industrial empires.[22] Before the recent waves of economic globalization spurred on by the new free trade regimes, Canada's economy was actually beginning to move in an alternative direction. In addition to being a major resource supplier, in the 1960s, Canada began to build a diversified and productive industrial base by spawning and nurturing higher-value industries and more sophisticated products.

Three significant value-added manufacturing industries — automotive, aerospace and telecommunications — emerged during this period. By the mid-1990s, for the first time in this country's economic history, unprocessed or barely processed resources accounted for less than half of total Canadian exports. By 1999, Canada was producing as much manufactured output as the country consumed, thereby providing the basis for balancing imports and exports of manufactured goods.

Over the past three to four decades, however, extractive economies have been revitalized, accelerated and intensified through the processes of economic globalization (deregulation, privatization and free trade) briefly discussed in Chapter 2. The Harper regime contributed greatly to reviving this country's heritage as an extractivist economy.[23] In his first international speech as prime minister in July 2006, Harper addressed a blue chip audience of investors at Canada House in London and announced that his government "intends to build . . . a global energy powerhouse," the centrepiece of which would be the tar sands of Alberta, his home province.[24]

Suddenly, elites in Washington saw the development of the Alberta tar sands as a strategic priority for U.S. energy security and a counter to their continuing dependency on imports from the Middle East, notably Saudi Arabia. Instead of heeding the threats of climate change by focusing on developing Canada as a powerhouse in renewable energy, Harper proceeded to lock the country into a political and economic trajectory for the twenty-first century based on the extraction and export of fossil fuels. As a consequence, this was the moment when the tar sands industry became Canada's fastest-growing global warming machine.

Ten years later, the tar sands industry had slipped into a bust period due to the nosedive in global oil prices while, at the same time, U.S. demand for Canadian oil had diminished as a result of the discovery of new technologies, such as hydraulic fracking for the extraction and production of shale oil and gas. As a result, thousands of workers in Canada's tar sands were laid off.

Apart from the Harper government's focus on extracting natural resources, other factors contributed to Canada's reorientation as an extractivist economy. Although a shift toward more industrialization had taken place, compared to other industrialized countries, Canada's economy remained relatively dependent on the extraction and export of raw materials during the first decade of the twenty-first century. With increasingly high commodity prices after the turn of the century, conditions were created for both an expansion of resource exports and a decline in value-added exports.

By 2011, the proportion of Canada's total exports consisting of unprocessed or barely processed resources had risen to almost two thirds from 40 percent in 1999. By 2012, Canada had become a major net importer of manufactured goods, with a national trade deficit in manufactured merchandise of $90 billion. In other words, the country's merchandise trade balance had been undone and the nation's economic evolution had more or less been reversed.[25]

Spurred on by Stephen Harper's economic vision of this country as the world's next energy superpower, Canada's economy effectively fell backwards into its traditional role as a resource colony for industrial empires and powers. The cornerstone of the Harper economic vision, the mega-development of the Athabasca tar sands, had to be protected at all costs. Possessing the second largest hydrocarbon deposit in the world, the tar sands industry had planned to expand production threefold from roughly two to six million barrels a day for export by 2030. Working closely with the petroleum industry, the Harper regime attempted to somewhat diversify its options as Canada's imperial masters now included China as well as the United States. The Keystone XL pipeline was to be the new delivery mechanism for bitumen to the United States, whereas the Northern Gateway was to serve the same purpose for China.

As economist Jim Stanford has shown, the priority put on developing, expanding and protecting the tar sands industry generated several disturbing distortions in the Canadian economy (see Table 3.1) during the bitumen boom. More recently, these became further magnified under more bust-like conditions.[26]

Table 3.1 Economic Distortions

Employment impacts: Over the decade ending in 2011, the highly capital-intensive petroleum industry accounted for less than 1 percent of all new jobs created. For every new job created in the petroleum sector, 30 were lost in manufacturing. Shifting $1 billion of GDP from manufacturing to petroleum production has the effect of losing 9,000 net jobs in the Canadian economy.

Income disparities: Although petroleum workers are generally well paid, they do not capture a fair share of the wealth they produce in terms of wages, salaries and benefits. As a share of the industry's total output, labour incomes are uniquely low, whereas corporate profits are disproportionately high.

International trade: Despite considerable increases in bitumen exports during the boom period, Canada's overall trade export performance declined substantially. Measured as a share of GDP, the decline in non-petroleum exports was 8.5 times greater than exports of petroleum products, thereby generating a chronic current accounts deficit.

Currency effects: Expanding bitumen production, coupled with high commodity prices and rising profit margins for the petroleum industry, caused the market value of Canadian petroleum (and mining) companies to surge, which inflated the value of the loonie on world money markets. Compared to other currencies, the loonie's purchasing power was overvalued by 25 percent.

Manufacturing crisis: Between 2001 and 2011, the manufacturing sector lost 520,000 jobs, dropping to 10 percent of total employment, the lowest level in postwar history. In 1999, Canada was the fourth largest auto assembler in the world, with a $15 billion trade surplus in auto parts. By 2011, more than 50,000 well-paid jobs were lost as auto plants shut down; we also developed a chronic automotive trade deficit of $15 billion.

Foreign investment: Over a third of the assets and more than half of the operating revenues in Canada's petroleum industry are held by foreign companies. Yet inflows of foreign finance reinforce links between world oil prices and Canada's currency, which impacts manufacturing exports, whereas outflow payments of interest, dividends and profits to foreign owners cause a deterioration in our current account balance.

These economic distortions have emerged during the latest bitumen boom and the restoration of Canada's extractive economy. The sharp decline in world oil prices during 2014–15 and the bitumen slide from boom to bust conditions served as a rude awakening to the pitfalls of reorganizing and restructuring Canada as an extractive economy mainly based on a single staple.[27]

Perhaps the most far-reaching impact of petro-governance occurred between 2011 and 2012 when the Harper government, now with a majority in Parliament, developed and enacted two omnibus pieces of legislation. Bill C-38, which was supposed to implement the 2012 federal budget, was broadened extensively to amend some 70 other pieces of existing legislation, most of which were environmental laws, programs and regulations that stood in the way of advancing the tar sands industry.[28] Bill C-45, designed to implement both the federal government's 2012 budget and its 2012 *Jobs and Growth Act*, included a series of amendments aimed at removing other laws and programs that, for example, protected the rights of Indigenous peoples but also posed obstacles to the tar sands industry. In other words, this legislative tool was deployed to advance the interests of the petro-state, overriding environmental protection and Indigenous rights. A subsequent study by the Polaris Institute, using data from the Office of the Commissioner of Lobbying, showed that the Big Oil producers and pipeline companies plus their industry lobbyists had direct access to cabinet ministers and senior government officials during this period — estimated to be 473 times that of environmental organizations and First Nations.[29]

Similarly, U.S. pipeline companies such as Kinder Morgan mounted a sustained and successful lobbying campaign to win federal government approval for their Trans Mountain project. According to research conducted by the corporate mapping project of the Canadian Centre for Policy Alternatives in British Columbia, officials from Kinder Morgan and its subsidiary Trans Mountain had 826 communications with key policy-making officials in both the federal and B.C. governments over the six-year period leading up to the prime minister's announcement of his government's approval for the proposed Trans Mountain pipeline. This amounts to approximately one contact with senior government officials every two business days during this period.

Between February 2011 and October 2016, spanning the Harper and Trudeau governments, Kinder Morgan and its subsidiary had 368 meetings with federal officials. In the crucial 10 months of 2016 prior to federal cabinet approval, "Kinder Morgan Canada initiated 47 meetings with ministry representatives, and Trans Mountain initiated an additional 14. The targets of these meetings included senior policy advisors within the Ministry of Natural Resources and the Prime Minister's Office, and the chiefs of staff for Fisheries and Oceans Canada, Environment and Climate Change Canada, and Natural Resources Canada."[30] Needless to say, nowhere near the same amounts of public resources were spent on consultations with affected communities, Indigenous peoples and environmental groups.

Trudeau's "Alternative" Solution

When the Trudeau Liberals came to power in October 2015, they initially showed a willingness to provide leadership on climate change issues, in contrast to the Harper Conservatives. In signing on to the Paris climate accord, the Trudeau government pledged not only to cut the country's total annual greenhouse gas emissions 30 percent by 2030 (as had the Harper government) but also to develop a concrete action plan with the provinces, territories and cities to get us there.

However, documents released by the Trudeau government at the First Ministers' Conference in early December 2016 were sorely lacking in concrete targets and benchmarks to be achieved by 2020, let alone between 2020 and 2030. Nor was any agreement with the provinces and territories reached on how such targets and benchmarks would be set and evaluated.

Moreover, just a few weeks before the conference, the Trudeau Liberals announced their decision to expand the fossil fuel industry in Canada by approving construction of a liquefied natural gas terminal in British Columbia, plus two pipelines to transport tar sands crude to refineries in the United States and to tidewater for delivery to Asian markets. When the construction of the Keystone XL pipeline (endorsed by then newly elected U.S. President Trump) was added to these approvals, the Trudeau government was, in effect, greenlighting the generation of almost 90 million tonnes of greenhouse gas emissions a year, wiping out whatever gains it claimed to have made elsewhere in reducing emissions.

In essence, the Trudeau government appears to be following in the footsteps of the Harper regime. The government has apparently decided that it can live with this fundamental contradiction: expanding the fossil fuel industry as the largest emitter of greenhouse gas emissions on the one hand, while appearing to reduce the country's national emissions annually in line with its commitments to international targets on the other. As Indigenous activist Clayton Thomas Muller from 350.org quipped, "Real climate leaders don't build pipelines." Rather than firmly commit to the urgent need of making the transition away from a fossil-fuelled economy to one fuelled by clean, renewable energy sources, the Trudeau government has seemingly opted in favour of maintaining our largely oil-based export economy. Under such leadership, Canada will remain locked into an economic model primarily based on extractivism, at least for the foreseeable future.

Meanwhile, domestic battle lines have also been drawn over multiple pipeline projects designed to move tar sands crude to markets elsewhere in Canada and internationally. Two pipeline projects stand out: TransCanada's Energy East project, cancelled by the company in October 2017, and Kinder Morgan's Trans Mountain project. Trans-Canada's project proposed to transport tar sands crude from northern Alberta across the prairies via existing pipeline networks into Ontario and Quebec, from which new pipeline extensions would be built to carry on moving the crude to markets in eastern Quebec and the Atlantic provinces. The Kinder Morgan project plans to transport tar sands crude from northern Alberta through the Rocky Mountain range down into Vancouver and the Burrard Inlet, where it will be loaded into tankers for shipment across the Pacific Ocean to markets in Asia.

Both pipeline projects faced stiff popular opposition from First Nations and organized community groups along most of their routes. Both were actively opposed by municipal governments, led by successive Montreal mayors Denis Coderre and Valérie Plante and Vancouver mayor Gregor Robertson.

In November 2016, the Trudeau government decided to greenlight the Kinder Morgan Trans Mountain pipeline, along with Enbridge's Line 3 pipeline, which would transport tar sands crude to Wisconsin for eastern U.S. markets. This has served to further revive Canada's role as an extractive economy and slide it back into the staples trap. The Trudeau government appears to have bought into the argument that the tar sands industry can be saved by building new pipelines and expanding production.

But as Jeff Rubin, former chief economist and strategist at CIBC World Markets, pointed out, oil sands crude is a very costly fuel to produce and transport, making it increasingly "uneconomic." Since bitumen requires being "mixed with diluent to move through pipelines" plus "significantly more upgrading and refining before it can be converted into finished products like gasoline or diesel," said Rubin, "oil sands crude is an inferior fuel" compared to its competition. Moreover, said Rubin, "overseas markets typically pay less for bitumen and other forms of heavy oil than the U.S. Gulf Coast, home of the world's largest heavy-oil refinery hub."[31] In other words, the contention that getting tar sands crude to tidewater will bring higher prices is largely false.

Rubin offered the example of Mexico's Mayan crude, which fetches significantly higher prices from the U.S. Gulf Coast than it does from European or Asian refineries. In short, there is no reason why European and Asian refineries would pay higher prices for Alberta bitumen, let alone more than Gulf Coast prices.[32] Furthermore, Rubin warned that "the price differentials for bitumen and heavy oil between overseas markets and the Gulf Coast could even worsen."[33] Even if the tar sands industry could capture the same world oil prices that light conventional oil does now, it would still not be enough to render economic the bulk of current production and "virtually all planned increases in oil sands production," especially in a carbon-constrained world. Only "a very significant and sustained recovery" in world oil prices could make the tar sands have a commercially viable future.[34]

Carbon Lock-in

The tar sands industry not only exhibits all the characteristics of a staples trap but also has become the prime example of a "carbon trap" in the country's economy.

Just before the Paris climate summit, the Alberta government released its "Climate Leadership Plan," worked out with the petroleum industry and several public interest groups, in November 2015. The Alberta plan projected a 41 percent increase in allowable greenhouse gas emissions by 2020 through expanded production and delivery. Consequently, bitumen production in Alberta's Athabasca region constitutes both the largest single sector and the fastest-growing sector of the Canadian economy emitting greenhouse gases.

This carbon lock-in or trap of bitumen production adds a whole new dimension to Canada's extractive economy and our understanding of the challenges we have to face. Let's examine a few characteristics and elements of this carbon lock-in[35]:

- The extraction and upgrading process for bitumen require burning natural gas, thus generating close to three times the quantity of greenhouse gas emissions per barrel of crude as conventional oil production.
- The tar sands industry's strip-mining operations have already destroyed much of the boreal forest in the region, nature's sink for storing carbon.
- Despite the production cap negotiated between the Alberta government and the oil industry limiting expansion on bitumen production to 100 million tonnes by 2020, greenhouse gas emissions from the tar sands are expected to grow, reaching 115 million tonnes by 2030. In effect, the tar sands industry is allowed to increase its emissions, whereas other industries are urged to reduce theirs.[36]
- The tar sands industry is expected to account for over 100 percent of Canada's projected increase in total greenhouse gas emissions between 2005 and 2020. As carbon emissions from the expanding bitumen production in the Athabasca continue to rise dramatically, they will effectively wipe out the gains made in other provinces and sectors of the economy, including important steps taken by Ontario and Alberta to phase out their coal-fired generators.
- Commitments by the petroleum industry to plough ahead with several of the big pipeline plans for bitumen delivery (especially Trans Mountain) will lock the country and the economy into a rigid cycle of bitumen production for export, resulting in ongoing carbon pollution. The staples trap basically ensures that there will be more and more built-in pressures to prioritize bitumen extraction and pipeline construction for delivery to markets.
- The carbon lock-in also basically nullifies traditional strategies for escaping from the staples trap itself, which usually entails secondary processing of the resource or staple for value-added production before export. Although Canada

could benefit from developing new industries to upgrade and refine bitumen for various oil products to sell here and in export markets, this strategy would do nothing to address the climate change challenge. We would still have the greenhouse gas emissions from extracting and upgrading the bitumen, along with added emissions from the new secondary processing sectors.

• The "staples mentality," which promotes the belief that bitumen production and export offer a golden opportunity for Canadian economic development, prevails in elite political and economic circles throughout the country. Those who advocate alternative strategies are often dismissed as being naïve, radical and even dangerous. This mentality continues to play a key role in minimizing, if not denying, the realities of climate change and the challenges it poses to our prevailing economic model.

In the age of climate change, when the entire global economy must take radical action to reduce greenhouse gas emissions to avert climate chaos, Canada's economy is tied to the production and export of one of the most carbon-intensive resources in the world. Instead of joining other countries in developing concrete strategies for transitioning to a low-carbon economic future, Canada has been and still is moving in the opposite direction.

A Costly Gamble

If there was any doubt about this assessment, it was dispelled by the Trudeau government's decision in late November 2016 to greenlight Kinder Morgan's Trans Mountain and Enbridge's Line 3 pipeline projects, in addition to earlier approvals granted to the PETRONAS liquefied natural gas terminal project in British Columbia and the Keystone XL pipeline. The amount of upstream greenhouse gas emissions from these projects added to Canada's total annual emissions comes to 88.9 million tonnes.[37] This more than cancels out all the gains made through measures taken by the Trudeau government and the provinces since the Paris summit, such as coal phase-outs, carbon pricing, fuel standard regulations and methane and hydrofluorocarbon regulations (81.7 million tonnes annually). When the downstream impacts are factored in, the four projects identified above will together generate greenhouse gas emissions amounting to well over 100 million tonnes.[38] Depending on both pipeline capacity plus the type of fuel being transported, the midstream and downstream emissions from oil or gas projects like this may account for over 80 percent of emissions. Thus, Canada's approval of these four projects alone sends a signal to the rest of the world, sanctioning the expansion of the fossil fuel industry in an age of runaway climate change.

A staples economy that plays the role of resource supplier in the global economy is linked to the development priorities and patterns of other national economies, notably the industrial powers. By approving more pipelines to get bitumen to tidewater (plus liquefied natural gas terminals and more fracking) while developing a climate leadership plan to reduce greenhouse gas emissions for the country, the Trudeau government has "betrayed" a lot of people who supported them in the 2015 election said environmental activist Tzeporah Berman. "I think a lot of us who knocked on doors for the Trudeau government," said Berman, "really believed them when they said they were going to bring evidence based analysis and science and democratic process back to pipeline reviews."[39] Yet, sooner or later, the negatives outweigh the positives — market opportunities to sell dirty energy in a carbon-constrained world soon dry up, leaving bitumen-producing countries such as Canada on the losing end, economically and environmentally.

In June 2016, Global Sustainability Research Inc. president David Hughes, an earth scientist and geologist who has written extensively on fossil fuel production, released a report called *Can Canada Expand Oil and Gas Production, Build Pipelines and Keep its Climate Change Commitments?*[40] In short, his conclusion was "no" given current measures and federal government approvals for pipeline expansion projects. According to Hughes's calculations, based on Environment Canada's own projections, by 2030, Canada's greenhouse gas emission levels will be 55 percent higher than the level it committed to in signing the Paris accord. This assumes that tar sands production is held at the 100 million tonne cap level by 2020, as negotiated by the Alberta government, and that the former B.C. government's plans for the liquefied natural gas industry proceed. If so, then by 2030, Hughes predicted that the oil and gas sector will account for 53 percent of Canada's annual emissions. The choice to safeguard oil and gas production would increasingly put enormous pressure on the non–oil and gas sectors to accelerate their emission reductions to close the gap leading up to 2030.

Not only does Canada remain out of step with many other countries in making the transition needed to become a low-to-zero carbon economy, but the rigidities of the staples trap also create blinders and obstacles for policy-makers. Despite a change in government, developing plans for more and more pipelines to deliver the bitumen extracted to markets remains a priority. The more investments are made in building up this infrastructure, the more the fixed costs are absorbed by the economy and the more bitumen must be sold to pay for these costs. As a result, it becomes increasingly important for the Canadian economy that the industrial centres of the global economy continue their dependence on fossil fuels.

When Justin Trudeau's Liberals won their majority government in October 2015, there was a considerable amount of excitement and optimism among concerned citizens who sought a better Canada — economically, socially, environmentally — in terms of both domestic and international affairs. The removal of the decade-old Harper regime evoked a sigh of relief. Gone from public policy–making, at least federally, were the climate change deniers who believed global warming was a great hoax or conspiracy and who therefore refused to develop serious programs and strategies to combat it. Gone too was the mythical dream of Canada becoming a global energy superpower through the expansion of its fossil fuel industries. There was much hope that the change would soon translate into substantial reductions in greenhouse gases. The newly minted Trudeau government fuelled these hopes as it made its first major international foray on the eve of the Paris climate summit in December 2015, declaring that "Canada is back!"

Since becoming prime minister, Trudeau has frequently signalled his government's desire to become a "leader" on climate issues. He's declared that Canada will do its part in keeping global warming to well below the 2-degree Celsius threshold. In signing the Paris climate agreement, he committed Canada to developing a roadmap for a 30 percent reduction in carbon greenhouse gases by 2030. In addition, this roadmap would include the complete phase-out by 2030 of coal to fire up electrical generators and the introduction of a national carbon tax to reach $50 per tonne by 2022.

He also pledged to cultivate a new relationship with Indigenous peoples in this country, keeping in mind climate challenges and resource development issues; revamp the role, composition and responsibilities of the National Energy Board in making decisions on pipeline proposals and submit each pipeline proposal to a climate test as part of evaluating and determining whether or not the projects were "in the national interest." Although the promises conveyed through these messages were initially welcomed by many Canadians as a sign of a new political era in Canada, the concrete actions taken thus far do not measure up to the lofty words.

Efforts to reduce greenhouse gas emissions in Canada continue to be cancelled out by the increase and expansion of fossil fuel production. The government simply has not come to grips with the fact that the prime cause of runaway climate change, the fossil fuel industry, is firmly entrenched at the centre of both the Canadian and the global economy. As long as this country's economy is primarily based on an extractivist model, producing and exporting oil and minerals to serve the demands of major industrialized and industrializing countries, we can expect to face major obstacles due to the built-in staples trap and carbon lock-in, reinforced by the apparatus of a petro-state. Moreover, these obstacles will further multiply unless multilateral trade and investment rules in the global economy (see Chapter 2) are revamped to promote and facilitate the transition to a carbon-constrained world.

CHAPTER 4
Net-Zero Challenge

The Paris climate summit upped the ante on the worldwide climate challenge in the twenty-first century. Instead of the previously adopted 2-degree ceiling on temperature increases above preindustrial levels this century, governments throughout the world shifted to a new threshold, declaring that global temperatures must be held to no more than 1.5 degrees Celsius to preserve life as we know it.

However, given the pledges currently made by nation-states for greenhouse gas reductions between now and 2030, the planet is on course for a global temperature rise of more than 3 degrees Celsius in that time frame. Furthermore, many countries, including Canada, have traditionally fallen short of realizing such pledges. If business-as-usual scenarios are maintained, global temperatures could well rise by intolerable levels of 4 or even 5 degrees Celsius by the end of the twenty-first century. Already by 2016, the hottest year ever recorded to that point, the global thermometer had risen by 1.2 degrees Celsius during the relatively short period since the beginning of this century. In other words, the planet's temperature rise is already rapidly closing in on the 1.5-degree danger zone. By 2020, with four fifths of the century still ahead of us, the heating process will have already entered the 1.5-degree red zone.

For Canada, the challenge is even more pronounced than for most other countries. Many have argued that Canada is, relatively speaking, a bit player in the climate change sweepstakes as we account for less than 2 percent of global greenhouse gas emissions. However, because of our dependence on the fossil fuel industry in terms of our economy (both production and consumption), along with our geographic proximity to the Arctic and its fragile ecology, Canada has an outsized overall impact on planetary heating. Given the extensive burning of natural gas for the extraction and upgrading of bitumen in northern Alberta, which, in turn, contributes greatly to melting the tundra in the Northwest Territories, that releases methane (a greenhouse gas 85 times more potent than carbon dioxide) — the Arctic ice caps are now losing 30 percent of their average sea ice every year.[1]

This Arctic meltdown threatens to result in rising sea levels, causing massive flooding of coastal cities worldwide. Characterizing Canada as a bit player also fails to acknowledge that it is locked into an extractive economy, which is now highly dependent on protecting and expanding the fossil fuel industry. However you look at it, Canada is a major player in the global warming sweepstakes.

No Credible Plan

Despite its rhetoric, the Trudeau government simply does not yet have a credible action plan for making the transition from a carbon-intensive economy to a net-zero carbon economy. The Trudeau Liberals are doing what Liberal governments have always done: playing the left and the right against each other before coming up the middle. But this strategy won't work in confronting climate change. As discussed in Chapter 2, climate change is unlike any other challenge faced by public policy–makers. It is nature's ticking time bomb, moving now at a pace that even confounds many climate scientists.

Nor, for that matter, does any other major Canadian political party have a credible action plan for moving forward in the coming decade, let alone between now and mid-century. Both of the major opposition parties were embroiled in leadership races in 2017 — normally an ideal time to develop and debate fresh ideas. Yet little or no real progress appears to have been made. The climate change challenge proved to be a non-starter for all but one of the 14 candidates for the leadership of the Conservative Party of Canada, the Official Opposition at the time, thereby more or less confirming that party's image as one largely made up of climate change deniers.[2]

By contrast, the New Democrats' leadership debates addressed the future of the fossil fuel industry and major pipeline projects such as Kinder Morgan's Trans Mountain and TransCanada's Energy East pipeline, with several leadership candidates expressing opposition to pipeline expansion.[3] But like the other parties, the NDP does not have a clear action plan with targets and benchmarks moving forward between 2018 and 2030. Undoubtedly, the NDP, perhaps reinforced by the Green Party, is in a better position than the Conservatives to move the Trudeau Liberals toward a more ambitious and progressive plan. Yet it is highly doubtful that the NDP will move in this direction by itself without a dynamic social movement mobilizing public pressure — and likely even more doubtful that the Trudeau government will do so.

Imagine for a moment what it would be like if a grassroots-based social movement were to emerge over the next year and collectively declare war on runaway climate change. And imagine that in the lead-up to the next federal election in October 2019, this social movement challenged all major political parties to join the struggle. Political daydreaming, you say — perhaps so. But something needs to be done to shake the complacency of the country's political institutions and processes so that we can elect a progressive government committed to authentic leadership on climate justice. Although militarized metaphors such as preparation for war are certainly not ideal, there is nothing quite like having a clear common enemy to rally against as a means to work together despite differences. In today's world, the most formidable common enemy is runaway climate change and the threat it poses to humanity and life on this planet.

The climate disaster clock is ticking away. According to that clock, we have, at best, just three full decades left to reach the goal of net-zero carbon emissions by 2050. After mainly dithering away the previous three decades, we now face a reckoning that we cannot escape.

If governments are going to be authentic climate leaders, then they must develop a credible action plan to get us to the goal line — which, as defined by the Paris climate accord, means keeping global temperature increases to below 2 degrees Celsius, or closer to 1.5 degrees, this century. To achieve this goal, signatories to the Paris accord must substantially reduce their annual greenhouse gas emissions to net zero. This means reductions of roughly one third for each of the three remaining decades leading up to 2050. In Canada's case, if we take the 2016 figure of 704 million tonnes of greenhouse gas emissions as the base point, the emissions reduction target for 2030 would be 234 million tonnes.

Yet, so far, the Trudeau government has not developed or presented, let alone implemented, a credible plan of action for Canada to effectively achieve these goals in collaboration with the other levels of government — provincial, territorial and municipal, plus Indigenous governance bodies where applicable. In effect, this is basically the same conclusion that Canada's environment commissioner reached, along with provincial auditors general, in their scathing report publicly released in early October 2017.[4]

The Trudeau government has made a commitment to reduce Canada's annual greenhouse gas emissions by 30 percent during the decade between 2020 and 2030. After the Paris accord was signed, the Trudeau government hastily convened a First Ministers' Conference in Ottawa, where it promptly announced its "Pan-Canadian Framework on Clean Growth and Climate Change." However, rather than presenting a concrete strategy, complete with targets, benchmarks and timetables or deadlines, the "framework" appeared to be a mishmash of projects or initiatives already underway, with little or no connection to one another. It did not indicate how they would function to achieve the goals set for greenhouse gas emission reductions, nor did it do the math to show what impact they would have on reducing the country's emissions.

Much attention was paid to what was achieved in terms of consensus (or lack thereof) around a national carbon tax. Although a carbon tax may well be an important policy tool for generating public revenues for, and regulating actions on global warming, it alone does not constitute a credible plan for mitigating climate change. Even more troubling is the government's failure to take account of its own analysis in relation to addressing the real causes of greenhouse gas emissions:

- Except for the continued decommissioning of coal-fired generators, there is nothing substantive in the government's climate plan to bring about an *energy shift* by phasing out the production and use of fossil fuels such as oil and gas (currently responsible for 26 percent of greenhouse gas emissions) and replacing them with a systematic plan for the production and use of renewable energy.
- The current climate plan does not do much more than is already being done to advance and accelerate the *transportation shift* needed — taking more combustion engine cars and trucks (which generate another 25 percent of Canada's greenhouse gas emissions annually) off the road by transporting more people and freight via public transit within urban areas and higher-speed rail between cities within urban corridors.
- Finally, the government's climate plan does little or nothing to boost a significant *building shift* by retrofitting the country's leaky building stock, which generates an additional 12 percent of Canada's annual greenhouse gas emissions through energy waste.

Moreover, the framework appears to ignore the increased warnings of some climate scientists that global greenhouse gas emissions must peak and stabilize by 2020 if there is much hope of staying on track to meet the Paris climate targets.[5] Although global emissions have not increased between 2015 and 2018 and are therefore potentially moving (however slowly) in that direction, Canada's emission rates are not stabilizing as they should to keep pace. Indeed, the federal government's current climate plan accepts as given decisions already made that substantially increase fossil fuel production and export. These include the construction and operation of the Keystone XL pipeline, the Kinder Morgan pipeline, the Line 3 extension pipeline and the liquefied natural gas terminals on the West Coast. Taken together, these projects, if developed, are expected to generate 90 million tonnes of emissions annually by 2020. As well, the Alberta production cap negotiated between the Big Oil companies in the Athabasca tar sands and Rachel Notley's NDP government allows for a 41 percent increase in bitumen production until 2020, when the cap finally comes into effect.

To make matters worse, the Trudeau government has also delayed previously announced actions on greenhouse gas emissions, notably regarding methane. After a spring 2016 joint announcement with the Obama administration of commitments to reduce methane emissions 40 to 45 percent below 2012 levels by 2025, the government announced a year later that these measures would be delayed by another two years because of mounting costs to the petroleum industry. All of this prompted some environmentalists and other observers to wonder whether the Trudeau government was now following the Trump administration's "race to the bottom climate policy."[6]

As well, the pan-Canadian framework allows SaskPower, the Saskatchewan government's public energy utility, to use expensive and as yet unproven new technology — carbon capture and sequestration — to achieve greenhouse gas emission reductions. A 2017 report by a U.K.-based think tank, Global Warming Policy Foundation, raised serious questions about the efficiencies of this technology for reducing emissions.[7]

On top of all of this, Canadian governments continue to subsidize fossil fuel industries by a whopping $46.4 billion annually, according to a 2015 report issued by the IMF.[8] Approximately $1.4 billion comes in the form of direct subsidies (e.g., pre-tax subsidies), whereas the remaining $44.6 billion is manifested through uncollected taxes on externalized costs, such as societal expenditures that result from air pollution, traffic congestion and climate change.

During the 2015 election campaign, Trudeau called for the elimination of public giveaways in the form of direct subsidies. But the IMF economists who wrote the report went much further in their recommendations.[9] They proposed that Canadian carbon-based fuels should be taxed an additional $17.2 billion annually to compensate for climate change, plus another $6 billion for air pollution, $14.9 billion for traffic congestion and $2.1 billion for traffic accidents, along with another $3.5 billion in uncollected value-added taxes, $1.4 billion in direct subsidies and $800 million for road damage. Predictably, the IMF report was roundly panned by Big Oil and business elites in this country but raised profound questions about the management of public revenues that need to be addressed in developing a credible climate action plan.

Canadians concerned about climate change need to focus their sights squarely on the Trudeau government, the opposition parties and key corporate players. To be sure, compared to its predecessor, the Trudeau government has shown a degree of climate leadership. Trudeau himself is not completely wrong when he says, "We don't have to choose between the economy and the environment." The fundamental problem, however, is that neither he nor his government has the right formula to do the job. You cannot fight climate change by propping up and expanding the fossil fuel industry. If Canada wants to be a climate leader, it must seize the moment to make the transition from a primarily extractive industrial economy to a new, more sustainable social economy. This means choosing both at the same time: prioritizing both the environment and the economy and making deep transformations on both fronts.

The public investment plans that the federal government has made for the coming decade barely include job creation targets to be achieved, let alone new jobs that are designed to contribute to the systemic reduction of greenhouse gas emissions and the transition to a more sustainable economic model. A real climate plan must demonstrate a determination by government to lead the way by making public investments designed to provide new forms of employment, decent-paying jobs that directly result in the reduction of greenhouse gas emissions.

A growing segment of the population sees climate change not as simply another policy issue but as a dynamic force in its own right, impacting both nature and society. This segment calls on people to make fundamental choices about their economies for the sake of the planet's future. Polls continue to show that most Canadians see tackling climate change increasingly becoming a top priority for governments, but they also want to see an action plan that's both measurable and accountable.[10] Canadians want and deserve to know where we need to be at each stage in this crucial journey.

Emission Targets

A key place to begin identifying targets, benchmarks and timelines is with the country's annual greenhouse gas emissions.

Although Canada's historical emissions vary from year to year, they have been steadily increasing since 1990. On average, Canada's annual greenhouse gas emissions grew from around 600 million tonnes in 1990 to well over 700 million tonnes during the first decade of the twenty-first century, including a high of over 745 million tonnes in 2007. They were steadily above 700 million tonnes almost every year since 2000, except 2009, which was at the apex of the Great Recession. Canada is now ranked seventh among all countries in the world when it comes to its share of total global greenhouse gas emissions. Moreover, it has become increasingly evident that Canada is not on track to meet either its 2020 or its 2030 commitments for emission reductions.

Meanwhile, several European countries, including Germany, Sweden and Norway, are leading the way in developing and implementing their own action plans to reach net zero in greenhouse gas emissions by mid-century. In Germany, the *Klimaschutz 2050* plan, which was originally designed to make that country carbon neutral by 2050, now has details on target industries, benchmarks and timetables.[11] The plan also has an intermediate goal of achieving a carbon reduction of 55 percent within the next 15 years. In June 2017, Sweden passed a climate law declaring that the country would become net zero in greenhouse gas emissions by 2045.[12] Not to be outdone, Norway, also in June 2017, pledged to become net zero by 2030 as its parliament approved a set of radical proposals for accelerating emission cuts and carbon offsets to reach this goal 20 years earlier than originally planned.[13] All three strategies potentially provide motivating, and hopefully inspiring, lessons for Canada.

So what has to be done in Canada to get to zero by 2050? Well, here's one scenario. We must find effective ways of reducing our total annual greenhouse gas emissions by more than 700 million tonnes over the next two to three decades. At first glance, this appears to be a monumental task. But it becomes more coherent and manageable if we take a closer look at the numbers. The recent drop in Canada's total annual greenhouse gas emissions from around 730 million tonnes in 2015 to 704 million tonnes may indicate this country's emissions are beginning to level off and go into decline. While this is still a big "if" and Canada will no doubt miss its 2020 targets, the trend line may be sufficient to indicate that emissions have dipped into decline mode. If this is the case, then the stage would be set for advancing a more ambitious agenda for 2030 and beyond.

Assuming Canada's greenhouse gas emissions have turned downward and are in a gradual decline, then emission reduction targets for the coming decade can be reset as follows. Using the latest *National Inventory Report* of Canada's total greenhouse gas emissions in 2016 as our base line, we then divide 704 million tonnes by three (for each of the next three decades). This means national targets of roughly 234 million tonnes of greenhouse gas emission reductions on average per decade. These targets may have to be readjusted upward if the science shows that the space left in the carbon budget is shrinking faster than anticipated.

To make an appropriate plan, we must identify and target those sectors of the Canadian economy that have made, and continue to make, the lion's share of greenhouse gas emissions annually. To do so, Environment and Climate Change Canada uses criteria provided by scientists on the Intergovernmental Panel on Climate Change, who study which economic sectors are generating large quantities of greenhouse gas emissions. Figure 4.1, taken from the latest *National Inventory Report*, summarizes their findings based on 2016 data.[14]

Figure 4.1 Annual Greenhouse Gas Emissions by Canadian Economic Sector 2016

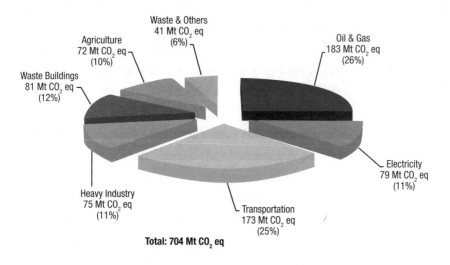

Waste & Others
41 Mt CO_2 eq
(6%)

Agriculture
72 Mt CO_2 eq
(10%)

Waste Buildings
81 Mt CO_2 eq
(12%)

Oil & Gas
183 Mt CO_2 eq
(26%)

Electricity
79 Mt CO_2 eq
(11%)

Heavy Industry
75 Mt CO_2 eq
(11%)

Transportation
173 Mt CO_2 eq
(25%)

Total: 704 Mt CO_2 eq

Note: Totals may not add up due to rounding.

Source: National Inventory Report of Environment and Climate Change Canada

As generators of annual greenhouse gas emissions, each of these sectors could be targeted as priorities for national action. However, some of these sectors are more regionally specific, such as agriculture and heavy industry, whereas others are more widespread, such as transportation and consumption of oil and gas. Although actions focused on any of these sectors would be helpful in reaching zero greenhouse gas emissions by 2050, three sectors together constitute the lion's share of Canada's greenhouse gas emissions: oil and gas (energy), transportation and buildings. As of 2016, oil and gas production amounted to 183 million tonnes of equivalent carbon dioxide (26 percent of Canada's greenhouse emissions), transportation contributed 173 million tonnes (25 percent) and energy waste from building leakages contributed another 81 million tonnes (12 percent).[15]

Taken together, these three sectors of Canada's economy constitute 63 percent of the country's annual greenhouse gas emissions. If electricity production currently powered by coal-fired generators is replaced by other, more decarbonated energy sources (which is already identified federally as a national priority reinforced by actions taken in several provinces), then another sector could be included, which brings the total to 74 percent. In other words, an action plan could be developed that targets those sectors of the Canadian economy that are primarily responsible for almost three quarters of this country's annual greenhouse gas emissions. The target could be further augmented by another 10 percent if heavy industry or agriculture was added to the list, but the focus here is on the top three economic sectors as the prime source of this country's greenhouse gas emissions. These sectors, however, must be our priority to break the back of rising emissions.

According to well-documented research by diverse groups in the climate justice movement, the goal of a 234 million tonnes reduction in greenhouse gas emissions by 2030 can be met if

- the country's remaining coal-fired generators are decommissioned and mothballed,
- tar sands production is effectively capped and is in the process of being gradually phased out by the end of the decade and
- major public investments are made in renewable energy production, green building construction and public transportation.

2020 Tipping Point

"When it comes to climate, timing is everything." So declared Christiana Figueres, the UN's leading driver behind the global campaign to mitigate climate change, along with five of her colleagues in the publication *Nature* in late June 2017.[16] She was using the findings of a report publicly released on April 1, 2017, to make the case for why 2020 was a critical year in the global campaign on climate change. The report, *Mission 2020: The Climate Tipping Point*, was prepared by a team of experts from organizations such as Carbon Tracker and the Carbon Action Tracker consortium in the United Kingdom, the Potsdam Institute for Climate Impact Research in Germany and Yale University in the United States. The *Nature* article itself was authored or co-signed by more than 60 scientists, public policy–makers, business leaders, economists and public communicators, along with representatives of organizations such as the International Renewable Energy Agency, Climate Tracker, World Resources Institute, the International Trade Union Confederation and the European Geosciences Union.

The initiative was designed to send a clear signal that despite a downward dip in global greenhouse gas emissions over the past three years, operating on the basis of "business-as-usual" scenarios will not move the world closer to achieving the Paris target. Rather, if emissions start to rise again beyond 2020, or even if they remain the same, "the temperature goals set in Paris become almost unattainable."[17] Instead, the time had come for countries and key sectors of their economies to raise the levels of ambition and action to bend the emissions curve downwards by 2020.

Proponents of this message formed Mission 2020 to highlight the importance of recognizing 2020 as the climate turning point and the urgent need to raise ambition and action on a nation-to-nation basis.

One of the main achievements of Mission 2020 has been to develop and apply a global budget for carbon emissions. In other words, how much room is there in the carbon budget to release and store greenhouse gas emissions before the temperature limit is breached? This requires calculating the amount of greenhouse gas emissions that have accumulated in the atmosphere over the centuries, subtracting that amount from the total volume Earth's atmosphere has the capacity to absorb. On the basis of its own calculations, the Mission 2020 team concluded that Earth has a carbon credit of between 150 and 1,050 gigatonnes left to meet the Paris temperature targets. The wide range is explained as largely due to the diverse ways of calculating these budgets using recent figures.

On the basis of the current global emission rate of 41 gigatonnes of carbon dioxide per year, Mission 2020 calculated that there were three scenarios:

- The lower-point scenario would not be feasible simply because it would pass in just four years, which provides too little time to do the necessary decarbonization of the economy.
- The second scenario provides a carbon budget permitting around

600 gigatonnes of greenhouse gas emissions (which amounts to 15 years of emissions at the current rate) before the heating of the planet enters the danger zone of a 1.5- to 2-degree Celsius temperature increase. Nevertheless, this scenario could potentially give us a 20- to 25-year period to reduce greenhouse gas emissions to zero.

- The third scenario involves stretching the global carbon budget by another 200 gigatonnes to a total of 800 gigatonnes, which could extend the timeline another 10 years, but at a much greater risk of exceeding the temperature danger zone.

There is a reasonable amount of uncertainty associated with such calculations given the development of the science to date. Figure 4.2 portrays the challenges of the 2020 climate tipping point in terms of these three scenarios.

Figure 4.2 Carbon Budget Crunch: Strategic Options and Potential Risks

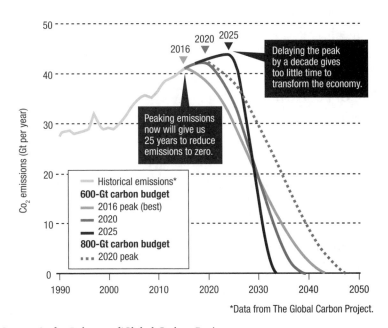

*Data from The Global Carbon Project.

Source: Stefan Rahmstorf/Global Carbon Project

Climate scientists associated with Mission 2020 have concluded that the carbon budget of the planet is shrinking rapidly. The year 2020, they say, marks the tipping point at which, at the latest, emissions must peak and stabilize worldwide and then decline dramatically thereafter. Otherwise, the world will not reach the Paris accord threshold of keeping global temperature rise to between 1.5 and 2 degrees Celsius this century.[18]

However, on the basis of updated data from the Intergovernmental Panel on Climate Change, it appears that the carbon budget is shrinking faster than previously anticipated. This means that the time left to reach the Paris goals is 20 years, not 30 years. In other words, for Canada and other countries to reach the goal of net-zero emissions, the target date is closer to 2040 instead of 2050. If emissions peak in 2025, or if we wait until 2050 to reach net-zero emissions, there is a significant risk of breaching the 1.5- and even the 2-degree Celsius threshold.

If Canada is going to be able to travel down this curve of decarbonization at the pace required to get to zero by 2040, it will have to take major strides to scale up its ambition and initiate bold action between 2018 and 2020.[19] Yet the UN's *Emissions Gap Report* for 2017 makes it clear that Canada is simply not on track to meet either its 2020 or its 2030 commitments — commitments that fall considerably short of what is now required to meet the climate tipping point challenge outlined above.[20]

Course Correction

There is no longer time to waste. Between 2018 and 2020, Canada needs to have in place and ready to go not only a revised and credible action plan but also much of the infrastructure to deliver it. Yet, as the environment commissioner's 2017 report and audit reveal, Canada is not even ready to meet either its 2020 or its 2030 commitments. Instead, Environment Minister Catherine McKenna and, presumably, the Trudeau government as a whole have decided to abandon Canada's 2020 targets and commitments, shifting their focus to the country's 2030 targets and commitments or, in other words, "kicking the can down the road" once again. In so doing, Canada's track record of never meeting its commitments and targets on greenhouse gas emission reductions will be sustained for yet another decade.

We find ourselves in a situation where we will undoubtedly have to redouble our efforts to measure up to the challenge at hand. Scientists will continue to investigate and debate what space remains in Earth's carbon budget for greenhouse gas emissions, thereby determining with more precision just how many years we have left for getting to zero. That said, it is better to be more than less prepared for the worst-case scenario. What Canada needs is a course correction: an updated plan that recognizes we have at most 20 years, not 30 years, left for getting to net zero and making the transition to 100 percent renewable energy.

Obviously, such a course correction would also necessarily include a revised set of targets for greenhouse gas emission reductions on a decade-by-decade basis. If the recent warnings of Mission 2020 scientists about the increasingly rapid pace of climate change taking place are correct, then the greenhouse gas reduction targets would have to rise from 234 to 352 million tonnes for each of the two decades between 2020 and 2040. In turn, the 352 million tonne target for greenhouse gas emission reductions would have to be broken down into sectoral and regional targets. So, for example, sectoral emission reduction targets could be set as follows: the energy shift at 110 million tonnes, the transportation shift at 25 then eventually 100 million tonnes and the building shift at 126 million tonnes.

Targeting these sectors will result in greenhouse gas emission reduction goals of 336 million tonnes per decade. The additional 16 million tonnes required to meet the 352 million tonne per decade target in order to reach net zero by 2040 could be achieved through greater efficiencies in agriculture, industrial and waste sectors of the economy. Similar kinds of calculations would also need to be carried out for a regional breakdown, which will be discussed in Chapter 8. Although the outcomes in terms of greenhouse gas reductions will no doubt vary from period to period, the targets will provide a set of goals from which progress can be more effectively measured and evaluated.

CHAPTER 5
The Big Shift

Taking up the net-zero challenge is imperative for overcoming runaway climate change. But how is this to be accomplished in a country such as Canada, which has an economy that is highly dependent on both the production and consumption of fossil fuels? Indeed, this deeply rooted economic and societal dependency needs to be simultaneously confronted and broken for the country and its people to confidently get on with the task of developing and implementing a plan of action that effectively stops and reverses the trend lines toward climate chaos.

Decisive action must be taken to substantially reduce heat-trapping greenhouse gas emissions, with a view to reaching the target of net-zero carbon emissions by, if not before, mid-century. This will require a fundamental societal shift in the kind of energy we use to fuel our economy. Burning fossil fuels (coal, oil and gas) has been scientifically established as the main human source behind the warming of the planet and related climate changes.

If climate change is to be effectively mitigated, then fossil fuel–producing nation-states such as Canada must adopt short-, medium- and long-term plans for phasing out the production and consumption of fossil fuels and prioritizing the transition to a clean energy economic future. This calls for a transformation in major industrial sectors of the economy. For extractive economies such as Canada's, this type of deep transformation poses a monumental challenge.

A prime target for recent industrial overhaul worldwide has been coal-fired electrical generators. Governments in many countries (including Germany, Australia, the United States and Canada) have led the way in initiating plans to mothball coal-fired electrical generation — a major cause of their greenhouse gas emissions — and replace coal with natural gas, along with wind and solar power. In Germany, Angela Merkel's government has developed and implemented a national plan of action called *Energiewende* ("energy transition"). With this plan, Germany hopes to reduce its greenhouse gas emissions by 40 percent below 1990 levels by 2020, 10 years ahead of the target date set by the European Union.

Meanwhile, public pressure was mounting in Australia to shut down 10 of its most polluting power plants. Whereas governments in Germany, China and the United States were taking direct action to close down carbon-polluting power plants, in Australia, governments were still spending taxpayer dollars to subsidize the operations of coal-fired electrical generators. Through their production and use of coal-powered energy, these plants were considered directly responsible for 158 million tonnes of Australia's total greenhouse gas emissions in 2013–14. In response, the Australian Conservation Foundation urged its government to impose the kind of direct regulations introduced by the Obama administration in the United States, effectively making these coal-fired plants untenable without using expensive carbon capture and sequestration technology.

In Ontario, the former Dalton McGuinty government also took decisive action to close down its coal-fired power plants in the province's electrical grid by the end of 2013. As a result, Ontario became the first jurisdiction in North America to go coal-free. Beginning in 2003, coal-fired power plants were gradually shut down and mothballed over a 10-year period. Coal was replaced by a mix of natural gas and wind power. This was made possible by a relatively aggressive energy law in

2009 establishing energy efficiency programs and a feed-in tariff providing generous financial benefits to renewable energy developers. As a result, greenhouse gas emissions from Ontario's energy sector fell from 40 to 10 million tonnes. As Alberta begins to implement its plan to decommission coal-fired electrical power plants, Rachel Notley's government can benefit from the insights and lessons learned from the Ontario experience, both positive and negative.

For Alberta and Canada as a whole, however, decommissioning coal-fired electrical power plants is by no means the only challenge related to industrial overhaul. When it comes to targeting industries that spew multiple millions of tons of greenhouse gas emissions into the atmosphere each year, the real elephant in the room requiring industrial transformation is the oil-based energy industry in the Alberta tar sands, the single largest industrial development of its kind on the planet.

Industrial Overhaul

We need to wean ourselves from our collective dependency on dirty, carbon-polluting fossil fuels while simultaneously building a new economy that is increasingly fuelled by clean, renewable sources of energy. This dual challenge calls for a twofold strategy for industrial transformation:

- declaring bitumen extraction for oil production from the tar sands a "sunset industry," to be gradually phased out over a set period of time, and simultaneously
- developing public renewable energy (e.g., solar, wind, geothermal) as a "sunrise industry," coupled with a national energy grid to equitably serve the needs of all peoples and regions in this country.

Although phasing out coal-fired generators for electricity across the country is an important step, Canada's single biggest industrial emitter of greenhouse gas emissions continues to be bitumen production for oil products from the tar sands in northern Alberta. Despite declining worldwide oil prices, the Alberta tar sands continue to be both Canada's largest and fastest-growing industrial emitter. New regulatory measures designed to limit the production and growth of the tar sands industry, along with corresponding greenhouse gas emissions, are therefore imperative.

Moving in this direction, however, entails clearly identifying the root cause of greenhouse gas emissions, the production and consumption of fossil fuels. As the Canadian Centre for Policy Alternatives documented in a recent report, virtually every Canadian jurisdiction — federal, provincial, territorial, municipal — depends on fossil fuels as its prime source of energy. If Canada continues to rely on current measures for reducing greenhouse gas emissions, then Environment and Climate Change Canada predicts that the country will miss not only its 2020 commitment but also its 2030 commitments under the Paris accord.[1]

As we saw in Chapter 3, energy specialist David Hughes estimated that Canada's greenhouse gas emissions will be 23 percent above our 2020 commitments and 55 percent above our 2030 commitments. It would be "extremely difficult," he said, to depend on making deep emission cuts (reductions of 47 percent or more) in other sectors, such as transportation and buildings, to make up for the slack. Hughes concluded that the only hope of meeting our Paris accord commitments for 2030 is to "demand real emissions reductions from the oil and gas sector."[2] This means calling for an overhaul and transformation of Canada's energy industry itself, starting with the tar sands. In short, this is the spearhead of the Big Shift that needs to be developed and implemented.

So how, then, to proceed? One way involves putting a cap on bitumen production; this would carry corresponding implications for limits on greenhouse gas emissions. The NDP government in Alberta has brought forward a so-called "cap" on greenhouse gas emissions, based on recommendations for a climate plan made by a commission chaired by the University of Alberta's Andrew Leach.

Rather than imposing a cap based on current levels of greenhouse gas emissions (70 million tonnes annually), however, the Notley government has increased the allowable annual tar sands emissions to 100 million tonnes, until 2020, before a cap is implemented.[3] According to Marc Lee, senior economist for the Canadian Centre for Policy Alternatives in British Columbia, although the cap of 100 million tonnes signals that there are limits on the greenhouse gas emissions that the industry can spew into the atmosphere, it also permits the industry to keep expanding its production. As a result, "the cap amounts to being no cap at all."[4]

We need a true cap on production. Before the worldwide slump in oil prices that began in 2014, the Canadian Association of Petroleum Producers predicted that bitumen production in Alberta would surpass 5 million barrels per day by 2035 — almost twice the current level of production. If this were to occur, the carbon budget for the tar sands would have been blown within a few short years. Before it's too late, we must recognize that bitumen production in a carbon-constrained world is a "dirty energy business" that must be phased out over a 10- to 15-year period at most. The same studies that enable us to determine how much room is left in the carbon budget could be used as the basis for determining how many barrels of crude oil could still be produced on a daily basis from the tar sands that would be considered allowable and acceptable during this 15-year transition period. In other words, the production cap would need to be adjusted on the basis of the tar sands carbon budget and associated science.

In a carbon-constrained world, a production cap spearheading a gradual phase-out of the industry would provide Alberta and Canada with the means necessary to keep greenhouse gas emissions from the country's largest and fastest-growing emitter under control. It would provide governments with an important tool for managing the production of bitumen, thereby further facilitating our economy's transition from dependence on fossil fuels to greater reliance on sources of renewable energy. It would also keep the industry and its workforce intact for the foreseeable future rather than risk the prospect of being compelled to suddenly and completely shut down all operations as a result of mounting political pressures generated by an intensifying climate crisis. Moreover, the ongoing operation of the industry would also provide a source for resource revenues that could be used for making the transition to a new economy increasingly based on renewable energy.

For the production cap to achieve these and related outcomes, it would need to be accompanied by additional regulatory and programmatic measures. For example, a regime designed to regulate greenhouse gas emissions from the tar sands industry would have to be put in place, one that regulated emissions both upstream (where the bitumen is processed for oil products) and downstream (where the bitumen is extracted and upgraded for delivery by pipeline). Putting a cap on bitumen production plus a cap on greenhouse gas emissions for the industry would also provide a twin set of policy criteria for evaluating the maze of pipeline proposals that were on the table in mid-2017, all designed to bring bitumen-based crude oil from the Alberta tar sands to markets, notably in the United States and Asia.

In effect, this is what happened in October 2017 when TransCanada suddenly cancelled its application to build the Energy East pipeline. In August 2017, the National Energy Board announced it was broadening the scope of its climate test to include both upstream and downstream impacts of the Energy East project on greenhouse gas emissions.[5] Normally, the climate test of a project focuses on the upstream impacts in terms of greenhouse gas emissions generated from "the point of extraction to the project under review," which generally includes extraction, processing, handling and transportation. By broadening the climate test to include the downstream impacts concerning greenhouse gas emissions, the scope was enlarged to include industrial activities from "the point of the product leaving the project to the final end-use," which generally includes further refining, processing, transportation and end-use combustion. The Trudeau government also mandated the National Energy Board to review whether or not the Energy East pipeline was still necessary given the introduction of new climate change rules that could reduce dependency on oil and gas in the future.[6]

Later, however, it also became clear that this expanded climate test would not be applied to other pipeline projects that had previously been greenlit by the Trudeau cabinet, such as Kinder Morgan's Trans Mountain project, Enbridge's Line 3 extension, or TransCanada's Keystone XL. As a result, the focus of public debate in the aftermath of TransCanada's decision to pull the plug on the Energy East pipeline has been on other issues:

- regional divisions that pit, for example, Alberta against Quebec (which strongly opposed the project), thereby fuelling a potential national unity crisis;
- political risk the Liberals could not afford to take by going against widespread public opposition to the project in Ontario and especially Quebec with a big election on the horizon in 2019 and
- the sheer business calculation that the project was no longer sustainable from an economic standpoint, with oil prices half of what they had been when the project was initially proposed.

If Canada is to become a climate leader, the same kind of climate test must be applied as a regulatory measure systematically and equitably to all proposed pipeline projects. This climate test must include both a production cap and an emissions cap, developed in keeping with the targeted reductions that Canada has committed to achieve by 2020 and 2030. Equally important, the dual caps should be set with a particular view to the carbon budget and the amount of space left in the atmosphere to absorb carbon emissions. As with Energy East, it must also be applied to both upstream and downstream impacts of all proposed pipeline projects (and related projects, including the proposed liquefied natural gas plant on the B.C. coast).

Moving decisively in this direction would help set the stage for the kind of overhaul of the energy industry this country needs. If the production and emissions caps are well managed over the next 10 to 15 years, bitumen could be creatively used as a transition fuel by phasing out exports to the United States and making environmentally innovative use of bitumen products for domestic needs that do not require burning and combustion. To do so, however, the Canadian government would also need to call for the removal or renegotiation of the proportional sharing clause in NAFTA that obligates Canada to maintain ongoing energy exports at current levels to the United States.[7]

Meanwhile, the increasing signs of decline in the Alberta oil sands may yet provide conditions and opportunities for a turnaround. In June 2017, Oil Change International released a briefing report showing evidence that the tar sands industry had reached the "end of growth" and was going into decline.[8] Since 2013, the oil price nosedive from roughly $100 to $50 (U.S.) per barrel, more or less, has created an atmosphere for disinvestment. International oil companies, notably U.S. and European, have been selling off their assets in the tar sands and investing their capital elsewhere. As Hannah McKinnon, the report's co-author, explained,

> Because tar sands projects are so capital intensive, take a long time to build, and produce for many decades, investors need to feel confident that oil prices are going to be sustained at high enough levels to make massive up-front capital expenditures worth it.[9]

Indeed, the oil industry landscape has dramatically changed, with U.S. shale oil production stabilizing global oil prices ranging from US$55 to $75 plus a barrel. Meanwhile, no commitments had been made to invest in new tar sands projects beyond 2020. In other words, "the golden era of the tar sands is over," according to Oil Change International. The challenge now becomes how to "manage the decline."[10]

As a result, more serious attention is being given to the prospects for diversifying Alberta's economy. "Diversification" does not necessarily mean further upgrading and refining bitumen before export or developing a secondary manufacturing industry such as petrochemicals (as Alberta did in the 1970s and 1980s). Such strategies may serve to liberate the economy from the staples trap (discussed in Chapter 3) but do little or nothing to address the problems of the carbon lock-in associated with bitumen production. Instead, the focus needs to be on what political economist Gordon Laxer has called "deep diversification." According to Laxer, author of the 2015 book *After the Sands*, "Alberta could become a leader in specialized green technology and services, like ultra-deep geothermal power."[11] Alternatively, he suggested that Alberta's economy could become more specialized in developing pathways to a new, more sustainable economy through

- other forms of renewable energy (e.g., wind and solar power),
- building retrofits for extreme cold and hot climates or
- expanding public transit and higher-speed rail to move people and freight over longer distances.

Such strategies for diversification prioritize decarbonization or reducing greenhouse gas emissions.

Financial Regimes

To be effective, an industrial overhaul strategy also needs to be rooted in at least one of the two major climate financial regimes operating internationally:

- cap-and-trade, whereby a cap is put on emissions in industrial sectors and emission credits can be bought or exchanged between sectors, or
- a carbon tax, whereby a levy is charged per tonne of emissions (e.g., $30 per tonne).

The challenge here is that each of these regimes has already attracted the buy-in of several key provinces. Quebec and Ontario (until very recently) have joined a cap-and-trade regime in collaboration with California, whereas British Columbia and more recently Alberta (2018) have instituted a carbon tax, which can be progressively raised every five years or so.[12] Thus, a patchwork quilt of rules has already emerged between these provincial jurisdictions and the federal government. The Trudeau government has committed itself to a revenue-neutral national carbon tax, which may tip the balance and provide a more common framework. Admittedly, however, the recent announcement by the newly elected Conservative government in Ontario to pull the province out of the cap-and-trade regime with Quebec and Ontario, leaves a gaping hole in this financial regime on climate issues.

Nevertheless, the slowdown and phase-out of carbon-intense bitumen production from the tar sands must be accompanied by a plan of action for developing clean, renewable sources of energy. Canada has tremendous potential to develop renewable energy sources, not only hydroelectric power but also solar, wind, geothermal and tidal. And Canada is not alone. According to Clean Energy Canada, recent global analysis shows that a record-breaking US$325 billion was invested in renewable power around the world in 2015 — nearly 50 percent more than was invested in power from fossil fuels that year.[13]

Despite these developments, some analysts have concluded that renewable energy growth is still being "crushed" by worldwide expansion in the fossil industry, particularly oil and gas. Fossil energy resources grew rapidly between 2009 and 2016 as we emerged from the global recession, to the point where they now supply 85 percent of global energy demand. Nevertheless, a boom of sorts continues in renewable energy as a result of declining costs of production in countries such as the United States, where the cost of utility-scale solar photovoltaic systems have dropped 82 percent and wind energy costs have declined 61 percent since 2009. Along with the United States, the biggest players in clean, renewable energy development include China, Japan, the United Kingdom and India, with Canada in eighth place.

Recognizing these new trend lines in energy investment, some of the U.S.-based Big Oil corporations have been hedging their bets by increasing their own investments in renewable energy. Tar sands players such as Suncor and Chevron have played a leading role. Diversifying its operations by investing in a range of renewable energy projects, Suncor's portfolio now includes eight wind farms in Canada, with a capacity for generating almost 200 megawatts of electricity.[14] Using its geological technical expertise developed in the Alberta tar sands and elsewhere, Chevron is becoming one of the largest players in the geothermal power industry internationally.[15] And Enbridge, the Canadian proponent of various pipelines to transport bitumen from the tar sands to tidewater, has invested close to $5 billion since 2002 in renewable energy projects such as wind, solar, geothermal and waste heat.[16] Some readers will likely applaud these and other Big Oil corporations for investing in renewable energy, but such moves are likely being made both to protect the petroleum industry's vested interests in extending the lifeline of fossil fuels and to secure control over the future of renewable energy.

As the boom in clean energy investment was taking place in 2015 around the rest of the world, Canadian investments in renewable energy went into a slump. In 2015, there was a significant drop in such investment, from $7.4 billion to around $4 billion — a 46 percent decline from 2014.[17] From Clean Energy Canada's perspective, there are several noteworthy reasons for this. Two in particular stand out:

- the patchwork of renewable power policies held by various provincial governments, which tends to undermine the long-term certainty that renewable energy developers need, and
- the lack of overall national leadership and policy support for the transition to a low-carbon energy future for Canada; so far, constructing pipelines still takes precedence over building power lines and clean sources of energy.

Unless a concerted national plan of action, with clearly defined targets and timelines, is adopted and nurtured through public investments, clean energy investments will remain in a slump, and the much-needed transformation of Canada's energy industry will languish. Fortunately, Canada has a proven tradition of developing and using Crown corporations as a policy tool to accomplish overarching public interest objectives.[18] Accordingly, the federal government could establish a pan-Canadian Crown corporation with a policy mandate and the tools required to co-ordinate the energy industry overhaul and facilitate the transition to a renewable energy future by 2050 if not sooner. Major energy-producing provinces such as Alberta may have corresponding interests in establishing their own provincial Crown corporation to work collaboratively, wherever possible, in accomplishing these public interest objectives.[19]

This proposed pan-Canadian Crown corporation, for example, could develop and implement a roadmap for the phase-out of the tar sands industry over the next 10 to 15 years. This could include setting a gradually decreasing production cap for each five-year segment, commensurate with targeted reductions in greenhouse gas emissions for the industry. The Crown corporation would be equipped to monitor and regulate adherence to the production cap and the greenhouse gas reduction targets. If necessary, a state-owned oil company could be established to play a more active role in the oil market to further facilitate this transition, operating in collaboration with the Crown corporation.

This Crown corporation could also be given a mandate to work collaboratively with provincial and territorial governments to identify and locate viable sites for wind, solar, geothermal, tidal, biomass and small-scale hydroelectric projects. This would include strategies for collaborating with existing manufacturing industries, or developing new ones, to produce component parts for renewable energy production. As well, provisions could be made to further support the development and refinement of "incubator programs" designed to facilitate collaboration between contractors, developers and unions involved in renewable energy solutions, such as the Energy Futures Lab and the Alberta-based Tundra Process Solutions' Acceleration Centre for Entrepreneurs.[20]

These are some of the initial challenges to be faced in transforming Canada's energy industry. If the private, largely foreign-owned, petroleum companies in Canada's oil patch actively resist such a transformation of the tar sands industry, then governments do have the option of, and the tools for, securing public ownership and control of their assets in the public interest.[21] Indeed, over 70 percent of the oil reserves left in the world are controlled by public or state-owned companies. Canada is the only one among the 10 largest petroleum-producing countries in which the oil industry is not dominated by state-owned firms.

Eco-pathways

The shift to a new economy calls for a transformative process, triggered by innovative strategies that are designed to fundamentally change the economy so that it functions in harmony with its surrounding ecology. These innovative strategies, or "eco-pathways," act as stepping stones toward building a more just and sustainable economy. The prefix *eco* encompasses both the *eco*nomy and *eco*logy and implies the interaction, interrelation and interdependence that needs to take place between them.

The foundations of the high-tech model of industrial capitalism that governs our economy and society need to be rethought and re-evaluated in light of challenges posed by climate change. We need to rethink how

- we extract natural resources to produce products and services for our economy;
- the economy provides the energy we need to run our industries and factories, heat our homes and industries and fuel our vehicles for transport;
- energy is wasted daily in heating and cooling our homes and buildings, especially in a climate with periods of extreme cold and heat and
- our society transports both people and freight safely and efficiently to multiple destinations within urban centres and between cities within urban corridors.[22]

Together these challenges require bold transformations in at least three industrial sectors of our current economy:

- energy,
- construction and
- transportation.

Environment Canada's *National Inventory Report 1990–2016*, published in 2016, reported that energy, buildings and transportation were responsible for 63 percent of Canada's total greenhouse gas emissions in 2016.[23] This is why it makes sense to start with these sectors in developing eco-pathways moving forward. These eco-pathways must strengthen and reinforce one another as foundation stones for building the new economy. Moreover, when coal-fired generators for electricity production plus heavy industry are also added as targets for emission reductions, the scope of the plan increases to potentially cover up to 85 percent of Canada's total annual greenhouse gas emissions.[24]

One approach for developing eco-pathways along these lines in Canada has been initiated by the Green Economy Network. Composed of 25 civil society organizations — labour unions, environmental groups, youth networks, public interest associations and faith-based communities — the network has been working since late 2009 on developing eco-pathways for transitioning to a new economy in response to climate change. In particular, the network has developed a challenge and an action plan for creating one million climate jobs in this country over a five-year period.[25] By "climate jobs," the network means new forms of work and employment that either

- contribute, directly or indirectly, to the reduction of greenhouse gas emissions causing climate change or
- enable people and their communities to be resilient in the face of the damage caused by extreme weather events resulting from climate change.

By focusing on these jobs, the Green Economy Network has prioritized making the economy simultaneously more sustainable and more just. The underlying strategy involves fighting climate change by fighting unemployment and poverty through putting people back to work in clean, decent-paying jobs that contribute to increasing harmony with nature. The network has argued that we need public leadership and investment by governments to open up these pathways and prepare for the transition rather than relying on markets and for-profit corporations alone. Although the private sector has a role to play, the public sector must lead the way by making substantial public investments and by establishing a pan-Canadian framework of ground rules and regulations. These measures will help ensure that workers and communities are able to effectively contribute to the reduction of greenhouse gas emissions and cope with the disastrous impacts of climate change.

The Green Economy Network's platform proposed three eco-pathways involving major public investments in the three priority sectors identified above, which together constitute the prime causes of Canada's greenhouse gas emissions:

- **Energy** — transitioning from fossil fuels as this country's prime source of energy to reliance on clean, renewable sources of energy such as solar, wind and geothermal power, plus tidal and small-scale or run-of-river hydroelectric power
- **Construction (buildings)** — dealing with the enormous amount of energy waste that is generated by burning fossil fuels to heat and cool our buildings — residential, commercial, public — and the corresponding need to retrofit our building stock for energy efficiency and climate resiliency
- **Transportation** — addressing our societal dependence on combustion engine vehicles for transporting people and freight and the corresponding need to take cars and trucks off the road by improving and expanding public transit in our cities, developing higher-speed rail transport between cities in urban corridors and promoting the use of electric vehicles

Public investments in these three sectors could put hundreds of thousands of people to work in new forms of employment designed to reduce the country's greenhouse gas emissions.

The strategic linkage and relationship between the economy and ecology make the network's approach unusual.[26] To fully grasp the significance of all three eco-pathways, it's important to closely examine the platform and each of its main components in terms of the

- public investments required,
- number of jobs that could be created,
- amount of greenhouse gas emissions that can be reduced over a five-year period and
- strategic linkages between job creation and greenhouse gas emission reductions.

This Big Shift plan and program can be evaluated in measurable terms and rolled over several times in five-year intervals to achieve and multiply results in key regions and sectors of the economy.

Energy Shift

If Canada is going to come anywhere close to measuring up to its commitments arising out of the Paris climate summit, let alone begin to effectively mitigate climate change, we must immediately embark on a path of making the shift to 100 percent renewable energy by, if not before, 2050.

The only way for Canada to become an energy power in this age of climate change is to become a producer of clean and renewable sources of energy. To date, however, only 3 percent of Canada's energy comes from these emerging, low-impact, renewable sources (excluding hydroelectric power).[27] To be sure, this country's greenhouse gas emissions from electricity generation have recently fallen below 1990 levels, due mainly to the achievements of hydroelectric power production and emission reductions in Quebec, plus some increased use of other renewable energy sources (e.g., wind, solar power) for electricity production in a few other provinces. Yet, as the Green Economy Network's platform noted,

> Canada has enormous potential for the production of
> electricity from clean, renewable sources of energy. Our
> coastal regions along with some inland areas provide major
> opportunities for wind power through wind farms; specific
> locations in this country rank amongst the best in the world

*in terms of direct sunlight for solar power production; and
regions in the west and northwest are particularly well
suited for large-scale geothermal energy.*[28]

Canada is also well positioned to develop tidal power in several coastal areas
as well as small-scale hydroelectric projects on remote rivers and lakes.

This historic transition will require committed and co-ordinated
public leadership across the board. Although the private sector and
markets will no doubt have an important role to play, we need the public
sector to signal the level of transition that must take place by using the
multipronged policy tools and strategies at its disposal, including

- public investments,
- ownership,
- regulations,
- programs and
- infrastructure.

In Canada, all levels of government — municipal, provincial, territorial
and Indigenous — need to play key roles in promoting and developing
renewable energy solutions in their jurisdictions, with active facilitation,
guidance and support from the federal government in advancing the
transition.

To facilitate this transition, the platform called on governments to
make specific and strategic public investments in developing all the
various types of renewable energy over a five-year period. The network
proposed public investments of $23.3 billion to stimulate development
of renewable energy sources to power the economy in a way that cre-
ates new jobs and reduces greenhouse gas emissions at the same time.[29]
Averaged over five years, this amounts to an annual public investment
of $4.65 billion. Applying the unofficial formula that is often used in
cross-government financing of joint projects — 50 percent federal, 40
percent provincial, 10 percent municipal — the costs become more
manageable. Under this formula, the federal government's annual share

would amount to $2.33 billion, which is less than 1 percent of its annual budget.

This kind of public investment would generate tens of thousands of new jobs. According to economic modelling developed by the Center for American Progress, an annual investment of $4.65 billion would generate 58,300 person-years of employment.[30] This would include

- 22,300 person job years in direct employment within renewable energy industries,
- 19,500 person job years generated in supply industries or indirect employment and
- 16,500 person job years created in retail and sales to service newly employed workers (or, in other words, induced employment).

The number of jobs created will vary by industry. For example, a $1 billion public investment in solar energy production would create 13,400 person–years of employment, whereas the same amount invested in geothermal energy production would result in 8,240 person job years. Table 5.1 provides more details.[31]

Table 5.1 Annual Employment Estimates from Renewable Energy Investments

	Millions/yr	Direct*	Indirect	Induced	Total
Wind Energy	$1,300	6,110	5,720	4,680	16,510
Solar Photovoltaic	$1,000	5,500	4,100	3,800	13,400
Geothermal	$800	2,400	3,520	2,400	8,240
Tidal	$666	3,596	2,531	2,464	8,591
Hydroelectric	$553	2,876	2,323	2,101	7,300
Biofuel	$333	1,798	1,265	1,232	4,296
Total	**$4,652**	**22,280**	**19,459**	**16,677**	**58,337**

*Employment is measured in person job years

Canada would want to ensure that the development plan includes domestic procurement provisions, requiring that a certain percentage of the component parts for wind turbines, solar panels, geothermal energy production and the like be produced domestically by Canadian workers rather than being imported from other countries. Such domestic procurement provisions in Ontario's *Green Energy Act*, however, were struck down by the WTO in 2013 as a violation of global trade rules. Indeed, these and related global trade rules will need to be modified, changed or eliminated if there is to be any hope of bringing about the energy shift required.

In addition to stimulating development of renewable energy sources, the Green Economy Network's public investments proposal would also gradually reduce Canada's annual greenhouse gas emissions. By the end of the five-year period, Environment and Climate Canada data suggest that this investment would have begun to reduce Canada's annual greenhouse gas emissions by between 44 and 110 million tonnes. At the high end of this estimate, 110 million tonnes in greenhouse gas reductions from renewable energy replacements, which may not be reached until the ninth or tenth year, would represent approximately 16 percent of Canada's overall annual greenhouse gas emissions of 704 million tonnes (2016). Once renewable energy components are constructed, installed and fully operational as part of the energy grid, greenhouse gas emissions are expected to decrease at an ever-faster rate as fossil fuels such as coal and natural gas are replaced by clean, renewable energy sources.

We already have living community-based examples of the transition to renewable energy power in action across Canada. For instance:

- **Sault Ste. Marie in northern Ontario** provides an excellent example of a city that has developed renewable energy (wind and solar power) to offset declining employment in steel and forestry industries in the region. The Sault has one of the country's largest wind energy farms, composed of 126 wind turbines, producing 189 megawatts of renewable energy, which is sufficient to power 60,000 homes — twice the number of houses in the city. As well, the Sault's 20 megawatt farm has been expanded and has the capacity to generate 50 megawatts of solar power for the community. The city has five hydroelectric stations in the area, which generate a total of 203 megawatts of renewable power, plus a co-generation power project that produces 70 megawatts of electricity for the Sault's largest steel mill.[32]

- **A social enterprise in Manitoba called Aki Energy** offers another living example of community-based transition to renewable power. *Aki* is the Ojibway word for "Earth," so Aki Energy translates as "earth energy," or what is often referred to as geothermal power. This refers to Earth's natural heating and cooling systems that lie below its surface. As a not-for-profit social enterprise, Aki Energy was initially organized to retrofit the heating and cooling systems of homes and public buildings in First Nations communities within Manitoba, removing fossil-fuelled systems and replacing them with geo-thermal systems for heating during the winter and cooling during the summer. Aki Energy employs some 125 workers from First Nations communities, who are trained and then work in teams retrofitting houses in communities such as the Peguis Nation north of Winnipeg. To date, Aki Energy has transformed 150 homes from fossil fuel systems to geother-mal power in First Nations communities, with funding sup-port from Manitoba Hydro, a provincial crown corporation. It has contracts to retrofit another 850 homes over a five-year period.[33]

As these and other examples illustrate, community-based power has a vital role to play in the transition to a renewable energy future. Although the various levels of government have key roles to play in facilitating, financing and co-ordinating this historic economic shift, there can be no effective transition without the active engagement and support of local communities and their groups. In some parts of the country, renewable energy projects such as windmills have been met with protests and fierce resistance, which should not be ignored. For these and related reasons, governments at all levels need to take a proactive stance, strengthening both incentives and benefits for community participation in the transition.

Building Shift

Canada has four distinct seasons and experiences extreme weather conditions, ranging from frigid cold in winter to blistering hot temperatures in summer months. Yet Canada's building stock remains woefully inadequate for dealing with these extreme temperature swings in an energy-efficient manner. Although conserving energy in the heating and cooling of our homes and buildings should be a top priority for Canadians, our present housing and building stock wastes a great deal of energy through walls, ceilings and furnaces. This energy waste compounds the release of greenhouse gas emissions into the atmosphere, reinforcing the dynamics of climate change. Although attention has been focused on reducing energy waste when heating homes and buildings in winter, extreme-heat weather patterns resulting from climate change also create increasing demands for energy-intensive cooling in the summer.[34]

As the chart from the Green Economy Network's platform shows (see Table 5.2), almost 30 percent of Canada's total energy use is dedicated to heating and cooling the country's building stocks, which is responsible for a quarter of greenhouse gas emissions from energy use. Energy conservation and efficiencies reduce emissions from fossil fuels used to heat and cool homes and buildings; additional emission reductions will come as clean, renewable energy replaces fossil fuels for these purposes. Establishing energy conservation and efficiency as a national priority would mean energy savings that also result in lower energy bills. Indeed, energy efficiency strategies are unique in that they can be implemented so that they can pay for themselves through savings over time.

Table 5.2 Energy Efficiency for Buildings in Canada

Building Sector	Percentage of Total Energy Used	Percentage of Greenhouse Gas Emissions
Residential	16%	14%
Commercial, Industrial and Institutional	12%	11%
Total	28%	25%

Source: Green Economy Network

Other countries (notably the United States and United Kingdom) have led the way in developing energy efficiency programs and strategies to renovate existing building stock. In 2011, President Obama launched his "Better Buildings Initiative" in the United States, which was preceded by the U.K.'s action plan on retrofitting buildings called "The Green Deal."[35] Both include programs to retrofit homes and buildings over a 15-year period, with targets set for every five years. Germany has also initiated a building retrofit program as part of its economy and climate change strategy. So far, however, Canada has been a laggard. Although previous federal programs, such as Energuide and ecoENERGY, offered financial assistance for building retrofits, barely 8 percent of the country's building stock has benefited.[36]

Drawing on the work done in the United States and United Kingdom, the National Energy Efficiency Initiative for Canada was proposed and developed by both the Canadian Energy Efficiency Alliance and the Canadian Renewable Energy Alliance in August 2010. At the national level, this initiative calls for expanding the Office of Energy Efficiency in Natural Resources Canada to maintain energy standards, building codes and benchmarking services. It would also include support for innovative "pay-as-you-save" financing programs. These allow home and property owners to make energy efficiency improvements through low-interest loans that are repaid over time by installments combined with guaranteed energy cost savings.[37] The Green Economy Network's platform proposed a strategy for both green homes and green buildings based on this model, which has been successfully test-run in the United States and United Kingdom. Table 5.3 summarizes the **green homes** strategy.

Table 5.3 Green Homes Strategy
(To be implemented over a five-year period)

Broad Goals	
40 percent of Canadian homes	Retrofit to an average level of 30 percent increased energy efficiency savings
150,000 low-income homes	Upgrade, reducing their energy bills by an average of 30 percent
All new homes	Increase energy efficiency by 2 percent per year until 2025 (new homes built after that date would be required to achieve net zero, generating as much energy as they consume)
Financing Programs	
Low-income housing grants	For retrofits, as part of a national initiative
"Pay-as-you-save"	Property tax financing for all major home retrofits
Loan repayment	For smaller retrofits through energy cost savings on utility bills
Additional	
A national home retrofit training and certification program	
Minimum building and housing retrofit standards to be phased in over five years within all provinces	
Universal mandatory home energy labelling at time of sale or new rental agreements	

Similarly, the **green buildings** strategy aims to improve the energy efficiency — both technical and operational — of all commercial, industrial, business and public buildings across the country by 50 percent over a five-year period and to ensure that all new buildings are at net zero by 2025. Table 5.4 shows how it would achieve these goals.

Table 5.4 Green Buildings Strategy
(To be implemented over a five-year period)

Action/Target	Goals
All commercial, industrial, business and public buildings nationwide	Improve energy efficiency — both technical and operational — by 50 percent
All new buildings	Ensure they are net zero by 2025
National database and benchmarking service	On building performance
Universal building labelling	At the time of sale or new rental agreements
Regional efficiency centres	Providing audit-to-implementation technical services to major institutional enterprises
"Pay-as-you-save" financing initiatives	Innovative financing such as loan guarantees for both major retrofits and green buildings where possible
Domestic procurement criteria	Ensure that job creation benefits, where possible, go to people in the region or the country at large

According to the Green Economy Network, this green homes and buildings strategy will require investments totalling $30 billion over the five-year period. A relatively small portion of this total would involve actual new government funding; for example, $1.5 billion may be required from the federal government for the Office of Energy Efficiency and $2 billion from the provinces combined for regional efficiency centres. Most of the remaining $26.5 billion could be covered through pay-as-you-save financing set up through loan guarantees based on the municipal tax base and local banking institutions, working in collaboration with local public utilities.[38]

This strategy could generate tens of thousands of new jobs for the Canadian economy. Based on the methodology developed by the Center for American Progress, a $30 billion investment over five years could generate 438,000 person-years of employment. Approximately 189,000 of these would be in the form of direct employment in the retrofit industry, whereas 123,000 would be newly employed in secondary industries, such as suppliers, plus another 123,000 in the form of induced employment generated by increases in retail sales and services due to the new investment.

During the same five-year period, this green homes and buildings strategy would make Canada's building stock significantly more energy efficient. Based on Environment and Climate Canada's method for calculating greenhouse gas emission reductions, the projected annual decrease in emissions would range from 32 to 126 million tonnes after ten years if the plan were rolled over and repeated. If, during this period, greenhouse gas emission reductions from this country's building stock were to decline by as much as 126 million tonnes per year, it would amount to a decrease of nearly 18 percent of Canada's total annual greenhouse gas emissions. Hence, this strategy would make yet another ongoing substantial contribution to reducing Canada's annual greenhouse gas emissions.

A nationwide effort to retrofit and renovate this country's building stock for energy efficiencies along the lines discussed above would provide concrete opportunities as an eco-pathway for greater social equity. Curbing climate change by radically reducing greenhouse gas emissions through energy efficiency also opens doors for combatting poverty and inequality in our society:

- Retrofitting homes and buildings provides opportunities for unemployed workers in our communities to secure decent-paying employment.[39]
- Special rebates for low-income housing retrofits plus renewed social housing development with energy-efficient units would provide additional opportunities for energy cost savings along with improvements in the quality of housing.

Transportation Shift

The third eco-pathway relates to the transportation sector and the importance of a public transportation strategy. In 2016, 24 percent of this country's greenhouse gas emissions, or over 170 million tonnes, came from the transportation sector. According to Environment Canada, a little more than half of the energy used in this sector is for transporting people.[40] Although significant portions of this energy use come via air travel, rail and buses, most of it stems from the widespread dependence on conventional private automobiles with combustion engines. If Canada is to make substantial reductions in its greenhouse gas emissions, clearly major public investments are needed in urban public transit and higher-speed rail between cities in metropolitan corridors, along with promotion of the manufacture and sale of electric-powered cars and light trucks.

Given the extensive urban sprawl surrounding cities such as Toronto, Vancouver and Montreal, we must urgently rethink how to transport people (as well as freight) within and between our major cities. The urgency stems not only from climate change but also from quality-of-life issues such as traffic congestion, long commutes and worsening air and water pollution. The process of addressing climate change effectively compels us not only to rethink how we transport people (and freight) within and between urban centres but also how we design or redesign our cities to be more humanly and environmentally habitable.

To take more cars and trucks off the road, the Green Economy Network proposed developing a national public transportation strategy. This strategy would have two basic components:

- **Public transit systems** — improving and expanding public transit for transporting people within urban centres across the country
- **Intercity rail systems** — developing new higher-speed rail systems to transport people between cities within metropolitan corridors such as the Windsor-Toronto-Montreal-Quebec City corridor, the Edmonton-Calgary corridor or the Vancouver-Seattle corridor

To successfully reduce dependency on private automobiles, the network maintained that such a national transportation strategy must be accessible, affordable and accountable.[41]

Public transit development in Canada has traditionally occurred in a piecemeal, even haphazard, way. Even though all Canadians benefit, one way or another, from improved and expanded public transit, municipal governments end up covering most of the costs. According to a study conducted for the Canadian Urban Transit Association, most of the operating costs for urban public transit are covered at the municipal level — 61 percent through ridership fees and the remaining 39 percent through funding from municipal governments.[42] Although 65 percent of the capital costs for urban public transit are generally covered by the provinces, municipal governments still pay for 18 percent, with the federal government contributing a mere 14 percent through 2015. This pattern of funding from federal and provincial levels of government has been insufficient to cover the costs of municipal transit systems across Canada.

There has been absolutely no public investment by any level of government to build higher-speed rail between major cities in the three major urban corridors identified above, even though repeated studies have demonstrated that higher-speed rail lines in these corridors would be both feasible and practical. Other countries, including China, France, Germany, Italy, Japan, Spain, the United Kingdom and the United States, have already developed higher-speed rail systems for intercity transport and have plans for expanding these systems.

The Green Economy Network has proposed public investment strategies for both public transit and higher-speed rail developments over the short, medium and long term.[43] The short-term plan calls for public investments in public transit systems amounting to $53.5 billion over the first five years, primarily for capital costs. Of this amount, only one third needs to be raised as the remaining two thirds has already been committed by provincial and federal governments for these purposes. The network's short-term plan for higher-speed rail projects requires an additional $10 billion over five years to initiate the design and construction of intercity rail for the largest urban corridor, the Windsor-Toronto-Montreal-Quebec City corridor. All told, the network's five-year short-term plan for public transportation calls for $27.6 billion in public investments. Studies such as the one done by HDR Decision Economics indicate additional public investments that will be required to bring Canada's urban transit systems up to an "optimal level" of supply and demand beyond the initial five years.[44]

It turns out that public investment in urban transit is very cost-effective. According to a national survey published as *The Economic Impact of Transit Investment,* public investment "reduces the amount of public money that must be spent on everything from health care to municipal services."[45] Estimates suggest that in 2007 alone, investments in urban transit saved Canadians some $115 million in related respiratory health costs, $2.5 billion in costs due to traffic collisions and $5 billion in the operating costs of household vehicles.[46] Add to this a range of other costs, such as parking and social costs, and urban transit ends up being one third to one half less expensive than automobile use. As well, urban transit systems in Canada contribute over $10 billion to the Canadian economy each year.

The Green Economy Network's short-term, five-year public investment plan would also create tens of thousands of decent-paying jobs in urban transit and intercity higher-speed rail transport. On the basis of the Center for American Progress methodology, public investments of $53.5 billion ($17.6 billion of which is new money) for improving and expanding public transit, spread over five years at $10.7 billion per year, would generate 136,000 person job years of employment. These jobs would be broken down as follows:

- 52,000 person job years in direct employment within the public transit industry where investments are made,
- approximately 45,000 person job years in secondary or supply industries and
- another 39,000 or so person job years in induced forms of employment.

A further investment of $25.7 billion to stimulate intercity higher-speed rail in designated corridors over five years ($5.14 billion per year) would annually generate another 65,300 person job years — nearly 25,000 in direct employment within the railcar industry, close to 22,000 in secondary or supply industries and 18,500 in induced forms of employment.[47]

The reduction in greenhouse gas emissions from this public transportation strategy will be gradual and less dramatic than from the energy and building strategies. The reason lies in the difference between direct and indirect effects. The direct effect is referred to as the "ridership effect," involving the shift from private automobiles to public transit use, whereas the indirect effect has to do with land use in the form of more compact development and greater urban density achieved through better urban planning. Greenhouse gas emission reductions are generally four times greater from the land use effect as a result of more compact communities and shorter trip distances, whereas emission reductions from the ridership effect usually take longer to materialize because of the time it takes to change behaviour patterns. Therefore, the direct greenhouse gas emission reductions over the five-year short-term plan would be between 12 and 25 million tonnes a year, but the long-term emission reductions are more likely to be between 48 and 100 million tonnes annually.

Such a public transportation strategy can be successful only if ridership in both urban public transit and intercity rail increases. To achieve this goal, public transit and intercity higher-speed rail must be made more affordable, especially for low-income and working people. As long as transit fares remain high, it will be difficult to encourage people to use public transit and thereby get greenhouse gas–emitting cars off the road. Indeed, emissions from transportation have continued to grow every year, amounting to a 31 percent increase between 1990 and 2013 and has remained at that level since. Unless transit fares are lowered and made more affordable (if not free), there is little chance of reversing people's use and dependence on the private automobile.

Implementing the Big Shift

The total five-year plan calls for public investments amounting to $80.9 billion (close to $16 billion per year), which in turn would generate over one million jobs and reduce Canada's annual greenhouse gas emissions by over one third, between 88 and 262 million tonnes. Table 5.5 illustrates the breakdown of anticipated expenditures, jobs gained and emission reductions achieved in each sector.

Table 5.5 Big Shift Campaign Overview: Inputs and Outputs

	$ Billion Invested over 5-Year Period	Total Person-Years of Employment Created	GHG Emission Reductions (Mt CO2eq)
Energy Shift	$23.3	290,000	44–110
Building Shift	$30.0	438,000	32–126
Transportation Shift	$27.6	324,600	12–25
5-Year Totals	$80.9 billion	1,052,600 person job years	88 to 261 Mt annually

Source: Green Economy Network

The plan can be rolled over and repeated after the first five years. Since the desired transformation in each of the three sectors will not be completed within the first five-year cycle, the plan could continue into a second and even a third or more rounds, subject to built-in evaluations and improvements. The objective would be to implement two cycles of the five-year plan in the 2020–30 decade, with the prospect of continuing into the next decade (2030–40), making necessary adjustments and improvements, until net zero in greenhouse gas emissions is reached.

Raising new public revenues to fight climate change should be a priority for all governments. One option, of course, is putting a price on carbon through a carbon tax. Another option is to eliminate direct and especially indirect subsidies granted to polluting industries. According to the IMF, Canadian governments (federal and provincial) provide indirect subsidies every year to resource industries (e.g., petroleum, mining) through clean-up services, roads and related infrastructure amounting to over

$46.5 billion annually.[48] Following up on both measures would allow governments to raise significant new public revenues to finance bold initiatives such as the three eco-pathways discussed above. The government could raise an additional $8 to $10 billion or more annually by clamping down on wealthy investors engaged in tax avoidance schemes such as offshore tax havens or by reinstating former tax rates on corporate profits and income. Such initiatives would go a long way to building the kind of financial war chest that governments are going to need to take on this monumental challenge.

In short, this three-pronged formula provides a workable transition formula for "getting to zero" by 2040. The plan

- features strategic public investments aimed at removing the prime causes of greenhouse gas emissions in the economy,
- opens up a new line of employment in the economy by creating hundreds of thousands of decent-paying climate jobs and
- establishes the infrastructure needed to continue the process of reducing greenhouse gas emissions and transitioning to a new net-zero carbon economy for the future.

Implementing such a plan would require reorganizing federal government departments. Each of the plan's three pillars — energy, buildings and transportation — would be headed by a cabinet minister who would oversee a corresponding department. To provide ongoing oversight, integration and evaluation of the overall plan moving forward, the three ministers and their deputies would constitute a special committee presided over by the prime minister or his or her designate. Furthermore, to ensure that progress is made and evaluated with respect to the equity shift and a just transition (discussed in Chapter 6), a specific position would need to be created with appropriate duties, resources and powers to work with this special committee. Moreover, recognizing the scope and depth of the effort required to make the Big Shift happen within the critical path and timeline leading up to 2040, a publicly owned Crown corporation will also need to be established with the necessary mandate and powers to facilitate the transition.

Ongoing Challenges

If the Trudeau government or its successors were to develop and implement an action plan along the lines of the Big Shift, they would no doubt encounter numerous challenges and obstacles along the way. Here are three by way of example:

- **The increasing corporate takeover of the burgeoning renewable energy industry.** Today, the more than 100 mega–solar farms being developed in Ontario are constructed and operated by large domestic and foreign-owned corporations such as Enbridge, TransCanada and Samsung (to name a few).[49] These developments signal the resurgence of the old economic model of big corporate domination over energy matters and solutions. Although investment capital is certainly needed for the renewable energy shift to take place, it becomes increasingly problematic if for-profit corporations end up controlling the renewable energy industry — all the more so if oil corporations such as Exxon and Suncor or pipeline companies such as Enbridge and TransCanada are positioning themselves to control the future of renewable energy to protect their vested interests in the fossil fuel industry. The proposal to insert a Crown or public corporation to facilitate the transition could provide a much-needed counterweight.

- **Goals for organizing campaigns to advance the Big Shift.** In official international circles, the goals related to climate change action are framed in terms of limits on the rise in global temperature this century. However, since the temperature-focused goal does not specify the amount of greenhouse gas emission reductions a country is to make, "it is therefore relatively easy," wrote Oliver Geden, research director at the German Institute for International and Security Affairs, "for governments to support ambitious global targets while doing little against national climate change in practice."[50] As Geden put it, focusing on the goal of achieving zero greenhouse gas emissions rather than temperature thresholds is "noticeably more precise, easier to evaluate, politically more likely to be attained and ultimately more motivating too." According to Geden, "whoever ignores the target will not be able to deceive others" as "it is relatively easy to ascertain whether the respective emissions are going up or down." The Trudeau government has so far been caught up in temperature-focused goals, but the Big Shift campaign should set its focus on the goal of "getting to zero" or achieving net-zero greenhouse gas emissions by 2040.

- **The price tag.** An investment of $80.9 billion is a hefty one for governments to make, even if it is spread over five years. However, as noted earlier, this can be mitigated by implementing pay-as-you-save financing for building retrofits, using the 50/40/10 formula for governmental financing of common projects and raising revenue through a new national carbon tax. Naturally, additional costs associated with developing and delivering a program such as the Big Shift will arise. Some of these may be absorbed by the new infrastructure that would be created, but new revenues would also likely need to be raised. Two other potential methods of raising new public revenues would be

  - collecting taxes from corporations that generate ecological and social costs for governments in the form of wildfires, air pollution, traffic congestion and climate change, as advised by the IMF (such costs currently amount to nearly $45 billion annually in Canada alone),[51] and
  - reviving the Bank of Canada's original mandate to operate as a public bank for governments by providing access to the public capital needed to finance medium- to long-term action plans such as the Big Shift program.

These are but a few of the challenges in developing and implementing the Big Shift strategy in Canada. Before focusing too much on the challenges, we need to consider one more necessary shift: an "equity shift."

CHAPTER 6
Just Transition

In the previous two chapters, we have addressed some major components of the Big Shift that must take place to meet the challenge of runaway climate change. The shift to a new economy requires a deep transformation in major sectors of Canada's economy. But this kind of societal transformation also needs to be facilitated by a process that is fair and just, as well as sustainable.

After all, people and their communities lie at the heart of the needed deep transformation. Since the Industrial Revolution, Indigenous peoples, workers and their communities have paid a heavy price for many of the major economic transitions that have taken place. It is hard enough when workers lose their jobs in the normal boom-and-bust cycles of resource industries. But when companies that extract coal and bitumen are designated as sunset industries for generating greenhouse gas emissions, the impacts on tens of thousands of coal mine workers and well over a hundred thousand workers in the bitumen industry, along with their families and communities, will be devastating.

Increasingly, workers in the fossil fuel industry are speaking out about the threats of climate change and the transition challenges they face. Ken Smith, a 57-year-old heavy equipment mechanic from Fort McMurray who works for Suncor and heads the Unifor union local of 3,500 oil workers in the tar sands, spoke from the floor during a public forum at the Paris climate summit on the "one million climate jobs" challenge.[1] "We hope we're seeing the end of fossil fuels for the good of everybody . . . but how are we going to provide for our families?" Smith told the audience. As he made his plea, newscasts from Alberta were reporting that the suicide rate in the province had risen 30 percent as a result of mounting job losses.

Smith went on to say that whereas 10 years ago oil workers resisted the idea that climate change is real and dangerous, they are now beginning to "get it." The fires in northern Alberta and northern Saskatchewan and strange weather patterns have had their effect. However, "if slowing down or dismantling the industry is part of Canada's response, then don't leave workers behind in the process," he pleaded. "Our employers will move on to the next shiny thing they see and make another billion dollars — but where are our workers going to go?" We're going to need some kind of transition, he said. Otherwise, "when it ends, we're going to be the ones holding the bag."

So, for the Big Shift plan to work effectively, it must include one more shift: an *equity shift*. In the past, major restructurings of the economy have all too often left people such as laid-off workers from sunset industries, poor and racialized communities and Indigenous peoples marginalized. The immediate challenge here is to ensure that the economic restructuring generated by the three-pronged Big Shift program leaves no one behind by providing effective tools for a just and sustainable transition. This includes targeting investments for the creation of new, decent-paying jobs (climate jobs); ensuring that displaced workers and other marginalized peoples (such as Indigenous peoples, the working poor and racialized communities) have equitable access to these jobs; providing real opportunities for skills training or retraining as needed and programming income supports during the transition for displaced workers and their families.

To date, just transition strategies have been based on the principle that the "costs of environmental adjustments" should be shared across society rather than shouldered alone by those most affected by them. In other words, no workers should be left behind. In terms of public policy, this generally means a twofold approach of minimizing the social impacts on workers and involving workers in decisions about their livelihoods. Moreover, in its 2008 document *Green Jobs: Towards Decent Work in a Sustainable Low-Carbon World*, the United Nations Environment Programme broadened its approach to a just transition by including workplaces and local communities as follows:

> *Issues of protection, retraining and relocation of workers*
> *displaced by declining industries, the generation of good*
> *quality green jobs that are available to all communities*
> *and the question of fair trade, technology transfer, and*
> *ensuring sufficient funds for adaptation to climate*
> *change. Meaningful worker and community participation*
> *is seen as an essential feature of the transition, as is social*
> *dialogue at all levels of decision-making.*[2]

In 2000, the Canadian Labour Congress adopted a broad policy position on a just transition that called for "the fair treatment of workers and their communities when employers close their facilities."[3] This implies the "continuation of employment without loss of pay, benefits or seniority" where possible and, if not, then the provision of "just compensation." This vision of a just transition prioritizes "quality employment in a [new] economy based on sustainable production and infrastructure." It also assumes a plan of action and programs for transition. Two years later, the Canadian Centre for Policy Alternatives produced a report entitled *Making Kyoto Work: A Transition Strategy for Canadian Energy Workers*, which played a role in building labour union support in Canada for the Kyoto Protocol.[4]

The call for just transition strategies, however, is sometimes greeted with sighs of skepticism on the part of workers and activists — and for good reason. After all, the proposals outlined in the transition strategy for Canadian energy workers mentioned above have not, for the most part, been actively and widely promoted by the labour movement in this country, let alone adopted by any federal or provincial government. Moreover, no government to date has come up with a plan of action for financing just transition strategies along the lines identified above. Even more importantly, the scope of just transition is still too narrow. To be sure, the Trudeau government has struck a task force on "just transition" that includes representatives of labour unions, but it is not yet clear what position and influence they will have on the outcome. Initially, the main focus was on a "just transition" for coal workers since priority was being put on the de-commissioning of coal-fired generators. But, the task force so far does not specifically include and involve Indigenous communities whose land and people have already been impacted by Big Oil projects and will be further impacted, both directly and indirectly, by additional industrial transformation and the transition to a new economy called for here. Nor does it include poor communities with high unemployment that have been left out of the old industrial economy and urgently require access to decent job and training opportunities in the eco-pathways to a new economy. The equity gap looms large.

What is needed now is a collective commitment by governments to develop a deeper and broader approach to just transition strategies. In particular, priority should be put on displaced workers, Indigenous peoples and poor communities. This calls for a threefold approach: a workers' contract, an Indigenous covenant and community pacts.

Workers' Contract

The whole idea of developing a social contract with displaced workers who lose their jobs, through no fault of their own as a result of a major societal shift, dates back at least to the post–World War II era. When the war-based economy came to an end in the mid-1940s, giving rise — temporarily at least — to a new peace economy, a smooth transition was needed for tens of thousands of soldiers returning from overseas as well as those workers displaced by dismantling the war economy at home. Revenues from taxes paid by corporations and workers during this postwar era flowed back through a wide range of public services. At the same time, this social contract provided opportunities for unions to organize on behalf of working people and negotiate with corporations and governments, which, in turn, led to improvements in wages, benefits and working conditions. Now, however, after more than four decades of neoliberal public policies emphasizing deregulation, privatization and free trade, that social contract has been substantially eroded and dismantled.

The great transformation from an oil-based, carbon-intensive, industrialized economy to a largely zero-carbon economy based on renewable energy sources represents a societal shift no less massive than the one that took place in the 1940s. This time we need to develop a "green social contract" to enable displaced workers from the tar sands industry, along with new and unemployed workers, to make the transition to a new economy based on sustainable production and infrastructure. Recent studies show that although there will be significant job losses in fossil fuel industries in the coming decades, there will be new, decent-paying job opportunities opening up in emerging clean energy and related industries. The key is to develop strategic linkages between displaced and unemployed workers and these opportunities opening up in the renewable energy development sector, the area of green homes and building retrofits and public transit and higher-speed rail.

In this process, a green social contract must be guided by basic principles such as justice and sustainability, along with solidarity and transformation, to ensure that a truly fair transition takes place. What follows is an outline of some of the key components that could be incorporated into a just transition program for workers in sunset industries, based on a Canadian Centre for Policy Alternatives report directed toward the largely resource-extractive economy of British Columbia[5]:

- **A just transition fund.** A stand-alone fund, at the provincial or federal level, would offer a financial base for the programs and initiatives required to help workers through the transition.

Federally, a comprehensive fund could be established through revamping the Employment Insurance (EI) program, which currently has a healthy surplus that is projected to continue for several years. Even so, EI has its limitations. As a national Canadian Centre for Policy Alternatives report noted recently, the current maximum payout is only $543 per week for 45 weeks — a precipitous drop in income for high-paid oil workers. For fossil fuel workers facing the extinction of their industry, 45 weeks with such a reduction in income is likely insufficient for reskilling or relocation to find another job. Resource revenues from increased royalty rates or a carbon tax could be used to enhance the financial base of a federally administered just transition fund. Any revamping of the EI program for these purposes, however, must include worker and employer representatives.

- **Advanced skills training.** All the changes we are discussing will require new skills among workers. This calls for long-term planning and investment in appropriate and accessible skills training programs in colleges and related training facilities across the country. This, in turn, necessitates collaboration between government, labour and employers, along with co-ordinated investments in credited training programs.

- **Apprenticeship investments.** To increase the number of skilled workers overall, apprenticeship training is a key component of any just transition strategy. This is especially important for attracting young people to a new, emerging industry, such as the development of renewable energy, or the revival of older industries, such as building retrofits for energy conservation. Being certified as apprentices through training programs for these and other eco-pathway industries increases the number and types of skilled workers available for the transition to the new economy. In Canada, most of the apprenticeship training authority lies with provincial governments. In various provinces, there are industry training organizations responsible for administering and updating the types of training for programs they have been assigned. In Quebec, for example, employers are compelled by law to pay a training levy through their payroll taxes if they do not make a concrete commitment to train their own employees. To make a smooth transition to an economy based on more sustainable production, we will need greater collaboration and co-ordination between the various industry training organizations.

- **Transition income security.** A secure source of income during periods of unemployment or training comprises a necessary part of a just transition plan. Workers who are suddenly displaced may require income protection for between one and four years through measures such as continued qualification for EI and the Canada and Quebec pension plans. For older workers, options with creative flexibility may be needed, such as bridging their pension and full retirement rate. As well, Canada Pension Plan provisions need to be revised to ensure that older workers can retire earlier with dignity and without a major loss of benefits. In turn, early retirement would open up more job options for younger workers, which reinforces the need for training and retraining for new work opportunities in sustainable production.

- **Worker and family supports.** Beyond skills development, workers and their families often need short-term emotional supports to get through the transition period. Providing counselling services, for example, can help people weather the emotional turbulence that comes with job transitions. In some cases, workers may also require longer-term occupational support to enable them to plan ahead for their career development and build personal confidence to take on new challenges. A process is needed whereby workers can seek and attain extended counselling services and benefits. A just transition program must also consider what can be done to provide services to enable spouses and other family members to find good jobs in public sector fields such as health care and community development.

A just transition along these lines requires considerable public planning, management and oversight. The tar sands and the fossil fuel industry in Canada are largely controlled by petroleum corporations and their investors who reside elsewhere, usually outside the country. As a result, policy decisions affecting the economic and social security of workers during a transition are mainly driven by the vested interests of distant shareholders and by the fluctuations in global commodity markets. A coherent public planning and management regime is therefore required if an abrupt displacement of workers is to be averted during periods of industrial transformation.

In its January 2018 review of just transition policies and programs in Canada, the Canadian Centre for Policy Alternatives made a useful distinction between two types of transition policies: "reactive" and "proactive."[6] Reactive just transition policies "are focused on the workers and communities negatively affected by the shift to a zero carbon economy," such as displaced workers in coal and bitumen industries and communities affected by decarbonization policies and programs. Such programs are designed mainly to provide direct financial support to individuals and communities affected by the transition, especially enabling displaced workers to find new jobs. On the other hand, "proactive" just transition policies are more focused on "job creation and workforce development measures" in relation to "a planned expansion of zero-carbon industries." Proactive policies and programs are primarily aimed at promoting investment in the creation of what we call "climate jobs" or, more broadly, "green jobs" in the transition to a new, more sustainable economy and the training of new workers. Both reactive and proactive tracks are essential for a comprehensive just transition in Canada.

The Canadian Centre for Policy Alternatives concluded that Canadian governments are in a mixed state of readiness to undertake a just transition. For example, "the federal government already has social security and workforce development policies in place to facilitate a reactive just transition." In some provinces, notably Alberta, measures are now in place to provide additional targeted support. But "the scope of these programs is inadequate to prevent undue hardship in the areas most affected by decarbonization policies," said the centre. Also, the various levels of government in Canada "lack a coordinated plan for the transition of affected workers into new jobs and industries."[7] At the same time, the Trudeau government has begun to make proactive public investments in the creation of green infrastructure, which includes new job creation and workforce development policies such as the skills training needed for the emerging zero-carbon economy. However, the Canadian Centre for Policy Alternatives contended that "the scale of funding is inadequate given the scope of the challenge." What's more, there is "no comprehensive industrial strategy to tie these spending and training programs together." As a result, "it is not at all clear that the workers being trained and the jobs being created will overlap with the jobs and industries being lost in certain parts of the country."[8]

Essentially, we lack co-ordination and strategic direction. Perhaps here's where the proposed creation of a Crown corporation comes into play. A Crown corporation — say, in the bitumen industry — with a mandate to ensure that displaced workers in the industry get a just transition, could provide a concrete example of this kind of transition in the oil patch, using appropriate tools of public ownership and control of the resource to carry out its mandate.[9] Creating such a corporation requires an action plan that provides concrete institutional linkages between individual displaced oil sands workers and new job opportunities in solar, wind, geothermal and related renewable energy industries. Such a plan must also include provisions for the various support mechanisms outlined above — advanced skills training, apprenticeship investments, transition income security, worker and family supports — along with the just transition fund to finance it all. The

Crown corporation would function in collaboration and co-ordination with these mechanisms. It could also ensure that whatever resource developments continued during the transition period would include new partnerships respecting the rights and entitlements of neighbouring Indigenous communities and a much more balanced approach between conservation and extraction.

Furthermore, if one of the goals of a new economy is inclusiveness, then more attention needs to be paid to the equity shift. The fossil fuel industry is one of the most skewed of all sectors in the Canadian economy when it comes to inequities — gender, racial and economic.[10] Fossil fuel workers in this country are predominantly male (77 percent) and comparatively very well paid: an average of $68 an hour, twice the Canadian average of $35 an hour. According to the recent Canadian Centre for Policy Alternatives report, fossil fuel workers are also disproportionately born in this country, so only 12 percent are immigrant workers in the oil and gas sector compared to 23 percent across all other sectors. Because women are much more likely to get jobs in lower-paid services than in more lucrative fossil fuel production, the gender pay gap is more extreme in the province of Alberta than in the rest of the country. And Indigenous workers, although well represented in fossil fuel industries compared to most other sectors of the economy, tend to end up with lower-income and precarious jobs. When it comes to extractive projects, the Indigenous experience is largely "last hired, first fired." In short, there cannot be a just transition unless the equity shift is made imperative.

Indigenous Covenant

Developing a just transition strategy does not begin and end with enabling workers displaced by industrial transformation to make the shift to clean, decent-paying jobs in a new economy. Whether or not a transition strategy is just will also be judged on the basis of what is done to respect the rights and improve the livelihood of Indigenous peoples. Therefore, not only a workers' contract, but also an Indigenous covenant with First Nations, Inuit and Métis people, needs to be developed and implemented so that they can play a more effective role in the new economy. This calls for, among other initiatives, a whole new approach to forming partnerships between Indigenous peoples and governments, not only federal but provincial and municipal as well.

The foundation for such a covenant has been laid in recent decades both nationally and internationally:

- The 1996 Royal Commission on Aboriginal Peoples recommended a new Royal proclamation for Aboriginal peoples, a new order of Aboriginal government, an Indigenous peoples parliament and the extension of the Aboriginal land base and natural resources.[11]
- These recommendations were reinforced in 2007 by the adoption of the *United Nations Declaration on the Rights of Indigenous Peoples*, which now requires signatories such as Canada to recognize the economic, cultural, social and political rights of Indigenous peoples; renegotiate extensions to their traditional lands, along with the corresponding development of a land-based economy and realize their rights to "free, prior and informed consent" before any industrial development projects take place on (or affect) their lands and territories.[12]
- The 2015 report of the Truth and Reconciliation Commission concerning the struggles of residential school survivors in this country captured the moral imperative for urgent action on a range of priorities, including the political and economic ones identified in the other documents.[13]

Indigenous values and wisdom contain important ingredients for the vision needed to guide this country toward a post-industrial economy and society. Although the Royal Proclamation of 1763, enshrined in the *British North America Act*, was to ensure British protection of the rights and cultures of Indigenous peoples, the subsequent process of making treaties with First Nations was a sham. Instead of the

Indigenous understanding of the treaties as "peace and friendship" agreements on a nation-to-nation basis, Canadian government officials viewed the treaties as "tools of power" and "commercial mechanisms . . . for land ownership transfers."[14]

Despite Indigenous peoples' rights to their traditional lands embodied in these treaties and more modern land claim agreements and further enshrined in the Canadian *Constitution Act* through provisions adopted with repatriation in 1982, the cultural divide remains. On the one hand, these lands are valuable because they contain deposits of money-making oil, gas, minerals, timber and hydroelectric power; on the other, they stand in the way of the delivery of these resources to markets by pipelines, railways and cargo ships. The concept of Indigenous land-based economies is ignored, lost and forgotten. More recently, those Indigenous lands containing valuable resource potential have been labelled by some entrepreneurs and commentators as forms of "dead capital" that need to be freed up.[15] Moreover, the rights that Indigenous peoples hold over these lands are in the form of collective ownership, frozen as "stranded assets" in the *Indian Act*. To free up this capital, they say, collective ownership needs to be replaced by individual private property rights for Indigenous peoples. Collective property, it is argued, is the path of poverty, and private property is the path of prosperity.

However, attempts during the Harper regime to bring in legislation to replace collective ownership with a private property regime on Indigenous reserves and territories were steadfastly rejected. In July 2010, for example, the country's 600-plus band council chiefs, meeting in Winnipeg as the Assembly of First Nations, unanimously voted against establishing a private property rights regime on Indigenous lands through federal legislation.[16] Although this rejection seems to have put a damper on such strategies for the time being, maintaining the status quo does nothing to break the deadlock, let alone resolve historical injustices. In advanced industrial societies based on the pursuit of profit, buying and selling land through real estate transactions has been a key factor in the accumulation of wealth and power. To accumulate wealth, therefore, priority has been put on plundering the land to exploit the natural resources used to manufacture products demanded by industrial society. In other words, the land, and therefore nature, must be conquered and dominated. However, for most Indigenous communities, the land is understood as "Mother Earth" and the "source of life itself." There is a strong spiritual identity with the land, which nourishes and preserves life. The land belongs to the Creator, the Great Spirit; it should not be bought and sold but rather looked after by the people as its guardians and caretakers.

The Indigenous view does not mean that the land must not be developed for its resources. However, the model of development must respect and be in harmony with nature, and the land must be returned to future generations in as good a condition as it was before being developed. From this perspective, some Indigenous peoples have envisioned their own land-based economy and land use plans.[17]

Take, for example, the Dehcho First Nation located north of Alberta in the Northwest Territories, with links to the tar sands through the Mackenzie and Athabasca rivers.[18] After extensive consultations with their elders and collecting the stories of their ancestors, the Dehcho leaders developed a comprehensive land use plan as the cornerstone of their land claim negotiations with Ottawa. The plan divided the Dehcho land base into three zones. The first are the *conservation zones* (by far the largest of the three, also including Nahanni National Park Reserve), designated as areas where no new non-renewable resource developments would be permitted. The second are the *development zones*, where non-renewable resource development projects would be permitted under special management to meet certain specified environmental and social criteria. The third are the *mixed zones* for general use purposes, where both conservation and development projects would be permitted. At its core, the Dehcho land use plan is based on the Dene way of life — "our land is our life."

In 2007, the Dehcho fully ratified the land use plan, but it was subsequently rejected by the federal government on the grounds that it "protected too much land from development and added uncertainty to the existing regulatory regime."[19] After nearly two decades, the Dehcho land claim negotiations remain at a standstill. Meanwhile, the Dehcho land use plan has been heralded by other Indigenous peoples and nations as a major breakthrough in establishing the foundations of an Indigenous land-based economy rooted, in this case, in the Dene Nation, based on Dene values and traditional knowledge.

The Dehcho land use plan presents a real test case for this country. If Canada is serious about bringing about reconciliation with Indigenous peoples, as well as fulfilling its commitments to combat runaway climate change, the federal government could show leadership by ratifying the Dehcho plan, which provides a living alternative model for a land-based economy. Doing so would go a long way toward laying the foundations for an authentic Indigenous covenant and send a clear message about reconciliation moving forward.

In the meantime, Indigenous peoples have been and continue to be on the front lines of resistance against the construction of pipelines to bring carbon-polluting crude from the tar sands to U.S. overseas and domestic markets.[20] In addition, they are playing a leading role in facilitating the transition to a clean, renewable energy future for some of their communities. A notable example is the Indigenous-owned and run social enterprise Aki Energy, which has retrofitted more than 200 homes and buildings to switch from the burning of fossil fuels to geothermal power, Earth's natural underground heating and cooling system.

Also notable is the Lubicon Lake Nation community of Little Buffalo in northern Alberta, where a group of local community members developed the skills to set up a 20.8-kilowatt solar panel installation to power their community's health centre and provide surplus energy to the community electrical grid. They are now ready to use these skills to enable more homes and buildings to make the switch to solar power. Then there's the Pukwis Community Wind Park in Georgina Island, Ontario, a joint venture between the Chippewas of Georgina Island First Nation and the Windfall Ecology Centre, which is a community-owned enterprise that, in its first phase, produced enough electricity to power 7,500 homes.

Although many more examples could be cited, these three illustrate how Indigenous peoples are on the cutting edge of reducing green-house gas emissions by developing clean, renewable sources of energy for their communities. Across the country, wind, solar and geothermal power on traditional Indigenous lands has considerable potential to be developed as sources of renewable energy for Indigenous and perhaps neighbouring rural communities. By forming partnerships with appropriate levels of government along similar lines, Indigenous nations and communities could help play a leading role in the transition from a fossil fuel–driven economy and society to a new economy based on clean, renewable sources of energy for the future.

In doing so, the best practices of these Indigenous community partnerships for renewable energy transition could constitute the basis for developing an Indigenous covenant. Such a covenant would provide the framework for developing a renewed relationship between the descendants of the original peoples and the descendants of the settlers who came to occupy this land we now call Canada. The cornerstone of this covenant would be the recognition of the contribution made by Indigenous knowledge and the recognition that Indigenous peoples are essential players in making the transition to a new economy and society for an ecological age.

The vision, principles, values and strategies required for the framing of this covenant have already been documented by the Royal Commission on Aboriginal Peoples, the *United Nations Declaration on the Rights of Indigenous Peoples* and the Truth and Reconciliation Commission. The core principles would include recognition of the economic, social, cultural and political rights of Indigenous peoples; the obligation to reassess and renegotiate the extension of Indigenous peoples' traditional land base and the realization of Indigenous peoples' rights to "free, prior and informed consent" before any industrial development projects take place on their lands and territories.

One obvious place to begin implementing such an Indigenous covenant is the federal government's process for developing Canada's Climate Action Plan in response to the Paris Agreement through First Ministers' Conferences. First Nations and representatives of other

Indigenous peoples need to be at the table as players, along with premiers, territorial leaders and the prime minister plus relevant cabinet ministers, to develop short-, medium- and long-term plans of action to drastically reduce greenhouse gas emissions to meet our targets; spur on the transition to a clean, renewable energy future and usher in the development of a new, more just and sustainable economy and society.

Community Pacts

If the kind of transformation we are discussing here is going to tackle climate change not only by substantially reducing greenhouse gas emissions but also by dramatically reducing unemployment and poverty, then the eco-pathways identified in Chapter 5 need to be even more targeted than has been discussed so far. The realities of unemployment and poverty in this country have become more and more concentrated over the past three decades or so. Although high levels of unemployment and poverty continue to prevail in rural areas and northern regions of the country (in the north largely because of the busts that follow boom cycles of an extractive economy), perhaps the most dramatic shifts lately have come in major metropolitan areas. Poverty and unemployment have become heavily concentrated in certain neighbourhoods and regions of our major cities, increasingly home to particular racial groups.

In Toronto, the country's largest metropolitan area, a more than 15-year-old, city-wide program called Toronto Strong Neighbourhoods Strategy 2020 has been set up to improve the "health and wealth" of the city's poorest districts. One of the poorest districts is the Jane-Finch community near York University in the northwest corner of the city, 70 percent composed of visible racial minorities.[21] The community has one of the highest unemployment rates in the city and profound levels of poverty. Two of its neighbourhoods, Black Creek and Glenfield–Jane Heights, had the lowest scores in the metro area's neighbourhood improvement survey in 2015 in terms of "health, well being and social equity." Meanwhile, the extensive public housing in the community is in need of major repairs, along with much of the private apartment stock. Many of the community's residents rely on precarious forms of employment with no health benefits. Moreover, the combination of few jobs and poor transit means that residents are compelled to use cars to get to work, thereby adding more greenhouse gas emissions. Also, Jane-Finch schools have the highest expulsion rates in the city and more children in child welfare. And given the scarcity of child care services, young mothers are unable to pursue decent employment opportunities by going back to school to upgrade their skills.

Similar patterns of concentrated poverty have also emerged in neighbourhoods of Montreal and Vancouver, as well as other major cities across the country.[22] In Vancouver, for instance, the east side generally has had higher unemployment rates than the west side. More recently, however, neighbourhoods such as Strathcona have been recording the highest unemployment and poverty rates, followed by Arbutus Ridge and Kerrisdale, whereas the highest concentrations of wealth and employment are still found in Shaughnessy. New trend lines of concentrated poverty and unemployment are emerging in the surrounding municipalities, such as Richmond, Burnaby and Surrey. These trend lines are what is now frequently called the "suburbanization of poverty," with new immigrants, refugees and non-white populations increasingly concentrated in the suburbs.

In Greater Montreal, pockets of poverty and high unemployment have become more and more corralled in the inner suburbs and, to a lesser extent, in the outer suburbs. Montreal's unemployment rate is above the national average, hovering around 10 percent. Non-white populations, composed largely of Haitian immigrants, have become increasingly located in the inner suburban ring.

Given these relatively new geographical concentrations of unemployment and poverty, what can be done to ensure that strategies such as the "one million climate jobs" plan create concrete employment opportunities for jobless people currently living in these communities? Are there ways of targeting the creation of climate jobs to more effectively serve the needs of local communities and neighbourhoods, both within metropolitan areas and in outlying rural communities and territories? One way to proceed is for community residents to negotiate and form "community benefit agreements" when new industrial, commercial, public or institutional developments are proposed. In the United States and the United Kingdom, community benefit agreements have a proven track record of providing jobs and other benefits to community residents.

Signed by representatives of the parties to a particular construction project, a community benefit agreement is a legally enforceable agreement that contains clear monitoring and enforcement mechanisms. It is designed to provide an inclusive, collaborative and accountable process whereby a community can leverage a specific construction project to achieve a range of community policy objectives, such as social equity, environmental sustainability, poverty reduction, local employment and economic development. It is also intended to outline in writing a series of benefits to be received from the project by the community, such as equitable hiring practices, training funds, support for social enterprises and specific neighbourhood improvements. The document can also provide assurances for substantial community participation in all phases of the agreement, such as the design, implementation, performance monitoring, enforcement and overall evaluation of the construction project with regard to mutually agreed on matters of community benefit.

In effect, community benefit agreements are a strategic tool for negotiating agreements between a private or public development agent and a coalition of community-based groups. This coalition may include neighbourhood representatives, single-issue advocates, labour unions, social service agencies, faith-based groups and others. Together they give a voice to people in infrastructure planning and land development processes — especially those who have been historically excluded or marginalized from these processes and decisions that affect them. These coalitions generally draw on their own membership and build their base of advocacy from neighbourhoods that directly surround the proposed development projects. By focusing on economic activities such as institutional purchasing and infrastructure, their strategies provide an alternative approach to the reduction of poverty and unemployment. What community benefit agreements do is ensure that the wealth generated by these development projects is shared more broadly and equitably through building community assets, strengthening local business incubation and creating specific opportunities for decent work and pay in the community.

In Canada, legislation could be proposed and passed requiring that all development projects using federal funds include community benefit agreements. Under such legislation, the minister of infrastructure would be empowered to ensure that bidders for federal funds meet this demand for community benefit agreements and that progress reports be made to Parliament. Since most publicly funded development projects include a mix of federal, provincial and municipal funding, provinces and municipalities would have to comply with this demand in their contract to receive federal funding. For provinces such as Ontario, whose Liberal government passed legislation in 2015 calling for community benefit agreements as part of its new legislation for infrastructure planning and development, this would likely be welcome. In other provinces with conservative governments such as Saskatchewan and Manitoba, which expect federal dollars for infrastructure to come with few strings attached, there could be significant resistance.

Community benefit agreements can be further fortified by other legal measures, such as project labour agreements. Under an agreement that includes a project labour agreement, any construction project proposed for the community that makes use of federal government funding can be obligated to ensure that a specified percentage of the jobs generated by the construction project go to local residents. An example is the community benefit agreement negotiated regarding the completion of the Eglinton Crosstown public transit construction project, requiring that 10 percent of the work hours for the remainder of the project go to disadvantaged youth, women and minorities who live in the area.[23] The deal struck by government, business and labour will create 300 jobs and pump money and skills training into the community, thereby setting a precedent for infrastructure projects in Canada. Meanwhile, the project itself will make a significant contribution to the reduction of Toronto's greenhouse gas emissions. It will also serve as a test case for what can be achieved under a community benefit agreement. Other legal tools and measures, such as obligations to pay a "living wage" or "prevailing wage," could conceivably be added in some jurisdictions.

Community benefit agreements provide a potentially useful strategic tool for ensuring that the climate jobs and eco-pathways outlined previously are pursued in a way that reduces both unemployment and poverty. Government funding for improving or expanding public transit development projects in major cities and towns, for example, could be required to include a community benefit agreement ensuring that a percentage of the new jobs created go to people in one or more low-income communities. The same could be said of building-retrofit strategies for homes and buildings to reduce greenhouse gas emissions in cold winters and hot summers, which involve not only direct government funding but also the use of the municipal tax base for pay-as-you-save financing by owners and occupants of residential, public, industrial and commercial building stock. Moreover, community benefit agreements can be used as a strategic tool by Indigenous peoples and family farmers to leverage economic benefits for their lands being used for the development of clean, renewable energy in the form of wind and solar farms.

To be effective, community benefit agreements could be strengthened with regard to securing good jobs for marginalized people by forming alliances with social enterprises to provide goods or services as benefits to the community. Social enterprises are "non-profit organizations that employ business methods and practices to create training opportunities and employment for low income and marginalized individuals."[24] A variety of social enterprises that have been developed in recent years provide services for marginalized people in obtaining skills training and employment opportunities. For example, Green Jobs Calgary is "designed to help lower income people in Calgary move into environmental jobs that offer opportunities for advancement and good wages in fields such as green construction, renewable energy, environmental remediation and recycling."[25] In Manitoba, a range of successful social enterprises have been developed to train unemployed workers from marginalized communities for green jobs, largely financed by the Crown corporation Manitoba Hydro. Their constituencies comprise unemployed and marginalized workers from Indigenous, immigrant and poor communities.[26]

Together these and related measures could further set the stage for a just transition to a more sustainable future.

Eco-social State

In these last few chapters, we have been discussing three long-range plans of action that need to be undertaken if Canada is going to achieve the goal of becoming a zero-carbon economy by 2040. They include strategies for deep structural changes: *industrial overhaul* of the energy, transportation and construction industries to substantially reduce this country's greenhouse gas emissions; *eco-pathways* from an economy based on fossil fuels to one based on a clean, renewable energy future through the development of solar, wind and geothermal power plus other renewables; green buildings and building retrofits for energy conservation and efficiency; public transit in urban centres plus higher-speed rail between cities in metropolitan corridors and *just transition* measures to enable previously marginalized peoples to make a relatively smooth transition to a more just and sustainable economic future by developing a new social contract with workers, a covenant with Indigenous peoples and community pacts to dramatically reduce unemployment and poverty. These three strategies are interdependent to the point where one cannot function, let alone succeed, without the other two. Together these are the ingredients for a deep transformation to be undertaken and implemented before mid-century.

Although these are not the only strategies that can be or need to be undertaken, they constitute some of the cornerstones on which a new political economy can be built. Yet little of the kind of deep transformation that has been outlined here can be achieved unless corresponding changes take place at the same time in our prevailing political and economic system. One of these has to do with the role of the state itself.

Given the magnitude of the transformation that needs to take place within a relatively short period of time, the direction, oversight and co-ordination of this system change cannot simply be left to the ebbs and flows of the market. On the contrary, governments and the public sector must step up to the plate and provide the leadership that is urgently needed. Although industries and the private sector will have key roles to play in bringing about the transformation required, they will need to operate within the basic framework and plan of action co-ordinated by the state and the public sector.

To accomplish this task, governments and the public sector will need to be recalibrated and revitalized in the process of getting to zero greenhouse gas emissions. The social state that emerged in Canada during the postwar period of the twentieth century has largely been dismantled over the past 40 years or so with the adoption of a series of neoliberal policies and strategies. As noted in Chapter 2, the processes of economic globalization gradually transferred many of the state's sovereign powers to transnational corporations, global markets and free trade regimes. In effect, national governments were stripped of their role, resources and tools to intervene in and regulate their own national economies in the public interest. Instead, the development and fate of domestic economies were largely left to markets that were increasingly dominated and controlled by and for the interests of transnational corporations, reinforced by global trade rules. As a result, the social state was gradually dismantled and replaced by more corporate models of governance, such as the petro-state and its extensive lobbying machinery.

The Trudeau government appears to recognize the need to recover and recalibrate, to some extent, the role and capacities of the state. Some initial steps were taken to review and redirect the powers of the National Energy Board in making decisions and recommendations to cabinet regarding pipeline proposals such as Energy East and Trans Mountain. This includes the application of a climate test and requirements for broader consultations with the Indigenous peoples and front-line communities affected. Soon thereafter, however, TransCanada withdrew its Energy East project proposal, in part at least because it either could not or would not do what would be required to meet the new, more rigorous measures. Meanwhile, it is not at all clear that Kinder Morgan was obligated to satisfactorily meet the climate test standards or fully carry out consultations with Indigenous peoples and front-line communities

— presumably for fear that Kinder Morgan would follow TransCanada by withdrawing its pipeline proposal rather than comply with the new regulations.

In February 2018, the Trudeau government tabled Bill C-69 in the House of Commons, an omnibus piece of legislation designed to enact the *Impact Assessment Act* and the *Canadian Energy Regulator Act* while at the same time repealing the *National Energy Board Act* and the *Canadian Environmental Assessment Act.*[27] Although the proposed legislation may well serve to streamline the approval process for pipeline and other infrastructure projects and include more rigorous regulatory measures, it may also run the risk of enshrining the Liberal government's mantra of "growing the economy and protecting the environment" at the same time. If anything, it leaves a false impression of Canada doing more to rigorously mitigate against environmental impacts while expanding and strengthening this country's role and destiny as an extractivist economy. Moreover, it does little or nothing to curb the corporate power wielded by the fossil fuel industry to control public policy–making in Ottawa (recall examples from Chapter 3). What is missing here is a comprehensive strategy for dismantling the unwanted remnants of the petro-state coupled with a clear vision of what kind of alternative model of governance is needed to deal with the twin eco-crises of the economy and ecology.

In other words, the government must seize the opportunity to recalibrate the role and powers of the Canadian state to get us to a zero-carbon economy by 2040. Doing so requires developing, promoting and implementing a new vision of the role and capacities of government — an eco-social state that aims to build a more just and sustainable future by transforming the economy to function more in harmony with ecological priorities and challenges, starting with climate change. Its initial set of objectives would be to develop a concrete plan of action to operationalize the threefold Big Shift program outlined in the last three chapters — phasing out the tar sands industry over the next 10 to 15 years (maximum); greatly multiplying community-based and public renewable energy developments plus building retrofits for energy efficiency to reach 100 percent clean energy goals by 2040; making the transportation shift to improved and expanded public transit in our cities and moving people and freight more efficiently between cities within urban corridors through higher-speed rail, combined with a just transition strategy to enable workers and communities affected by the burdens of transition associated with these structural changes. Moving in this direction, the government would need to be mandated and empowered both to create a new line of employment for the next economy (i.e., climate jobs) and to substantially reduce greenhouse gas emissions toward net zero.

At the end of the last chapter, we discussed the fact that undertaking and implementing the Big Shift are monumental tasks that would require major changes in our model of governance in this country. In particular, a tripod of federal departments was proposed, with each department focused on one of the three main targets identified for greenhouse gas reductions. To move in this direction requires rethinking the role and capacities of the state to provide ongoing leadership in response to the climate change challenge. In a provocative paper published by the Broadbent Institute in 2016, policy analyst Brendan Haley proposed that serious attention be given to revitalizing the role of the state in promoting innovation in the economy or, in other words, "the process of putting new ideas into practice."[28] The key message is that governments can play a fundamental role in changing economies by promoting innovation. Drawing on the work of Mariana Mazzucato, Haley argued that this requires that the state play a more entrepreneurial role in the economy by promoting innovations that can "change economic directions by creating and shaping markets."[29]

According to Haley, historically, Canada's most impressive innovations have come in the energy sector when governments have played the key role of promoting innovation. When the energy crisis of the early 1970s erupted, two Canadian governments responded with two very different innovation initiatives. On the one hand, in 1974, the Alberta government started promoting innovation in extracting oil from sand as its ongoing mission, using steam-injected in situ methods and technology to bring the bitumen-laden crude from beneath the sedimentary rock basin to the surface, where it could be further upgraded and refined.[30] A Crown corporation was set up, the Alberta Oil Sands Technology and Research Authority, which took on many risks investing in technological research and development along with initial manufacturing and commercialization.[31] These and other initiatives set the stage for the oil sands boom of the early 2000s, when oil prices took off and new markets were found, notably in the United States, which had the refinery capacities to turn bitumen into oil.

On the other hand, a lesser-known example of energy innovation was the building of Conservation House in northwest Regina in 1977 by researchers from both the national and Saskatchewan research councils.[32] Using a combination of superinsulation and novel designs, Conservation House achieved such high energy efficiency standards that it effectively eliminated the need for a built-in winter heating and summer cooling system. However, unlike the tar sands innovation, government support for Conservation House never took off. Two decades later, a German research institute picked up the idea and became a global leader in this type of super–energy-efficient construction.

There are many lessons to be learned from these two historical examples of energy innovation, not the least of which is what happens when governments drop the ball and fail to use all the tools at their disposal to promote creative energy-saving innovation such as Conservation House. Knowing what we do today about runaway climate change and its causes, we can see that the mission and priority of a hypothetical eco-social state in the early seventies could have been to promote major energy innovation through green building construction and building retrofits, using Conservation House as the model. In doing so, the government's role would have included investing in risky research initiatives; supporting innovative manufacturing, promotion and commercialization and developing or shaping new markets for green buildings and building retrofits.

Today, viewed in the context of an eco-social state, governments would be called on to take a leadership role in transitioning from a dirty fossil fuel–based economy to a clean, renewable energy–based economy by 2040. Governments have a range of public policy development tools at their disposal, such as the use of public procurement for developing appropriate green technologies and stimulating markets for new technologies plus the creation of new Crown corporations to facilitate this process.

According to Haley, today "we find ourselves locked into a carbon-intensive economic structure," largely because of the successful promotion of previous (and continuing) innovations such as the automobile and oil refining and business strategies promoting mass consumption.[33] Moreover, most government investments in energy today continue to be in the fossil fuel industry. To escape this carbon lock-in, he argued, we need a green entrepreneurial state "directing innovations towards reducing greenhouse gas emissions."[34]

In terms of the Big Shift, the role of governments would be to promote creative innovations designed to advance the energy shift, the transportation shift and the building shift (as noted above in the case of Conservation House). In doing so, governments are generally capable of mobilizing public investment and working with public organizations to explore innovative projects that the private sector finds too risky. Hence, they are positioned to take on risks at research and development stages and at stages of technological diffusion by supporting manufacturing and commercialization. Because of the numerous roles the state plays in the economy, Haley maintained that the state also "influences the direction of innovation when it manages training and educational institutions, produces information, sets regulations, supplies funds (with conditions attached), purchases goods and services, and sets targets."[35]

At the same time, governments today are up against a ticking clock when it comes to climate change. Urgent calls for action on climate change often evoke comparisons with the measures of a wartime economy. Although many understandably have difficulties with the use of militaristic language in this context, there are some useful lessons to be learned from Canada's wartime experience during the last century. As John Dillon noted several years ago, the Canadian Parliament granted Minister C.D. Howe and his Department of Munitions and Supply sweeping powers to transform Canada's economy for wartime production in August 1940.[36] Howe's mandate was to "mobilize, control, restrict or regulate to such extent as the Minister may, in his absolute discretion, deem necessary, any branch or trade or industry in Canada" to promote the war effort. As a result, "while some manufacturing facilities were redeployed, more than half of Canada's war production came from plants that had not existed in 1939."[37]

With the climate clock ticking away, it becomes increasingly doubtful that this deep transformation agenda can be developed and implemented in sufficient time to avoid a planetary catastrophe without some form of more centralized authority and power being invoked to carry out and complete the mission. This is perhaps the prime lesson in governance to be gleaned from this country's wartime experience for our collective struggle against runaway climate change.

Finally, no matter how enlightened the political leadership of governments may become, the kind of dramatic shift in the institutional capacities to bring about the bold transformation outlined above will simply not happen of its own accord. Certainly, one way of prompting and facilitating this kind of deep transformation in a democratic society is to ensure that there is a vibrant, strong and mobilized civil society movement, capable of acting as an effective counterweight to powerful corporations and their industry associations that are actively resisting the system change that's needed. It is imperative that such a mass social movement also be grounded in the vision and principles of climate justice.

CHAPTER 7
Movement Building

Clearly, neither the governing Trudeau Liberals nor the major opposition parties can alone provide the kind of progressive climate leadership urgently needed to move the country to a new economy. We also need a dynamic civil society movement — one that has the capacity to push all governments and indeed all political parties to take the actions needed to achieve a net-zero carbon economy by 2040. Such a movement must be rooted in climate justice principles and have the capacity to act as an ongoing watchdog of government policies and programs. Indeed, building a dynamic climate justice movement, in this country and elsewhere, may be the best hope we have left.

Bill McKibben noted that North Americans are very used to thinking of themselves as individuals. But as individuals, we are powerless to alter the momentum and trajectory of climate change in a way that is both effective and meaningful. Although it may be possible to get a small segment of the population to take action on climate change as individuals (e.g., by reducing consumption of oil or gas for heating and cooling their homes, driving less, installing solar panels), at most such individual actions would reduce greenhouse gas emissions by 5 or 10 percent. McKibben therefore suggested that individuals join a social movement committed to fighting climate change.[1]

The real underlying question here, said McKibben, is not so much what "I" can do to make a difference but what "*we*" can do to make a difference. It is through social movements "that people organize themselves to gain power" — perhaps, in this case, enough power to take on and overcome the economic clout of the fossil fuel industry.[2] Through social movements, sufficient public support can be generated to mobilize government, for example, to

- put a price on carbon that provides sufficient revenues for governments to act,
- compel politicians to keep fossil fuels such as bitumen in the ground and
- set up subsidies and other measures to encourage more people and institutions to install solar panels on their roofs.

If McKibben is essentially correct in his assessment of the purpose and role of movements, then how do these movements become known to the broader public as vehicles for individual action and participation? One answer is through special public events such as marches and demonstrations. Take, for example, the People's Climate March in New York City in September 2014, a little more than a year before the Paris climate summit, when more than 400,000 people (including many Canadians) marched through the city demanding that the United Nations and governments take bold action. Millions more people followed the event on television and the Internet, which portrayed the diversity of constituencies involved, whereas social media reproduced the multiple messages of the march to people all over the world. In the year that followed, there were smaller — but growing — marches and demonstrations demanding more climate action organized in various cities in Canada, including Quebec City (April 2015, 10,000 people), Toronto (July, 15,000 people) and Ottawa (November, 25,000 people).

Another way to follow the activities of the emerging climate movement in Canada is to plug into the lobbying campaigns and events waged by environmentalist and other non-governmental organizations on Parliament Hill, organized by Climate Action Network Canada every year. Other ways include checking in with some of the core constituencies that have their own climate action strategies, such as

- Indigenous organizations or First Nations themselves (plus those organizations that provide authentic support and services, such as RAVEN);
- specific environmental organizations, such as the David Suzuki Foundation, Environmental Defence, Équiterre, Greenpeace and 350.org;
- labour unions, federations and labour councils that are active on climate issues at local and regional levels and
- other local and regional networks, such as ecology action centres organized in places such as Ottawa and Halifax, as well as regionally based climate jobs and green economy networks organized in Alberta, British Columbia and Prince Edward Island.

These and related groups (identified in the following pages) provide further entry points for concerned individuals to plug into emerging movements.[3]

Given the challenge outlined in Chapters 4, 5 and 6 of bringing about a "great transformation," Canada needs an organized movement that will advocate for structural changes in the economic system. We need a social movement, involving a common front of civil society organizations, committed to gradually dismantling the fossil fuel industry and paving the way over the next three decades for developing a new, more just and more sustainable economy through new climate jobs combined with just transition policies and programs.

A movement entails active participation of people from diverse walks of life coalescing around a common cause (or common set of causes) in their local communities, in their regions, nationally and internationally. Once a movement-in-the-making reaches this stage, it may be in a position to exercise sufficient clout to effectively hold "feet to the fire" when it comes to governments and even corporations.[4] A close look suggests that such a movement to address climate change has indeed been developing in Canada. The following section examines this movement's emerging vision and organizing principles, its core constituencies and what needs to be done to strengthen them and grassroots momentum evident in different regions across the country.

Movement Vision

A pan-Canadian climate justice movement has gradually been taking shape over the past several decades. In part, its roots go back to campaigns waged by Indigenous peoples plus environmental and church groups, such as the successful campaign by the Dene Nation in the 1970s to stop construction of the Mackenzie Valley pipeline, a mega-energy project to transport natural gas from the Beaufort Sea in the Arctic to southern Canada and the United States. By the 1992 World Conference on the Environment and Development in Rio de Janeiro, global warming and climate change had become a common rallying point for environmental groups and their allies. In the late nineties, Canada collaborated with such groups as it officially joined negotiations among nation-states on the Kyoto Protocol.

Following the Montreal Conference of the Parties in 2005, the major Canadian environmental organizations came together to found Climate Action Network Canada, mainly as a civil society coalition pressing for positive governmental action on climate change policy. What made the network somewhat unique among similar bodies in other countries was its outreach to include other civil society groups, such as Indigenous peoples, labour unions and faith-based organizations.[5]

Around the same period, another network, called Tar Sands Solutions, appeared on the scene, primarily to challenge the expansion of the bitumen industry. The Tar Sands Solution also has a mixed membership base, including Indigenous peoples and other community-based front-line groups on both sides of the Canada-U.S. border, plus environmental groups.[6] Yet it has played a pivotal role in building and co-ordinating grassroots resistance to the tar sands (or bitumen) industry for over a decade.

By 2009, a third leg of allied groups with a common focus on climate action was being formed, led by labour unions along with environmental non-governmental organizations and social justice, public interest and faith-based groups. This network leg includes the Green Economy Network, which, as discussed in Chapter 5, has since mounted its "one million climate jobs" campaign as a pathway to a new economy.[7]

The main elements of this climate justice movement in Canada have, for the most part, evolved organically. They have not been commandeered in a top-down way; rather, the pieces have gradually emerged through a bottom-up process, largely in response to a growing awareness of the scope and depth of the climate change challenge. Priorities stem from community processes such as

- incubator hubs for forming analysis and strategies,
- consensus forms of decision-making and
- networking methods and creative use of tools for organizing action, such as social media.

Neither the movement nor its component parts are governed or directed by an overarching hierarchical structure. It is a movement of people and groups who fundamentally share a common vision and set of principles for taking on what is arguably the most pressing challenge of our times.

Rallies, with their placards and signs portraying the issues and themes of climate justice, have generally been organized through such organic processes. Similarly, campaigns related to the three pillars of the Big Shift are generally initiated, developed and implemented using organic methods and tools. Although it could be argued that the kind of deep transformation required would proceed more rapidly and efficiently if it were driven by a command centre, movement activists would likely counter that decentralized campaigns emerging from diverse hubs of activity are more effective and more democratic in the long run.

Indeed, this is perhaps one of the movement's great strengths. It is true that a non-hierarchical structure renders it harder to make and execute quick decisions on actions that need to be taken in response to changing circumstances. On the other hand, this approach accords with the aspirations of a participatory democracy for social change and allows for a greater diversity of tactics, which have often proven highly effective in generating public policy changes.

Operating Principles

This climate justice movement has also organically evolved a set of operating principles, primary among them *justice* and *sustainability*. Since the movement was initially driven by environmental groups, the emphasis on sustainability comes as no surprise. As awareness and understanding of the climate change challenge broadened and deepened, the concept of justice also emerged as a primary guiding and operating principle. This piece came into focus through the increasing participation of two other social movements:

- the Indigenous peoples' movement, representing the original inhabitants of this land, and whose populations have historically suffered injustices through land grabs and related forms of exploitation concerning Mother Earth and
- the labour movement, representing workers who have far too often been left behind in the boom-and-bust dynamics of resource development and who now demand a just transition in the energy shift from dependence on fossil fuels to renewable energy.[8]

These two principles appear to be reinforced by two more: *solidarity* and *transformation*. Although these two principles may be less explicit in the various campaigns being waged, they have increasingly become implicit in the way many campaigns are organized and implemented. Although tensions surface from time to time, there appear to be increasing degrees of solidarity between Indigenous peoples and environmental groups, along with local front-line community groups. This can be seen, for example, in the Tar Sands Solutions campaigns against Kinder Morgan's Trans Mountain pipeline and TransCanada's Energy East pipeline project. Furthermore, by creating new types of employment that directly engage workers in the fight against climate change through work that reduces greenhouse gas emissions, a potentially new kind of solidarity between workers and Indigenous peoples, environmentalists and community groups is generated. As key players and their constituencies in the movement realize that justice and sustainability, reinforced by solidarity, cannot be achieved without some fundamental structural changes in the political economy itself, the principle of transformation becomes more and more evident.

Leap Manifesto

One way to capture the characteristics and challenge of any social movement-in-the-making is to develop a common narrative that inspires and motivates people to come together around a shared vision for transforming the economy and society. To a significant degree, the Leap Manifesto provided elements of a common narrative when it was released during Canada's last federal election campaign.[9]

Four weeks before Election Day 2015, leaders and representatives of First Nations, environmental organizations, public interest groups, labour unions and faith-based communities, plus an array of actors, musicians and artists, came together in a hotel room in downtown Toronto calling for a new agenda of economic and political transformation in response to the climate crisis. Largely inspired by the writings of author Naomi Klein and filmmaker Avi Lewis, the manifesto contended that Canada's record on climate change has been "a crime against humanity" and called for "a leap" to be made from this country's dependence on fossil fuels.

The manifesto outlined the broad strokes of a plan for making the transition to reliance on clean, renewable energy sources for 100 percent of our power within the next two decades plus a complete transition to a zero-carbon economy by 2050. The text emphasized that the movement for this transition must be led by First Nations and front-line communities in an effort "to correct historic wrongs." To get us there, the Leap Manifesto called for a major shift in public policies, including

- new regulations on oil, gas and mineral extraction;
- public investments in renewable energy development (wind, solar, geothermal);
- retrofitting buildings for energy efficiencies,
- improvements or expansion of public transit and higher-speed rail and
- a much more localized and ecologically based agricultural system to produce healthier foods.

According to the manifesto, priority should be put on achieving greater community ownership and control of energy sources and terminating global trade rules that enshrine the power of corporations over local economies. Recognizing that "caring for one another and the planet" could become the economy's fastest-growing sectors, the manifesto also suggested expanding low-carbon sectors of the economy, such as caregiving, child care, teaching, social work, the arts and public interest media. The document highlighted the project's urgency: "Climate scientists have told us that this is the decade to take decisive action to prevent catastrophic global warming." For these reasons, taking "a leap" is imperative: "Small steps will no longer get us where we need to go."

The Leap Manifesto has been endorsed by some 50,000 people as an expression of the principles and priorities for democratic social change that needs to be undertaken in Canada.[10] It serves a dual purpose for many co-signers, partly as a common narrative for the emerging climate justice movement and partly as a call to action.

Meanwhile, there are other pressing priorities and needs for building a climate justice movement that require attention. One has to do with a concrete roadmap with directions as to how we can make the transition to a net-zero carbon economy by 2050 or even 2040. As discussed in

Chapter 1, the shift in global ambition adopted at the Paris summit to contain the heating of the planet to a 1.5- rather than a 2-degree Celsius threshold this century calls for a viable plan of action and roadmap in every country to get us there. Indeed, it requires a series of five-year plans with built-in targets and benchmarks, beginning no later than 2020.

These and other measures will be needed to both broaden and deepen the movement-building process. In this regard, the Leap Manifesto instills a sense of hope, confidence and courage that ordinary people and their communities can build an alternative future together. But to do so, the movement must also have a platform of bold ideas and concrete proposals for institutional transformation, plus an action plan to get us there. Furthermore, that action plan must include proposed solutions that match the scale of the problems we need to address and the time frame in which we must address them.

Core Constituencies

As we saw in Chapter 2, climate change is a multifaceted phenomenon whose basic causes are deeply rooted in the dominant economic order, the way society functions and how it is governed. Consequently, the climate justice movement cannot be a single-issue alliance of civil society groups. To confront the challenge of climate change demands a multipronged strategy aimed at transforming several key sectors of the economy and society simultaneously. To be effective, therefore, the climate justice movement must either be cross-sectoral in its modus operandi or become "a movement of movements."

The Canadian climate justice movement's core constituencies so far have been threefold: the environmental movement (including scientists), the Indigenous peoples' movement and, more recently, the labour union movement. Each of these has made various contributions to this movement-building process, each has exhibited its own particular set of strengths in doing so and each has revealed its own weaknesses or limitations. These three core constituencies are further fortified by a network of other civil society groups that have helped to strengthen various components of the broader movement at key moments. Nevertheless, the effectiveness of the climate justice movement in this country rests a great deal on the capacities of these core constituencies and their ability to work together.

Environmental Movement

The environmental movement led the way in ringing the alarm bell on climate change in this country, reinforced by ongoing studies of greenhouse gas emissions and their impacts. For more than two decades, environmental non-governmental organizations — including the David Suzuki Foundation, the Pembina Institute, Environmental Defence, the Sierra Club, Quebec's Équiterre and many more have been at the forefront in pressing governments to adopt a range of climate policies to reduce greenhouse gas emissions.

However, the more it became evident that the climate change challenge had deeper and broader implications — such as the land rights of Indigenous peoples and demands for a just transition affecting workers in natural resource extraction — the more it became clear that environmental networks could not continue to lead the charge alone. Not only did they lack the capacity to authentically represent the historical claims of Indigenous peoples, they also had few tools to tackle the challenges of economic restructuring posed by the climate crisis and its solutions. Moreover, with the exception of Greenpeace and 350.org, the environmental movement's capacity for mass mobilization was somewhat limited.

Indigenous Peoples' Movement

By 2008, it was apparent that Indigenous people were exercising more and more leadership as a core constituency within Canada's burgeoning climate justice movement. Drawing on their ancient teachings, Indigenous peoples with land and communities close to extractive operations in the tar sands and pipeline construction on both sides of the Canada-U.S. border rose up against the violence being dealt to Mother Earth. The resistance manifested by Indigenous and First

Nations communities along the various proposed pipeline routes added new energy and dynamism to the climate justice movement.

During this period, First Nations communities won a series of court rulings that further defined, broadened and consolidated their rights under the Canadian *Constitution Act.* As noted in Chapter 6, the 2007 *United Nations Declaration on the Rights of Indigenous Peoples*, which Canada finally ratified in 2016, stipulated that all resource development projects on Indigenous lands must have "free, prior and informed consent of Indigenous peoples" before proceeding.[11] The Truth and Reconciliation Commission's report that came out in June 2015 with its 94 recommendations provided Indigenous peoples with additional moral and political clout.[12]

The increasingly proactive participation of Indigenous peoples has made a valuable contribution to the evolution of a climate justice movement in Canada. The ongoing pipeline resistance of front-line Indigenous communities, combined with recent court victories plus various governmental and programmatic initiatives, has provided a boost for this movement-building process and given it credibility with respect to both climate and justice issues.[13]

So, too, has the alliance between environmental and Indigenous peoples' networks. Although it has at times been an uneasy, tense and somewhat shaky process, there are signs that this alliance continues along a pathway toward becoming healthy and strong. This is due in large part to players from both camps who are committed to the principle of solidarity and campaign-building efforts by Tars Sands Solutions that prioritized facilitating this relationship.[14] In Quebec, environmental groups such as Équiterre have worked with Indigenous groups to develop a new working relationship around mounting resistance to the proposed Energy East pipeline. Similar efforts were made in British Columbia between Indigenous and non-Indigenous peoples in mobilizing resistance against the Kinder Morgan pipeline and Northern Gateway projects. Indigenous and environmental groups in Canada have also found ways to collaborate with their U.S. counterparts via resistance campaigns against the Keystone XL pipeline, largely through the work of the Indigenous Environmental Network in the United States and the Indigenous Tar Sands Network in Canada.

Labour Union Movement

Meanwhile, a third core constituency of the Canadian climate justice movement has been gradually coming on stream: labour unions and the labour movement in general, where there has been a new awakening about the impacts of climate change on, and its relationship to, the economy and its implications for workplaces and the communities in which workers work and live. Many workers in the fossil fuel industry are organized in unions. Some of the component parts of the labour movement have been prioritizing climate justice issues:

- The Canadian Labour Congress played a key role in organizing the Green Economy Network that developed the climate jobs campaign.
- United Steelworkers, whose workers produce steel for pipelines, has been the organizational convener for Blue Green Canada, which promotes, among other priorities, the transition of workers from building pipelines to building windmills.
- Unifor, which represents the bulk of workers in the tar sands industry, has publicly opposed and even campaigned against Kinder Morgan's Trans Mountain pipeline and TransCanada's Keystone XL pipeline.[15] In the auto sector, Unifor has been organizing workplace environmental representatives through courses provided at its Port Elgin Family Education Centre, which range from learning about household and workplace toxins to understanding the basics of climate change.[16]
- Public sector unions such as the Canadian Union of Public Employees, with respect to municipal governments, and the Public Service Alliance of Canada, with respect to the federal government, have played key roles in promoting

action on climate justice issues.[17] The Canadian Union of Postal Workers has made some notably innovative proposals. Member organizations of the Ontario Teachers' Pension Plan have also led by example with their own pension fund and by encouraging other institutional investors to consider divesting from fossil fuel industries.

• The Toronto & York Region Labour Council has created a network of "environmental advocates" presumably to facilitate the climate justice agenda within workplaces and communities within its jurisdiction.

These and other unions and central labour organizations can bring critically important tools for promoting public policy shifts:

• **Collective bargaining.** Generally speaking, unions have collective bargaining powers that allow them to sit down across the table from their employer to bargain collectively on matters of importance to their employees. Such tools can be used creatively to advance economic restructuring priorities around issues such as climate justice. In effect, this is what the Canadian Union of Postal Workers has been doing in its collective bargaining with Canada Post to allow its facilities to be used for delivering community power to promote electric cars.

• **Effective mobilization.** Historically, the labour movement has also had a demonstrated capacity to mobilize its members to apply mass pressure for public policy change. Although this capacity has diminished in recent years, most unions still have tools and methods that could creatively be used to reach out to their own members and mobilize them on behalf of climate justice issues.

• **Solidarity building.** Finally, labour unions bring a long tradition and practice of solidarity building to the climate justice movement. Cultivating solidarity has been one of the hallmarks of the labour union movement in Canada and throughout the world. The challenge for unions and their members is to learn how to apply their understanding of solidarity to struggles for sustainability and for justice — a process that will require unions and their members to go through a major shift in consciousness about ecological issues.

This is where environmentalists and Indigenous peoples can help, through a working partnership with union members within a climate justice movement. Unions can exercise this broader understanding of solidarity through "solidarity pacts" with particular environmental groups or Indigenous peoples who are resisting pipeline or refinery projects. For their part, Indigenous peoples and environmentalists can broaden their practice of solidarity by forming similar pacts with unions and workers as they demand a just transition for workers affected by shutdowns of coal plants or pipeline construction.

In addition to these core constituencies, a variety of other groups and networks, real and potential, can make important contributions to building a climate justice movement in Canada. They include

- Unique Quebec based national ecological organizations like Equiterre along with local and community-based ecology action centres such as Ecology Ottawa and Ecology Action Centre in Halifax, which work with citizen groups in their communities on various issues of climate justice;
- national public interest organizations such as the Council of Canadians, which has been very active on energy and pipeline issues;
- faith-based organizations, such as KAIROS and Citizens for Public Justice, that do research and develop educational tools on issues of Indigenous, climate and economic justice;
- public policy research institutes, such as the Canadian Centre for Policy Alternatives and the Parkland, Pembina

and Polaris Institutes, that work on climate policies, pipeline projects and related economic policy issues and

- youth- and student-based organizations such as the Canadian Youth Climate Coalition, which develops educational tools and organizes public events on youth issues related to climate justice.[18]

Other key networks also see climate justice issues as having a direct or indirect impact on their constituencies. These include

- revitalized women's action groups making links to climate issues,
- racialized minority groups, particularly in urban communities,
- anti-poverty organizations fighting against increasing inequality and
- related social and economic justice networks.

Together these civil society groups have a vital role to play in current and expanding operations of the climate justice movement.

Finally, it's worth keeping in mind that this climate justice movement in Canada mirrors similar movements popping up in other countries. In some industrialized and developing countries, within both the global North and the global South, like-minded movements are taking shape in response to growing awareness of the planetary emergency, the call for justice and sustainability and the need for corresponding structural transformation. They may not all call themselves "climate justice" movements or coalitions, but they do largely identify with the Canadian movement's underlying vision and set of principles. This means that people can now be part of a more holistic and systemic approach, joined across regional and national borders, throughout the world.

Grassroots Momentum

Meanwhile, at a more grassroots level in this country, there are increasing signs that individuals and communities are moving ahead to make some of the critical transitions required, both within and outside the core constituencies. Numerous diverse and often innovative projects have sprung up across the Canadian landscape. Local and provincial governments have also played a role. Over approximately the past two decades, groundwork has gradually been laid by some provincial governments (notably Quebec, Ontario, Manitoba and, more recently, Alberta) and several major cities (notably Toronto, Montreal, Vancouver, Edmonton and Calgary) through various regulatory measures and programs. Through this process, many people have acquired crucial skills and learned to pool and share their expertise and experience in developing demonstration projects within their own communities. These diverse demonstration projects are emerging as visible symbols in local communities, showing the way to a more renewable energy future and a new economy. Here are just a few examples (in no particular order):

School Boards

In some regions of the country, school boards are leading the way in showcasing the energy shift that communities must make. An agreement signed between the London Catholic School Board, the Aamjiwnaang First Nation and a regional energy company offers a prime example.[19] Drawing on provisions in the Ontario *Green Energy Act*, the 20-year contract will see solar panels installed on the rooftops of 13 schools in the Sarnia area of southwestern Ontario; the process began in 2016. In Alberta, 25 school boards collectively leveraged their purchasing power to switch over to wind-powered energy generated by the Bull Creek Wind Project in Provost, near the Saskatchewan border.[20] The project will provide long-term carbon-free electricity for 500 schools, which will then be exempt from Alberta's new carbon tax, which came into effect in January 2018.[21]

Both projects constitute community-based demonstrations and symbols showcasing the shift from dependence on fossil fuels to renewable solar power. Both projects provide considerable savings in energy use and costs, with the cost savings being allocated to enhance the quality of education in their schools. More importantly, both projects in and of themselves exhibit major educational value for their students, their parents and their community. Imagine what could happen if many more schools followed suit across the country.

Indigenous Communities

Elsewhere, Indigenous peoples and nations are leading the way in making the energy shift from fossil fuels to renewable electric power. Some 200 northern, mostly Indigenous, communities currently rely on dirty diesel generators for their main power source. Although subsidized, diesel remains expensive and is often accompanied by blackouts, fuel spills and shortage of capacity.[22] But now, some Indigenous communities, such as the Lubicon Cree in northern Alberta, inspired by the teachings of their elders about Mother Earth, are forging a new future by becoming "powered by the sun." In Little Buffalo, the band council has erected solar panels to power its new health care facility and has begun to put some of the community's households on the electrical grid as well. Indigenous Climate Action was formed to develop the capacities of Indigenous communities and leaders to engage in the climate justice movement. Led by a group of inspiring women, Indigenous Climate Action uses Indigenous knowledge and methods of decolonization to enable Indigenous leaders to become "agents for change and climate change solutions."[23]

Faith-Based Communities

On another front, faith-based communities in urban centres from a variety of religious traditions have been installing solar panels on their buildings of worship — churches, mosques, synagogues, temples and convents — while also renovating these buildings to conserve energy. Acting in response to the so-called Green Rule — do unto Earth as you would have it do unto you — these faith-based communities have been taking up the fight against climate change as "one of the most urgent moral challenges in human history."[24]

Through a program called Greening Sacred Spaces, green audits are conducted on buildings owned by religious institutions. These audits cover matters such as the heating and cooling of buildings, insulating to reduce energy waste, ventilation, lighting and use of hot water and cleaning products. On the basis of such audits, recommendations are made for renovating the buildings to meet the standards of a "green sacred space." Once solar panels are installed or the building renovations are completed, the buildings are often "blessed" to commemorate the work done and the changes made, thereby becoming a symbol for the community at large to follow.[25]

Social Enterprises

Among the more creative agents for climate justice have been social enterprises such as Aki Energy, discussed earlier.[26] These are non-profit organizations using business methods and practices with a clear social purpose. Often formed by progressive governments in collaboration with community groups, these social enterprises are able to use Crown corporations such as Manitoba Hydro to finance their operations, without having to worry about profit margins. Two other climate-oriented social enterprises in Manitoba, BEEP (Brandon Energy Efficiency Program) and BUILD (Building Urban Industries for Local Development), combine a building shift and an equity shift in their approaches by hiring unemployed workers (often Indigenous men but also women and immigrants) to renovate buildings for energy conservation.[27] The trainees are paid slightly above minimum wage through the provincial government's Training and Employment Services agency and often move on from there to earn higher wages by working with another social enterprise, Manitoba Green Retrofit, which conducts energy renovations for Manitoba Housing. Although more could be done to advance the equity shift, these social enterprises provide a potential bridging mechanism for training and employment to make the Big Shift.

Postal Workers

Canada's postal workers are making their own creative contribution. In response to the new age of electronic mail and the dwindling demand for posted mail, they have come up with an innovative strategy: using

Canada Post facilities to help build local capacities to respond to the increasing challenges of climate change. As a Crown corporation, Canada Post has more than 6,200 post office facilities from coast to coast to coast. Focusing on the goal of "delivering community power" in response to the impending climate crisis, the Canadian Union of Postal Workers proposed that Canada Post's vast network of postal facilities and outlets be recalibrated to provide a range of services, including the following[28]:

- an alternative form of public banking and community financial services,
- a community-based charging station for electric vehicles,
- a fleet of electric vehicles to power community and neighbourhood mail delivery,
- an expanded role for door-to-door mail carriers to include strengthening the community's social fabric,
- a local community hub for the green revolution that connects businesses and customers and
- farm-to-food delivery programs in communities across the country.

Through widespread circulation of its illustrated booklet, *Delivering Community Power*, union members have been actively promoting its vision at public forums and rallies. Although the union's platform has provoked debate in some quarters, it has also sparked people's imagination in others, especially among those who recognize this as a time to transform key institutions in our economy and society.

Farmland Energy

Increasingly, farmers are providing land for large-scale solar and wind power projects.[29] According to European reports, it's best to build solar energy systems in rural areas that have low pollution levels, thereby making solar power collection more efficient. Southern Ontario and parts of Saskatchewan, for example, have relatively high solar potential, and solar arrays in these farmlands are becoming much more commonplace.[30] There are different ways that farmers can harness solar energy, including

- photovoltaic systems for electrical generation,
- hot air systems and
- hot water systems.

Wind turbines also require wide-open spaces in areas that have an ongoing consistent wind resource. Thus, farms in regions such as southern Ontario, Quebec and Alberta are becoming prime locations for wind energy generation. The wind farms in these areas are developed by private investors as well as co-operatives that include local farmers. Although farmers are free to use their land for small-scale wind energy projects for domestic purposes on their farms or lease their farmland to commercial wind power developers to generate income, it makes sense to encourage more communal ownership through co-operatives so that local communities can reap the economic benefits.

Community Benefit Agreements

As discussed in Chapter 6, community benefit agreements can provide marginalized communities with legally enforced contracts to ensure that projects designed to bring about a transportation shift are constructed in ways that benefit local residents. All too often, major public transit expansion projects are constructed without any local community review and involvement, especially those affecting low-income and marginalized communities. For example, toxic wastes are commonly dumped on land bordering low-income neighbourhoods during the construction phase of a project.

But when the Toronto Community Benefits Network negotiated its community benefit agreement concerning the construction of the Eglinton Crosstown Light Rail Transit system, it was able to incorporate legal clauses preventing this from happening.[31] Moreover, the Eglinton Crosstown community benefit agreement includes specific provisions for enhancing both job training and job placement opportunities pertaining to the construction and operation of the light rail system. The agreement also contains provisions involving procurement of goods and services from local social enterprises and businesses. It is designed to ensure that the transportation shift taking place also includes an equity shift by making it accountable to the interests and needs of the marginalized communities affected. Presumably, this community benefit agreement could also have included legal requirements limiting and reducing greenhouse gas emissions during construction and operation of the light rail system.

Fossil Fuel Divestment

On another front, the campaign to pressure institutional investors to divest from fossil fuel production and reinvest in renewable energy production has been slowly but surely gathering momentum. Led by Canadian-based environmental and church organizations, the fossil fuel divestment movement has been going through three waves[32]:

- In the first wave, those Canadian organizations with investments in fossil fuel companies that had already decided to divest did so and then deposited hundreds of millions of dollars into what is called the Genus Fossil Free CanGlobe Equity Fund.
- The second wave emerged when institutions such as universities, foundations and municipalities decided that divesting their stocks in fossil fuel industries was not only financially viable but also "prudent from a risk and reward perspective."
- The third and final wave, now in its early stages, is taking shape. In this stage, banks, pension funds and global institutions with large investment portfolios involving tens of billions of dollars are making their moves. This wave will likely be slower because the players involved usually wait until the financial advantages of divesting have been widely accepted within the investment community.

One key player to watch is the Ontario Teachers' Pension Plan, which is reportedly being pushed by some of its member bodies to divest up to $171 billion from fossil fuel industries. If successful, this move would remove $20 billion of capital annually from Canada's traditional energy industries. Once this third wave is fully in motion, observers agree that the energy shift to clean, renewable power will be "normalized, cost-effective, and commonplace."[33]

This is but a brief sampling of what is happening at more grassroots levels in response to the climate change challenge. Taken together, these responses demonstrate considerable momentum across the country. People and communities seem to understand that climate change will not go away without some fundamental changes to our economy and society. These initiatives are key elements of this movement-in-the-making and offer important contributions to the climate justice movement and the Big Shift campaign. They demonstrate the value of making conscious efforts to stimulate working relationships and partnerships among these and other grassroots initiatives and among the various components of the movement.

CHAPTER 8
Moving Forward

Now that we have the broad strokes of a plan for getting to zero, along with a profile for a climate justice movement in the making, we can consider how to operationalize these for success. First, it will be crucial to generate the level of political will required. This means we will need to

- urge the federal Liberal government to play a much more ambitious and progressive role in confronting runaway climate change,
- counter the Conservatives' denial of climate change,
- challenge the New Democrats to provide much more progressive leadership for climate justice and
- stimulate and mobilize more direct participation and action by concerned citizens and communities to generate bottom-up pressure and support for the Big Shift described in Chapter 5.

As discussed earlier, the Trudeau government has so far proved to be inadequate to the task of stemming climate change, all of which has potentially propelled the NDP into a more pivotal position, both federally and provincially. On the federal level, the Liberal government's failure to develop a credible plan for greenhouse gas reductions over the short, medium and long term that would put Canada on track with its national targets and international commitments for 2020, 2030 and 2040 has opened the door for the NDP to win back voters who abandoned them for the Liberals in the 2015 general election. On the provincial level, the NDP's razor-thin victory in the 2017 British Columbia election threw a monkey wrench into the alliance that had formed between Christy Clark's B.C. Liberals and the Trudeau government in Ottawa. How long this turn of events lasts depends on how well the NDP–Green Party alliance holds together in propping up a progressive minority government in Victoria and moving forward with its legislative agenda on hot-button issues, notably the construction of Kinder Morgan's Trans Mountain pipeline.

In response to Kinder Morgan's demands for guarantees that the pipeline project would proceed, the Trudeau government's decision, announced on May 29, 2018, that it would buy out and take over the Trans Mountain project came as a surprise to people on both sides of the issue. Cast in terms of protecting the "national interest," the public announcement of the buyout carried all the overtones of a "nationalization" initiative in the energy sector. No doubt the Liberal government's strategy was largely designed once again to tilt to both the left and the right of the political spectrum. Certainly, Premier Notley's announcement that the Alberta government was interested in buying a piece of the Trans Mountain project reinforced this perspective. Moreover, the prime minister was quick to point out once again that this strategy would allow his government to both "grow the economy" and "protect the environment" at the same time.

The subsequent public debate over the economic costs of the buyout nevertheless revealed ramifications. Although opinion polls taken before the federal announcement showed a small majority of Canadians in support of the project, this support soon evaporated amid speculation about the "real" economic costs involved. In making its announcement, the Trudeau government repeatedly declared that the cost of purchasing the Kinder Morgan pipeline asset would be $4.5 billion. It did not specify, however, that the asset to be purchased was a 65-year-old pipeline, initially built back in 1953, nor did it reveal the cost of extending the pipeline to tidewater — an additional $7.4 billion. These calculations did not include contingencies such as insurance expenditures and cost overruns. As a result, some analysts were warning that the economic costs would likely surpass $15 billion and could potentially go as high as $20 billion (given the Trump tariffs on steel).

So what does the Trudeau government (or, more precisely, Canadians as shareholders) get in return for public investments of $4.5 billion, or $12 billion or perhaps $15 to 20 billion? What will this investment deliver in terms of job creation and greenhouse gas reductions? According to Kinder Morgan's own calculations, some 12,000 person-years of work will be required during the construction phase. Once the pipeline extension is completed and operational, 50 new permanent jobs will be created. As to the project's impact on emissions, the answer is that not only will it not reduce them, it will actually increase them by quite a bit. It's estimated that if and when the Trans Mountain pipeline becomes fully operational, it will increase Canada's annual greenhouse gas output by an additional 30 million tonnes.

Canadian shareholders would get a much better return by investing in clean, renewable energy. If public investments of $4.65 billion, for example, were made annually in renewable energy development, some 58,300 full-time jobs would be created for one year (or person job years). Of these, 22,300 jobs would involve direct employment in renewable energy industries, another 19,500 jobs in indirect employment in secondary industries and an additional 16,700 induced jobs generated by workers in retail and wholesale (see Table 8.1). As the Green Economy Network platform put it:

> If $1.3 billion of these public revenues were invested in wind energy each year, 16,510 person year jobs (direct, indirect, and induced employment) would be created.

*Similarly, if $1 billion was publicly invested in solar energy
production, 13,400 jobs would be generated each year while
another 8,240 jobs would result from an annual investment
of $1 billion in geothermal energy production.*[1]

Table 8.1 Job Creation from Public Investments in Renewable Energy

	Investment	Direct	Indirect	Induced	Total
Wind Energy	$1,300	6,110	5,720	4,680	16,510
Solar Photovoltaic	$1,000	5,500	4,100	3,800	13,400
Geothermal	$800	2,400	3,520	2,400	8,240
Tidal	$666	3,596	2,531	2,464	8,591
Hydroelectric	$553	2,876	2,323	2,101	7,300
Biofuel	$333	1,798	1,265	1,232	4,296
Total	$4,652	22,280	19,459	16,677	58,337

Source: Green Economy Network

Unfortunately, it remains a basic fact of political life in Canada that neither the governing Liberals nor the NDP opposition is likely to move forward with progressive climate leadership and action along these lines without a major outpouring of grassroots mobilization. The period leading up to the October 2019 federal election is a critical time for building and mobilizing the climate justice movement to put increasing public pressure on the Liberals and the NDP. Imagine citizen brigades organized in regions across the country demanding bold leadership and action on climate change along the lines of the Big Shift. Simultaneous strategic actions could also be undertaken to challenge the Conservatives as the party with no intention of even trying to address the mounting climate crisis.

This campaign would need to mobilize bottom-up pressure on all levels of government to increase their ambition over the next two or three decades concerning reductions of greenhouse gas emissions to net zero. The climate justice movement could play a pivotal role in mounting such a campaign by cultivating the conscious develop-ment of a new breed of citizen activists — *eco-warriors*, fighting for fundamental transformations in the dominant *eco*nomic model so that the *eco*logy of the planet can be sustained.

Gearing Up

Despite the diverse array of creative grassroots initiatives taking place in communities across Canada, we still lack a cohesive plan that unites these and other exemplary cornerstones. This is what we know:

- The climate challenge facing Canada requires a deep decarbonization of the economy, starting with an overhaul of the energy sector.
- Our country has built and thrived on an extractivist economy that now must undergo a fundamental transformation.
- Canadians occupy a space next door to what is perhaps the most fragile ecosystem on the planet, the Arctic, which has been rapidly warming and melting as a result, in no small measure, of the tar sands industry in Canada.
- Meanwhile, under the Trump administration, our powerful neighbour on the other side, the world's second largest greenhouse gas emitter, has now officially abandoned the international fight against climate change.
- The climate clock is ticking, there is a planetary emergency and the moment calls for urgent and concrete actions to mitigate against runaway climate change.

Moreover, as declared in a new report from the Stockholm Environment Institute, the plan pursued by the Trudeau government to simultaneously "grow the economy" and "protect the environment" is both "contradictory" and "counteractive."[2] Canada has pledged to reduce its fossil fuel consumption, thereby reducing its annual greenhouse gas emissions 30 percent below 2005 levels between 2020 and 2030. At the same time, the oil industry plans to more than double its fossil fuel production, mainly through expansion of the tar sands during this period, adding another 1.2 billion more barrels a day, for a total of 2.1 billion barrels, mainly for export. Based on simple supply-and-demand economics, adding more oil to the global market daily "means more oil consumption and more emissions."[3] According to the Stockholm Environment Institute, adding 1.2 billion barrels of oil generates another 50 to 150 million tonnes of incremental carbon emissions annually, the equivalent of putting another 32 million more cars on the road each year.[4] In effect, this not only undermines but also counteracts Canada's bid to become a climate leader.

Hopefully, active responses to this challenge will lead to a new and more just and sustainable economy for future generations and the preservation of life on Earth.

Fortunately, many subnational governments — cities and units such as provinces or states — are playing leading roles in developing and implementing climate action plans within their jurisdictions. According to track0.org, by March 16, 2016, some 198 cities and regions around the world had pledged to get to zero greenhouse gas emissions or 100 percent renewable energy by 2050. Of these, 75 represented new pledges (an increase of 39 percent) following the Paris accord at the end of 2015 and the beginning of 2016. Just how realistic these pledges are, of course, remains to be seen. Nevertheless, it demonstrates a growing bottom-up momentum coming from progressively minded leadership in cities, towns and regions of nation-states. Since President Trump pulled the United States out of the Paris climate accord, we have seen increasing support for it from U.S. cities and states. Building alliances and partnerships with these cities and states may well be one of the best hopes for moving forward with an effective action plan.

So what can be done to kickstart development of a coherent and credible Canadian action plan for getting to zero before mid-century, beginning with the first decade, 2020–30? All levels of government have vital roles to play, working collaboratively, with the federal government holding responsibility for oversight and co-ordination. We know what needs to be done by way of substantial reductions in greenhouse gas emissions. The main economic sectors and industries requiring fundamental change have been identified, along with the primary ingredients of a viable plan. We simply lack a sense of urgency to get on with the task of developing a credible plan and graphically presenting it to the public as a collective challenge and undertaking.

The climate justice movement therefore needs to take the initiative and outline a transition roadmap for the first decade.[5] This would involve

- developing two five-year plans along the lines of the Green Economy Network's proposal, including targets for public investments, job creation and greenhouse gas emission reductions;
- showing how these targets could be achieved through proposals for the energy, building and transportation shifts, reinforced by the equity shift and
- outlining the mandates, targets, benchmarks and timetables regarding what needs to be accomplished for each of these four pillars of the Big Shift: energy, transportation, buildings and equity.

For example, the energy shift roadmap should include proposed mandates, targets, benchmarks and timetables for

- phasing out the bitumen industry,
- phasing in production of electric vehicles to replace the combustion engine,
- an authentic just transition strategy for displaced workers that includes skills retraining and compensation and
- substantial increases in clean, renewable energy development with the capacity to replenish between one third and one half of Canada's energy grid during this period.

The transition roadmap would provide a similar breakdown of targets and timetables for the transportation, building and equity shifts.

This is where concerned citizens and communities come into play. These challenges must first be confronted at the local level. To stimulate a sense of urgency, citizen brigades could be organized in local communities to challenge locally and regionally elected officials to develop credible plans for reducing between one third and one half of current annual greenhouse gas emissions through targeted actions related to energy, transportation and buildings over the coming decade (2020 to 2030) and the following decade (2030 to 2040).

Figure 8.1 portrays the potential growth in job creation over a decade (2020–2030) that would result if the Green Economy Network's five-year plan was fully implemented and then rolled over once more.

Figure 8.1 Job Creation and Renewable Energy Development Over 10 Years

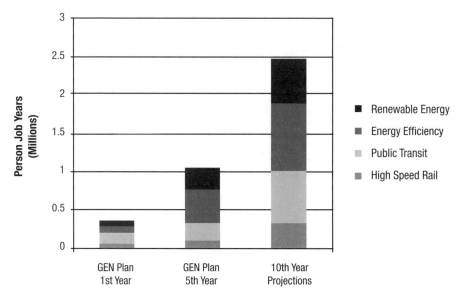

Source: Green Economy Network

Let's take a closer look at how a local area might tackle making the necessary sector shifts. Step one involves developing a profile of the particular sector, drawing on fairly recent sources that have been compiled. The Canadian Centre for Policy Alternatives' Tracking Progress and the Green Economy Network's Regional Backgrounders offer two excellent tools for this exercise.[6]

Energy Profile

To begin, the city or town will need an energy profile. Most cities and municipalities in the country keep up-to-date data that will be useful. Although most communities may be mainly energy consumers, some are both energy producers and consumers. Where possible, the profile should

- portray how dependent the city, town or region is on the consumption and production of fossil fuels;
- include an inventory of what types of clean, renewable energy development exist in the area and/or an assessment of the potential for such energy development;
- draw conclusions about the kind of energy mix that would be desirable and feasible by 2050 to feed into an integrated electrical grid and
- include data on public and private sector investments to be made, along with calculations on resulting job creation.

Armed with this and related data, concerned citizens and communities can press their locally elected officials to outline their plans for making a real yet ambitious energy shift in that area. (For a brief capsule summary of national priorities for Energy Shift 2020 to 2030, see Appendix 1-a.)

Transportation Profile

Once again, the starting point involves a transportation profile, either newly developed or existing. The profile should

- provide data on whether the most used mode of private transportation is car or truck;
- tell what percentage of the population makes use of public transit and whether the expansion of public transit in the past has resulted in ridership increases;
- include information on any plans for immediate improvements in local public transit and their expected impacts on reducing greenhouse gas emissions;

- include up-to-date information on the availability of electric vehicle production and sales in the area, as well as electric power stations and
- contain information about possibly building higher-speed rail (if the city or town is located within an urban corridor), along with data on the source and amount of public investments made and the number and types of jobs created as a result.

Again, having such a profile would enable concerned citizens and communities to demand publicly that elected officials provide a specific action plan designed to reduce greenhouse gas emissions by one third to one half in transportation between 2020 and 2030 — the transportation shift. (For a brief capsule summary of national priorities for Transportation Shift 2020 to 2030, see Appendix 1-b.)

Buildings Profile
Cities and towns will need building profiles as an important starting point. A report or profile on the local building stock may already exist in municipal offices, but it will need to be reasonably up to date and include

- data on residential, commercial, industrial, community and public buildings;
- any relevant data on the type of public investments made and the types of jobs that were and could be created through building retrofit projects;
- an assessment as to what percentage of the building stock would need to be fully renovated and retrofitted to become net zero by 2050 and
- an evaluation of what needs to be done to provide pay-as-you-save financing through public utility bills for these kinds of retrofitting projects.

Using these benchmarks as a guide, targets could be set for renovating old and developing new building stock for the coming decade (2020 to

2030) and succeeding decades with the aim of reducing greenhouse gas emissions in the building/construction sector by one third to one half by the end of each decade. (For a brief capsule summary of national priorities for Building Shift 2020 to 2030, see Appendix 1-c.)

These three shifts contain the ingredients of a platform we've been calling the Big Shift. Apart from the magnitude of the change required, the shift is "big" if it involves a *just* transition. This is where the fourth piece, the *equity shift*, comes into play.

A just transition addresses workers displaced by the phase-out of dirty industries such as coal and bitumen. It includes

- access to new, decent-paying jobs in the three sectors undergoing a transformative shift,
- retraining and skills upgrading where needed and
- a just transition fund for additional income support and compensation where needed.

As we saw in Chapter 6, a just transition inspired by an equity shift also casts the net wider to involve sectors of society that have been marginalized by previous waves of industrial development. These include

- Indigenous peoples who have lost their land-based culture and economy,
- low-income communities,
- racialized communities and
- the working poor who have been left behind.[5]

Table 8.2 Summary Goals for Three Phases of Transition Plan

Phase I (2020–30)	Phase II (2030–40)	Phase III (2040–50 or Less)
Develop a transition roadmap with a clear set of goals, targets and benchmarks — NOW	New transition roadmap needed based on what was (or wasn't) accomplished by the end of Phase I	Final transition roadmap based on what remains to be done to reach net zero

Making this happen will require that the movement develop a working partnership, wherever possible, with governments and political parties (at all levels) plus Indigenous peoples and First Nations. This working relationship should be developed and become operational before the October 2019 general election, when the country's political leadership could be tested in terms of its will to act on climate change through a climate justice lens.

Figure 8.2 compares the Green Economy Network pathway (green) to other options for reducing Canada's emissions during Phase I (2020–2030).7

Figure 8.2 Comparing Pathways to Net-Zero Greenhouse Gas Emissions

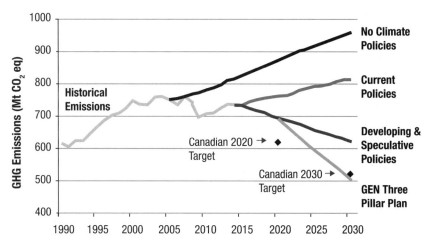

Regardless of whether the movement's transition roadmap is officially adopted by a government in office or an opposition party waiting in the wings, there is no substitute for a progressive social movement driving this agenda forward. A well-organized social movement — committed to the basic principles of climate justice — should be in the best position to make existing governments and opposition parties democratically accountable for their actions. History shows that such movements have, for the most part, been on the cutting edge of progressive politics.

Regional Campaigns

According to a 2016 report on global per capita greenhouse gas emission trends, Canadians emit four times as much greenhouse gas, on a per capita basis, as the rest of the world — a shocking statistic.[8] Our economy has become highly dependent on the production and consumption of fossil fuels, especially oil and gas products, which we rely on for transportation, industrial processes, electricity generation, home heating and a variety of other uses.

We all therefore bear a responsibility to become actively engaged in making the Big Shift happen. Although Ottawa has a key role to play in developing a credible action plan for the Big Shift and providing necessary oversight and co-ordination, much of the climate leadership must come through municipal and provincial governments. This will likely happen only if citizen activists and community groups organize campaigns to generate bottom-up pressure on a regional basis.

Armed with a profile and an action plan for the Big Shift in your region, a credible network of community groups (e.g., Indigenous peoples, environmentalists, labour unions, faith-based groups, public interest groups and many others) could be convened. The network can then organize

- meetings with key ministers and officials in the provincial government plus separate meetings with leaders and officials from the opposition parties;

- a public forum (or similar kind of public event) to present the profile and action plan for public discussion, debate and input from other concerned citizens and various community groups and
- a press conference or two at key moments to inform the media about the Big Shift platform for your region, the bottom-up call for urgent action and the response (or lack of response) from your meetings.

The Climate Jobs Council in Halifax exemplifies this type of regional organizing. This group (which incidentally grew out of a Green Economy Network roundtable co-sponsored with the Ecology Action Centre in Halifax in June 2016) has taken the lead in developing a regional profile and building a regional base of action relative to the provincial government on these issues.[9] Basically, it aims to mount bottom-up public pressure on and support for Nova Scotia governments to considerably increase their ambition with regard to reducing greenhouse gas emissions in their region. Such bottom-up public pressure through citizen brigades like this could be the spark needed to generate greater ambition and commitment at all levels of government across Canada.

Table 8.3 provides a brief sampling of the kind of relevant data that can be gleaned from both the Canadian Centre for Policy Alternatives' *Tracking Progress* and the Green Economy Network's *Regional Backgrounders* for developing regional profiles and plans of action. Readers inspired by the need to organize bottom-up campaigns in their region are encouraged to make use of both tools and data to develop their regional profiles and demands for governmental action.

Table 8.3 Collecting Data for Regional Profiles and Campaigns

Western Region

British Columbia	Alberta
• B.C. was an early climate leader, but momentum has stalled. The province missed its interim emission reduction targets in 2012 and 2016. It is now on track to miss its official target for 2020 by a large margin. • After Alberta, B.C. is Canada's largest energy producer — and a major consumer too. • The transportation sector accounts for one third of the province's total greenhouse gas emissions. • According to the Green Economy Network, B.C. could create 135,000 person-years of employment over a five-year period through a total public investment of $10.68 billion in public transit and high-speed rail, renewable energy and building efficiencies, which would reduce B.C.'s greenhouse gas emissions by up to 12.9 million tonnes yearly. • The Canadian Centre for Policy Alternatives reported that thousands of fossil fuel workers are facing job losses, including many coal communities, yet the province does not have a just transition strategy in place.	• Alberta accounts for two thirds of Canada's energy production. • As the biggest greenhouse gas-emitting province (by far), Alberta accounts for 38 percent of Canada's total emissions. Alberta's per capita emissions are 3 times the Canadian average and 13 times the global average. • For Canada to meet its targets, said the Canadian Centre for Policy Alternatives, Alberta would have to reduce its annual emissions from 274 million tonnes now to 193 million tonnes by 2020 and 163 million tonnes by 2030 by means such as a gradual phase-out of the tar sands. • The Green Economy Network calculated that Alberta could create 141,046 person-years of employment over five years by investing $10.89 billion in climate jobs (e.g., renewable energy, public transit, high-speed rail, building efficiencies), simultaneously reducing its greenhouse gas emissions by up to 25.7 million tonnes yearly. • Alberta has also been developing a just transition plan for displaced workers.
Saskatchewan	**Manitoba**
• Approximately 33 percent of Saskatchewan's greenhouse gas emissions are generated by the province's oil extraction industry; fossil fuel–based electricity generation accounts for a further 19 percent of emissions and agriculture is responsible for 24 percent according to the Canadian Centre for Policy Alternatives. • To bring its greenhouse gas emissions in line with national targets, Saskatchewan would have to reduce from 75 million tonnes in 2017 to 58 million tonnes by 2020 and to 49 million tonnes by 2030. The longer the province waits, the more costly it gets. • According to the Green Economy Network, Saskatchewan could create 48,029 person-years of employment over five years through targeted public investments in renewable energy, public transit and building efficiencies totalling $3.62 billion and thereby reduce greenhouse gas emissions by 9.7 million tonnes on average per year.	• Manitoba has been a climate leader in the past, being the first jurisdiction in Canada to legislate reduction targets for greenhouse gas emissions. • Manitoba is not a Big Oil producer, but it is a significant oil consumer — for transportation, industry and heating/cooling of buildings. • In 2014, Manitoba's greenhouse gas emissions were only 21 million tonnes or 2.9 percent of Canada's total annual emissions. • The Green Economy Network calculated that Manitoba could create 52,690 person-years of employment in climate jobs over five years through targeted public investments of $3.86 billion in renewable energy, public transit and building retrofits for more efficiency. In doing so, Manitoba's annual greenhouse gas emissions could be reduced by up to 6.4 million tonnes annually.

Central Region

Ontario	Quebec
• As a huge energy consumer but a small energy producer, Ontario imports a large quantity of fossil fuels for transportation, buildings and industry. • Roughly 33 percent of the province's greenhouse gas emissions come from transportation, 22 percent from buildings and 18 percent from industry, according to the Canadian Centre for Policy Alternatives report. • Successful phase-out of coal-fired generators reduced greenhouse gas emissions from that sector sixfold, but Ontario is still on track to miss its 2020 and 2030 targets for greenhouse gas emission reductions. • Ontario has no just transition strategy in place for displaced Ontario oil workers from the tar sands. • The Green Economy Network calculated that Ontario could create up to 379,296 person-years of employment over five years by making a total public investment of $29.19 billion in public transit and high-speed rail, plus renewable energy, building efficiency and conservation. • Such a targeted public investment would reduce Ontario's greenhouse gas emissions by up to 38.1 million tonnes per year. • Of course, given the June 2018 election results, it remains to be seen how far the new Conservative government will go to dismantle Ontario's current climate agenda.	• Compared with the rest of the country, Quebec has been a climate leader in both greenhouse gas emissions reduction (lowest per capita emissions in Canada) and clean energy production and exports (i.e., hydroelectric power). • Yet Quebec is also very dependent on fossil fuel imports to meet demands in transportation, industry and other sectors of the economy. • Despite significant progress, according to the Canadian Centre for Policy Alternatives report, Quebec's greenhouse gas emissions are projected to rise rather than drop further in the next two decades, largely because of increasing demand in transportation and industry. • Hence, the province will miss its 2020 and 2030 targets. • Quebec has policy infrastructure in place to drive further emission reductions, but deeper economic restructuring is needed. • According to the Green Economy Network, Quebec could create 203,258 person-years of employment over five years through targeted public investments totalling $15.2 billion in climate jobs, thereby further reducing its annual greenhouse gas emissions by up to 16.3 million tonnes yearly and closing the gap to meet its 2020 and 2030 targets.

Eastern Region

Nova Scotia	New Brunswick
• Although Nova Scotia's emissions have decreased by 17 percent since 1990, the province still has the sixth highest emissions per capita in Canada. • Nova Scotia imports large amounts of coal and petroleum products for electricity generation and transportation use. • Fossil fuels generate three quarters of the province's electrical power, which accounts for 42 percent of the province's total greenhouse gas emissions. • Fossil fuels for transportation use account for another 28 percent of the province's emissions, the Canadian Centre for Policy Alternatives reported. • The Green Economy Network calculated that Nova Scotia could create 30,753 person-years of employment over a five-year period by making targeted public investments totalling $2.28 billion in climate jobs, thereby reducing Nova Scotia's annual greenhouse gas emissions by up to 4.4 million tonnes yearly as well as reducing high unemployment (especially among youth) in the province.	• Although New Brunswick's contribution to the national greenhouse gas emissions is low (14.9 million tonnes in 2014 or 2 percent of the total), the province's per capita emissions were still ranked fifth highest in the country. • New Brunswick is highly dependent on burning fossil fuels to generate electricity. This accounts for 27 percent of the province's total greenhouse gas emissions, whereas the transportation sector accounts for another 28 percent and petroleum refining for another 19 percent of emissions according to the Canadian Centre for Policy Alternatives. • New Brunswick has been successful in driving down greenhouse gas emissions, particularly in the electricity sector, and is on track to meeting its 2020 and 2030 targets for greenhouse gas emission reductions. • According to the Green Economy Network, New Brunswick could also reduce its greenhouse gas emissions by up to 4.5 million tonnes a year and create 23,478 person-years of employment if it invested $1.73 billion in climate jobs, simultaneously reducing unemployment.
Prince Edward Island	**Newfoundland and Labrador**
• As the smallest province, PEI also has the lowest total of greenhouse gas emissions in Canada at 1.8 million tonnes annually. • Most of the energy produced in PEI comes from wind power, but the amount produced only serves about a quarter of energy demand. • According to the Canadian Centre for Policy Alternatives, two thirds of the energy consumed in PEI comes from petroleum products, with the result that the transportation sector accounts for almost 50 percent of all emissions. The remaining PEI emissions are generated by buildings and agriculture, approximately 20 percent each. • According to the Canadian Centre for Policy Alternatives, PEI should be able to meet its 2020 target of 10 percent below 1990 levels, but its 2030 target of 35–45 percent below 1990 levels will be more difficult to achieve.	• Although the province's contribution to the national greenhouse gas emissions is low, Newfoundland and Labrador has the fourth highest emissions per capita in Canada. • The province has a large oil industry, which includes both extraction and refining, and produces approximately three quarters of the province's primary energy. • Two thirds of the energy consumed involves refined petroleum products such as gasoline and diesel. As a result, one third of the province's total greenhouse gas emissions come from the transportation sector. • Newfoundland and Labrador developed an initial climate plan in 2011 that focused on energy efficiency and renewable energy infrastructure. • To date, the province has not come up with strategies to tackle those sectors of the economy that comprise the primary causes of greenhouse gas emissions in the province. • A new climate plan was due in 2017, but it remains to be seen how ambitious it will be. Understandably, oil workers in the Atlantic, as well as Alberta and elsewhere, are increasingly worried about their future, so it's imperative that this and other climate plans include a just transition strategy.

Northern Region

Yukon, Northwest Territories and Nunavut
• In all three territories, the local impacts of climate change are already apparent. • During the past 50 years, the NWT climate has warmed at a rate four to five times faster than the global average. • Arctic ice coverage has also been decreasing at a rate of 6.8 percent per decade since 1979. • Observable changes include frequency of extreme weather, thinner sea ice, earlier and faster sea ice breakup, melting permafrost and changes in wildlife distribution patterns. • These climate changes are having a profound impact on the people living in the territories, especially Indigenous peoples and their traditional activities. • The NWT is the biggest emitter of the three territories, which accounts for less than 1 percent of Canada's total emissions. • Since 1990, the annual greenhouse gas emissions of the NWT and Nunavut have risen steadily, with short dips and then rising again, whereas Yukon's emissions have been in steady decline. • Of the three territorial governments, Yukon appears to have been the most ambitious so far in setting sector targets for emission reductions in transportation, buildings, electricity and industrial operations. • All three territorial governments have developed climate plans. Yet all three focus mainly on adaptation rather than mitigation. This is understandable because the territories are located next door to the Arctic, where the drama of climate change is playing out. • The NWT set an economy-wide goal of stabilizing greenhouse gas emissions at 2005 levels in the long term, but the emphasis was still on adapting to a rapidly warming climate instead of reducing greenhouse gas emissions.

In developing these regional profiles, targets and plans of action, it is important to keep several factors in mind:

- National greenhouse gas emission reduction targets could range between 250 and 375 million tonnes per decade (between one third and one half of Canada's annual average greenhouse gas emissions) depending on how much space is left in the carbon budget.
- The five-year Green Economy Network action plan for the Big Shift is designed so that it can be rolled over several times consecutively in terms of targeted public investments, job creation and greenhouse gas emission reductions, either nationally or regionally.
- An important tool for monitoring the signs of global *decline* in the oil industry and the need to *manage* it is Oil Change International's new bulletin for civil society organizations, *OilWire*.[10]

- Funding for public investments regarding the energy, transportation, construction and equity shifts would be apportioned according to the 50/40/10 funding formula (or agreed-on variation).
- Other potential funding sources could be tapped for this purpose, including
  - the new federal-provincial carbon tax,
  - reallocation of direct and indirect subsidies to fossil fuel industries for renewable energy and
  - revenues garnered through a clampdown on tax avoidance through tax havens.
- New jobs created constitute a new line of employment, which contributes to the ongoing reduction of greenhouse gas emissions, and this new line of employment opens up pathways to the creation of a new, more equitable and sustainable economy for an emerging ecological age.

These regional campaigns to generate and mobilize bottom-up public pressure for enacting the Big Shift plan of action would need to work in tandem where possible with lobby action strategies initiated by the climate justice movement to engage with federal government and political parties leading up to the 2019 general election.

Eco-warriors

There is one more fundamental shift that must take place over the next few decades. This is the underlying *paradigm shift* that goes hand in hand with the Big Shift plus the other four — energy, transportation, buildings and equity. For more than 200 years, Western society (and now most of the rest of the world) has become increasingly dependent on, and even addicted to, oil and its by-products. As a result, we find ourselves caught in a trap, an endless cycle of producing and consuming petroleum products, which, in many ways, has become the hallmark of our high-tech industrial civilization.

Our focus throughout our discussion here has been on oil as a combustion fuel that is *burned* to power our cars, trucks, trains, boats and airplanes or to heat and cool our residential, business, commercial, industrial and public buildings. When petroleum products are burned as a combustion fuel for these and related purposes, they generate the greenhouse gas emissions that primarily cause global warming and climate change.

But there's more to an oil-based economy than treating it as a combustion fuel. Petroleum and its oil by-products are used in a vast range of other products, such as tires, nail polish, plastic, golf balls, astroturf, gum, lipstick, shoe polish, crayons, candles, asphalt, textiles, garden hoses, house paint, sneakers, handbags, pesticides, herbicides, fertilizers, disposable diapers, calculators, transparent adhesive tape, latex gloves, electronics, credit cards, extension cords, antifreeze, cleaners and balloons, to name a few.[11] Petroleum is even used to manufacture wind turbines and solar panels.

To be sure, the central focus of this oil paradigm for us must remain the use of oil and gas as combustion fuels. But all the other uses of oil and petroleum by-products serve to protect against any threats or challenges to this paradigm, on which the foundations of Canada's economy and society now largely rest. As a society, our collective belief in this oil paradigm represents a major obstacle to making the Big Shift a reality. Therefore, efforts to advance the Big Shift to get us to net zero in terms of fossil fuel emissions must be accompanied by efforts to hasten a paradigm shift in people's thinking and awareness, institutional structures and public policies.

To move in this direction, the climate justice movement would need to cultivate a new breed of citizen activists — *eco-warriors* — equipped to both reflect and act for the sake of deeper transformation.[12] The term *eco*, used here as a prefix, is meant to have a dual meaning, namely, the *eco*nomy and the *eco*logy and the correlation between the two. Within this framework, the movement's eco-warriors would accompany the many people working through their respective civil society groups on the three dimensions of transformation — industrial overhaul, climate jobs, just transition — in identifying creative and viable ways of exposing, confronting and overcoming the dominant paradigm. They would have the capacity for transformative *praxis*, the discipline of "naming" the deeper structural changes that will be required to bring about the overall eco-transformation needed. Indeed, the lesson emerging from the twilight years of the industrial age and revolution is that Earth may not survive without a major overhaul and transformation of the dominant economic model, both globally and domestically.

Drawing on the insights of ecological educators such as Joanna Macy[13] and popular educators such as Paulo Freire,[14] it is possible to identify a narrative and a process of "action and reflection" that could be useful for eco-warriors. To stimulate the deeper transformation needed, this praxis would involve a series of "turnings" — cultural, economic, political — in people's consciousness, moving from an old to a new paradigm. Together these turnings would prepare the way for more fundamental shifts in the paradigm to come. The three sets of turnings are interrelated and interdependent to the point where one cannot be realized or fulfilled without the other two.

Cultural Turnings

The term *cultural turnings* here refers broadly to the vision, values and principles that motivate people's lives, work and actions in their communities, their country and the world at large. More specifically, cultural turnings have to do with the constellation of values and priorities that comprise the main organizing principles of a given economy and society. It makes a difference, for example, if the organizing principle of an economy is "prosperity" (defined as the "accumulation of wealth and power") or "the sustainability of life on this planet."

The reference to turnings relates to *rethinking* those motivational values that function as the organizing principles of our economy and society, as well as what needs to be done to change course.[15] The climate justice movement needs eco-warriors to help inspire and cultivate this shift, not only among political and social leaders but also among artists, musicians and entertainers, who can potentially reach a broader audience.

Take, for example, the contemporary Western mindset, which is largely geared to think in the present, with little regard for long-term consequences. We tend to think and act more in terms of the "now" than the "future." However, the ancient wisdom of Indigenous people offers an antidote. Indigenous people, through their elders and teachings, can show us how to think about our actions today in terms of their impacts on future generations. Indigenous wisdom offers a guiding principle to live in harmony with Mother Earth: to "take only what we need now, conscious of the impact our actions now will have on seven generations to come."[16] This principle could help us overcome this cultural obstacle posed by our Western mindset and aid in developing a credible and viable action plan with scheduled targets and benchmarks over the next 10, 20 and 30 years.

The oil-based paradigm that underpins our society has been reinforced by a culture of extractivism, which has permeated much of our history as a nation-state. At the core of this extractivist heritage is the notion of "taking and taking without giving back."[17] Indeed, this is as much a moral critique as it is a cultural one.[18] Historically, for the most part, Canadians have collectively neither learned nor heeded the ecological lessons of Mother Earth from Indigenous elders. Given the ecological damage generated by the relentless extraction of bitumen in the tar sands, the growing clamour to "leave it in the ground" makes more and more sense. But as long as the oil-based paradigm continues to permeate our cultural thinking, the interests of Big Oil rooted in this culture of extractivism will surely prevail.

The culture of extractivism and the oil-based paradigm have been reinforced by a constant bombardment of advertising sponsored by corporate players in the oil patch. Foreign-owned giants such as ExxonMobil and Shell have promoted these themes in their corporate advertising, as have major tar sands developments such as Syncrude and Suncor. Ongoing corporate advertising campaigns have been waged since 2010 by industry associations such as the Canadian Association of Petroleum Producers and the Canadian Energy Pipeline Association. In particular, the petroleum association has spent millions of dollars on a yearly basis in TV, print and online ads extolling the virtues of the bitumen industry and the role it plays as the centrepiece of the Canadian economy. Shown repeatedly on CBC and CTV national broadcasts, several of these television ads also portray a complex web connecting producers and suppliers, reinforcing the message that our whole economy and society depend on the petroleum industry. The latest round of ads features succeeding generations of Canadian settlers suddenly concerned about preserving nature. In effect, these ads serve to convey the belief and impression that this oil-based paradigm is not only "environmentally friendly" but also here to stay.[19]

Underlying this kind of consumer advertising in defence of the oil industry is the cultural force that generally drives capitalist societies: "the accumulation of capital and wealth," "maximization of profits" and "limitless economic growth" as the prime goal of society measured in terms of the GDP. Eco-warriors can stimulate constructive discussion and debate on the role and impact of this organizing principle on our economy and society. Critical discussion of these and related questions also uncovers and exposes the extent to which our economy and society prioritize "exchange value" (based on what a product generates in terms of accumulating monetary wealth) over "use value" (based on what utility a product contributes to achieving other societal goals).[20] By wrestling with these questions, people can begin the process of more critically analyzing and communicating how our economy and society have become more and more dependent on, if not addicted to, oil.

To stimulate a cultural turning, however, eco-warriors also need to identify alternative values and visions. Instead of accumulating capital and wealth, what would it mean to put a priority on "sustaining life" as the organizing principle of our economy? Rather than "limitless economic growth" or "maximizing profits," why not make "sustainability of life on this planet" our societal goal and replace the GDP with something such as the Genuine Progress Indicator?[21] Or what about the guiding principle drawn from ancient Indigenous wisdom: learning to "live appropriately so that others may live." By encouraging ongoing dialogue with those Indigenous peoples who are the keepers of this ancient wisdom, there could be a renewal of collective vision and values for reconstituting the organizing principles of our economy, politics and society.

With sustaining life as the societal goal, the transition from production of and dependence on dirty oil and fossil fuels to clean, renewable energy sources could be considerably accelerated and made more seamless. It would also underscore the need for new modes of production that demand

- a rebalancing of the economy between resource, manufacturing and service sectors;
- a public transportation system that dramatically reduces the use of private trucks and cars and
- development of innovative strategies that make appropriate use of green technologies to create new enterprises for an ecological age.

Economic Turnings

Globally speaking, there are certainly signs these days of *economic turnings* — amounting in some cases to economic turbulence — that relate directly to the issues we have been discussing. Unfortunately, these turnings have so far been moving in diametrically opposed directions. On the one hand, the transition from fossil-fuelled to renewable energy–powered economies has received a major boost from a "made-in-China revolution" that is taking place in solar power. In 2012, large solar companies were failing and investors fleeing because solar energy production costs were high and demand was low. By 2014, however, the trend line had shifted dramatically as annual investments in fossil fuel industries dropped by $50 billion and investments in clean, renewable energy sources rose by 13 percent over 2013, which had seen a 12 percent increase over the previous year.[22] On the other hand, the Trump regime has pledged to terminate tax breaks for renewable energy, which Trump claims is "so expensive," in favour of reviving the coal industry.

From the outset of his campaign for the presidency, Trump embarked on a trajectory of leading the United States into a showdown with both China and Mexico over the U.S. trade deficits with both countries.

Since the mid-1990s, China has undergone a major economic transformation, which resulted in "a massive inflow of export-oriented foreign investment" from the U.S.[23] Basically, China's interest in attracting foreign capital dovetailed with the desire of U.S.-based multinational corporations to globalize their production.[24] Meanwhile, the United States has also developed a merchandise trade deficit with Mexico through the production sharing arrangements under NAFTA, whereby manufacturers on both sides of the Mexican border work together to produce goods, such as component parts for autos.[25]

Although Trump blames this outcome on a poorly negotiated NAFTA, the fact remains that this is the logic of corporate-driven globalization (discussed in Chapter 2), wherein U.S. corporations and Mexican economic elites greatly benefit at the expense of workers and the impoverished on both sides of the border. That said, the Trump regime has thus far made both China and Mexico prime targets in its effort to turn around the U.S. economy. In doing so, the United States could well provoke an all-out trade war on both fronts. The U.S. Congress has already followed the Trump agenda by slashing federal corporate income taxes, deregulating the energy industry on environmental matters and introducing a range of protectionist legislation (including Trump's punitive border taxes on softwood lumber, aeronomics, steel and aluminum imports).

Canada, which currently has a relatively balanced trade account with the United States, could end up caught in the crossfire. Despite an exemption or carve-out from the Trump protectionist trade tariffs, the Trudeau government may yet risk realigning Canada's economic policies and strategies with those of the Trump regime. After all, the Business Council of Canada, which represents the 150 largest corporations in the country, has been insisting that Ottawa's "no. 1 job" now is to make sure that Canada stays "competitive" with the United States.[26] In other words, slash federal corporate taxes, deregulate the energy industry and adopt more protectionist legislation on this side of the border too.

For the Trudeau government to embrace the Trump economic plan and the strategy being advocated by the Business Council of Canada would amount to a reversal of election promises and a betrayal of the vast majority of the Canadian electorate. The climate justice movement must take stock of its strategic options. The movement's eco-warriors would do well to begin with developing and mounting a counteroffensive to the Trump agenda and its effects. A strategic assessment, for example, needs to be made of the collateral damage that could result if Canada pursued the strategy advocated by the Business Council of Canada.

At least two critical challenges face eco-warriors in Canada and the United States regarding the Trump agenda. The first has to do with the Trump pledge to revive the fossil fuel industry as the cornerstone of an oil-based economy and civilization. He started the process through restoring and increasing federal subsidies to the coal industry while withdrawing government incentives put in place by the Obama administration to stimulate the transition from fossil fuels to renewable energy. The next stage could well be focused on reviving the oil and gas industry, including the nascent fracking industry, which extracts oil and gas from rock basins; the offshore petroleum industry, which extracts oil from the ocean floor and the advance of drilling operations for oil and gas in other ecologically sensitive areas, such as the Arctic. Clearly, reviving the fossil fuel industry would likely be a death blow to the movement to stop and reverse climate change.

The second critical challenge involves the effort to ensure that Canada continues as a major energy supplier to the United States. Whether or not NAFTA survives at the hands of the Trump regime, the proportionality clause built into NAFTA (Articles 315 and 605) guaranteed the United States access to a long-term supply of bitumen from the Alberta tar sands for crude oil production. If NAFTA or its successor (e.g., a bilateral trade agreement) retains this proportionality clause, Canada would be compelled to continue providing an ongoing supply of bitumen for crude oil production to the United States. If the clause continues to be a legally binding instrument, it is highly unlikely that Canada could achieve its goals and targets under the Paris accord, let alone any more ambitious objectives. Thus, the climate justice movement and its eco-warriors need to become more aware of this critical challenge and be prepared to propose or demand solutions and an action plan.

In any scenario, Canada and its economy are most likely in for a considerable shakeup and turbulent period. Accordingly, the Canadian climate justice movement and its eco-warriors will have to be extra vigilant about the Trump economic agenda and its impacts. While Trump remains in office, the movement in Canada should be prepared to

- mobilize public pressure on the Trudeau government to ensure that it does not make further concessions to the Trump regime and its agenda (whether this be engaging in trade wars with China or Mexico or revitalizing the fossil fuel industry);
- identify targets and build beachheads of resistance to pipeline expansion and other projects in Canada that could advance the economic traction for the Trump agenda and
- take advantage of opportunities that may arise during this period to further develop and promote the main pillars of the Big Shift.

The movement must organize itself to be the vanguard of this vigilance leading up to the next Canadian election in 2019 and the next U.S. presidential election in 2020. During this period, economic turnings, both negative and positive, will continue, affecting the prospects for the deep transformation that is urgently needed. Being vigilant about the key economic turnings should be a top priority. The danger is that this period could slip by very quickly, with little or no mass resistance. In such a scenario, Canada could find itself locked in by a series of major economic blockages.[27]

Political Turnings

The kind of economic restructuring that needs to take place cannot possibly be achieved without a corresponding *political turning*. It would take a considerable amount of political leadership to turn around the policy-making agenda in Ottawa (let alone Washington) and follow through with the kinds of public investments necessary to measure up to this challenge. In Canada, to date, none of the major political parties at the federal level has developed an adequate or comprehensive action plan, along the lines of the Big Shift, to move Canada's economy forward in this direction. As discussed in Chapter 6, the kind of economic turning required calls for key transformations in our political institutions and model of governance, not just timid tinkering. Eco-warriors working within the climate justice movement need to be equipped with the tools and resources required to stimulate this kind of political turning.

The mechanisms of economic globalization have already done a great deal of damage to the role of the state and the capacities of governments. During the past four decades or more, neoliberal forces and policies adopted by governments have resulted in a largely deregulated economy, both domestically and globally. Through the rise in the power of transnational corporations, capital is now able to move freely around the world, unfettered by either intervention or regulation by national governments, let alone regional or local ones. Under the multiple global free trade regimes that now exist, transnational corporations have acquired a kind of sovereign-state status with powers such as investor-state dispute settlement mechanisms that allow them to sue governments directly for passing environmental and social legislation that hinders their profit margins. These global regimes cast a political chill on governments, which now have to ensure that the policies and laws they propose can meet the litmus test of trade rules designed to benefit the interests of transnational corporations.

Any action plan for political turning must include measures designed to at least begin dismantling the corporate capture of the state. Although this corporate takeover has come in various forms in Canada over the past 40 years, it is now largely manifested in the form of a "petro-state" dominated by the petroleum industry. The Harper government's quest for global energy superpower status through the Athabasca tar sands and related mega–fossil fuel projects has been a driving force in reinventing the role and powers of the federal state in Canada. A prime example of this political restructuring has been the increasing power and influence exerted by the federal lobbying machinery of the petroleum industry. Although the federal lobbying act and regulations have been in effect since the 1990s, the power and influence wielded by Big Oil corporations and their industry associations, such as the Canadian Association of Petroleum Producers, have grown exponentially during the past decade in particular. As a result, the petroleum industry was highly instrumental in drafting two major omnibus bills (C-38 and C-45) between 2011 and 2013 that effectively rewrote much of Canada's legislation governing economic and environmental matters related to energy and resource development — in favour of the petroleum industry.

Dismantling this petro-state apparatus in Canada must be a top priority for any real political turning. In a globalized industrial economy where the "accumulation of capital" and "limitless economic growth" are prioritized, the corporate security state may thrive while doing a great deal of ecological and social damage. If Canada is to make the transition from an industrial to an ecological age, the state's focus should be redefined toward defending the sustainability of life on this planet. Just as the social welfare state emerged out of the 1930s' Great Depression as a new form of governance with a new mandate and new powers and tools, so the new eco-social state must be equipped to intervene in, and redirect, the economy where necessary to accomplish its goals. The social welfare state relied on Keynesian economics as its basis for intervening in the domestic economy; the new eco-social state must acquire the tools necessary to intervene in both the domestic and the global economy. In Canada, this requires a relatively strong centralized state, infused with a healthy dose of co-operative federalism, along with sufficient powers to navigate the turbulent waters of globalized capital effectively.

The climate justice movement, guided by its eco-warriors, can play an important role by developing and advocating for an action plan that could help reframe the mandate and role of an emerging eco-social state along these lines. An overarching ministry, for example, needs to be established in Ottawa with the mandate to stimulate, guide and implement the Big Shift to a net-zero carbon economy by 2050 if not earlier. The composition of this ministry (or "super"-ministry) and its departments could be largely based on a reallocation of talent and resources from existing government departments, reinforced by an additional sprinkling of creative talent from civil society organizations. Ultimately, this super-ministry would be primarily responsible for co-ordinating and overseeing the Big Shift action plan. Mandated by an act of Parliament, this ministry would include, among other priorities, responsibilities for working with counterpart ministries in provincial governments and major cities in gradually developing a new model of governance. The time frame for this new ministry would be the next 30-plus years leading up to net zero before mid-century, with the prospects of renewal based on a comprehensive review.

New institutions will also be necessary if this new model of governance is going to be effective in carrying out its mandate. For example, to make the critical transition required by the energy shift, it would be advisable to establish a Crown corporation with a mandate to gradually phase out bitumen production and reinvest its assets in publicly owned renewable energy production. Such an initiative could be undertaken by Ottawa or, if possible, jointly with the Alberta government, drawing on an established Canadian tradition of relying on Crown corporations to achieve public goals and priorities in the marketplace. Given the track record of Crown corporations generally, however, steps should be taken to counterbalance the powers of a state-owned oil company with forms of social ownership, perhaps by communities at a regional level.

Established regulatory bodies such as the National Energy Board need to be completely overhauled and transformed with a new mandate that includes, among other priorities, a comprehensive climate test for both upstream and downstream greenhouse gas emissions. To its credit, the Trudeau government has taken a step or two in this direction with its replacement of the National Energy Board and elements of its Bill C-69, before Parliament in 2018. To achieve the energy shift required, however, the new body's mandate must be explicitly devoted to facilitating the transition from a fossil-fuelled to a renewable energy economy before mid-century.

These three principal disciplines of a transformative praxis — cultural, economic and political turning — form the interdependent moving parts of the great transformation that needs to take place over the next 20 to 30 years. These disciplines should not be viewed in a linear fashion but rather in a circular one, operating simultaneously and interacting with one another. Ideally, concerned individuals will engage with the movement's eco-warriors in this type of reflection and in so doing will gradually develop a deeper consciousness of what needs to be done and can be done to transform the system. We must truly *rethink* our current system and dominant paradigm before the paradigm shift we so urgently need can take place.

There is, of course, a powerful built-in wild card that needs to be factored into implementing the Big Shift plan of action, namely, U.S. President Donald Trump. At the halfway point of his first term in office, it has become increasingly clear that Trump envisions a new and radically different world order. Not only does he reject the findings of climate science and corresponding threats to the planet, but it appears that his main aim is to restore "America's greatness" by building a new world order in which the United States occupies centre stage. As we've seen, a key piece of the grand Trump plan is to revitalize the U.S. fossil fuel industry, not only coal but also the petroleum industry, wherein Big Oil is destined to play a prominent role. In effect, this means once again putting a priority on fossil fuel consumption and production as the prime source of energy.

Needless to say, his agenda runs completely counter to the analysis and strategies discussed here to stop and reverse runaway climate change.

If the Trump regime succeeds or is only partially successful, the impact on Canada could be profound. Indeed, several scenarios are possible. One involves mobilizing a counteroffensive that ends up triggering a trade war with the United States, which results in not only the termination of NAFTA but also a blitz of escalating tariffs on steel, aluminum and autos plus other commodities that pushes Canada's economy into a recession. Another scenario entails a series of compromises to placate the Trump regime, which would end up further entrenching Canada's role as an extractivist economy and a major supplier of fossil fuel energy to the U.S. empire. Either way, the United States, not Canada, comes out on top.[28]

Meanwhile, Donald Trump is not the only "wild card" the Trudeau government has to face, negotiate and deal with on a regular basis. Closer to home, the June 2018 election of Doug Ford as Ontario's new premier poses a possibly formidable challenge. Within days of being sworn into office, Ford moved swiftly to take Ontario out of the cap-in-trade program with Quebec and California to fight climate change by providing incentives to industries for reducing their greenhouse gas emissions; cancelled the Ontario government's GreenON Program, which provided retrofit rebates for energy conscious homeowners in the province; and signaled its intention to take the federal government to court over the constitutionality of its actions to impose a carbon tax on the people of Canada. In response, Environment and Climate Change Minister Catherine McKenna declared that without a plan to take climate action, Ontario is effectively "withdrawing from the national climate change plan."[29] Suddenly, given Ontario is Canada's largest province, mitigating climate change has been turned into a test of the Canadian federation and its viability.

In any case, this is the challenge of the great transformation that progressive governments, inspired and motivated by a proactive eco-social movement, are called to make at this moment in history. To do so, the climate justice movement, guided by its eco-warriors, must carve out an alternative pathway to a just and sustainable future. In large measure, this is what the call to mount campaigns for mobilizing concerned citizens and communities to join in a common struggle for making the Big Shift happen — in energy, transportation and construction — is all about. In doing so, we must learn to navigate the turbulent waters of the Trump era and its worldview by confronting the new politics of "dangerous unpredictability."

This is where the vision and principles of climate justice come into full play. Not only do we have to mobilize to make strategic changes in key sectors of our economy, but we also have to do so in a way that dismantles and replaces this country's extractivist economy. In other words, the movement must aim to transform and build a new economic (and political) model for a more just and sustainable future. Moreover, this transformation must be carried out with equity, fairness and justice if the planet is to truly heal as the "giver of life" itself. "Getting to zero" really entails being mindful of this climate justice vision and its guiding principles.

Appendix

Energy Shift
2020 to 2030

Overall Goal:
Transform Canada's energy system from its current 77 percent dependence on dirty, polluting fossil fuels to 100 percent dependence on clean, renewable energy sources by 2050.

Strategic Objectives
To reduce Canada's greenhouse gas emissions one third to one half by 2030 (requiring the fossil fuel industry to cut its annual emissions between 61 and 91.5 million tonnes).
(Note: On average, the energy industry is responsible for 25 to 26 percent of Canada's total annual greenhouse gas emissions. Calculations here based on Canada's 2016 National Inventory Report.)

1. Develop and implement a 10-year plan for the gradual phase-out of coal production, the tar sands and hydraulic fracking for liquefied natural gas production plus any other fossil fuel industries. Managed phaseout should begin before 2025 and be fully operational by 2030.
   + targeted action, benchmarks and timetable

2. Develop and implement a 10-year plan for creating
a clean, dynamic, renewable energy system in
Canada — wind, solar, geothermal, tidal and small-
scale hydroelectric power, plus promote electric car
production and a pan-Canadian electrical grid.

+ **targeted action, benchmarks and timetable**

3. Develop and implement a just transition mechanism
whereby laid-off workers in fossil fuel industries can
find new, decent-paying employment opportunities in
renewable energy, green building, public transportation or
green technology industries along with any skills retraining
necessary and related compensation to ensure a just
transition. Plan should also include provisions to ensure
that Indigenous people, women, the working poor, racial
minorities etc. have equitable access to opportunities for
skills retraining and decent paying jobs.

+ **targeted action, benchmarks and timetable**

Public Investments in Renewable Energy	Climate Job Creation in Renewable Energy	Greenhouse Gas Emission Reductions
$23.3 billion over 5 years	290,000 jobs over 5 years — could potentially double over 10 years	Between 44 and 110 million tonnes (after 5 years)
Funding coming from all three major levels of government: 50 percent federal, 40 percent provincial, 10 percent municipal	Includes direct, indirect and induced person-years of employment over 5 years resulting from $23.3 billion in public investment	Up to 200 million tonnes after 10 years or so

Note: *This is a 5-year action plan for the required energy shift, designed to be renewed and rolled over several times before reaching the goal of net-zero greenhouse gas emissions and a 100 percent renewable energy economy.*

Appendix 1-b

Transportation Shift
2020 to 2030

Overall Goal:
*Transform the mode of transportation
for people and freight from dependence
on cars and trucks to greater reliance
on public transit in urban centres and
higher-speed rail between cities in urban
corridors by 2050.*

Strategic Objectives
To reduce Canada's greenhouse gas emissions one
third to one half by 2030 (requiring the transportation
industry to cut its annual emissions between 57.6 and
86.5 million tonnes).
(Note: Transporting people and freight by combustion
engine cars or trucks accounts for another 25 to 28
percent of Canada's annual greenhouse gas emissions.)

1. Design, develop and implement urban transportation
strategies, in collaboration with municipalities and
provinces, to expand and improve public transit within
our cities. Transporting people by private automobiles
has become a quality-of-life issue involving considerable
personal stress, money and time. Investing in urban public
transit, therefore, can also be a major factor in redesigning
and rebuilding urban centres for greater density and
curbing urban sprawl.

+ **targeted action, benchmarks and timetable**

2. Design and develop higher-speed rail systems between cities within urban corridors. The longest, underdeveloped urban corridor for transporting people and freight is the Quebec City-Montreal-Toronto-Windsor-Detroit corridor. Others include Edmonton-Calgary and Vancouver-Seattle. Despite numerous studies demonstrating the practicality and feasibility of higher-speed rail, nothing has been done. Although the previous Liberal government in Ontario announced intentions to build the Toronto-Windsor leg, as of August 2018 it is not clear what the Conservative government will do.

+ targeted action, benchmarks and timetable

3. Develop and implement two 5-year action plans for improving and expanding urban public transit and for building higher-speed rail between cities in urban corridors: showing how it will be affordable, accessible and accountable; outlining benchmarks for what needs to be achieved in terms of new climate job creation by 2025 and by 2030 and for Canada to achieve its greenhouse emission targets for 2030. Note: the full impact of annual greenhouse gas emissions to come closer to ten year period.

+ targeted action, benchmarks and timetable

Public Investments in Urban Public Transit and Higher-speed Rail	Climate Job Creation in Urban Public Transit and Higher-speed Rail	Greenhouse Gas Emission Reductions
$17.6 billion over 5 years for urban public transit and another $10 billion for higher-speed rail	223,000 person-years of employment over 5 years in public transit and another 101,600 for higher-speed rail investments	Between 32 and 126 million tonnes (after 5 years)
Funding coming from all three major levels of government: 50 percent federal, 40 percent provincial, 10 percent municipal	Includes direct, indirect and induced person-years of employment over 5 years resulting from $27.6 billion in public investment	Variations in greenhouse gas emission reductions due largely to two major lag effects: the ridership effect and the land use effect

Appendix 1-c

Building Shift
2020 to 2030

Overall Goal:
*Transform the energy efficiency of
Canada's total building stock (residential,
public, commercial, industrial,
institutional) to achieve a target of net-
zero emissions for all buildings by 2050.**

Strategic Objectives
To reduce Canada's greenhouse gas emissions one third
to one half by 2030 (required targets for this would
range between 27 and 40.5 million tonnes annually).
(Note: Energy waste through poorly insulated buildings
accounts for 12 percent of Canada's annual greenhouse
gas emissions based on Canada's 2016 National
Inventory Report.)

1. Develop and implement — in collaboration with
   provinces, territories and municipalities — a national
   green homes program with more stringent national
   efficiency regulations; financing for building retrofits
   through guaranteed loans to municipal governments
   based on the property tax system; maintenance and
   expansion of national efficiency support services; a pay-
   as-you-save financing program; mandatory labelling for
   energy conservation plus a national model home retrofit
   code and a renovator training program for green homes.

   + targeted action, benchmarks and timetable

2. Develop and implement a green buildings program designed to substantially improve the technical and operational energy efficiency of existing buildings plus requirements that all new buildings be net zero starting in 2025. This program would include measures such as universal mandatory labelling at the time of sale or rental renewal, a performance-based conservation database, regional efficiency centres and loan guarantees for pay-as-you-save financing supports for new net-zero buildings.

+ targeted action, benchmarks and timetable

3. Develop and implement two 5-year action plans for green homes and green buildings, outlining benchmarks for what needs to be achieved in terms of new climate job creation by 2025 and by 2030 for Canada to achieve its greenhouse gas emission targets for 2030.

+ targeted action, benchmarks and timetable

Public Investments in Green Homes and Buildings	Climate Job Creation in Green Homes and Buildings	Greenhouse Gas Emission Reductions
$30 billion over 5 years	438,000 person-years of employment over 5 years	Between 32 and 126 million tonnes (after 5 years)
Funding coming from all three major levels of government: 50 percent federal, 40 percent provincial, 10 percent municipal.**	Includes direct, indirect and induced person-years of employment over 5 years resulting from $30 billion in public investment	

* Net zero = the amount of energy provided by onsite renewable energy sources is equal to the amount of energy used by the operations of the building.
** Mostly recovered through pay-as-you-save financing.

Endnotes

Introduction

1. See Brian J. Stocks and other scientists' comments linking the Fort McMurray fire to global warming in Justin Gillis and Henry Fountain, "Global Warming Cited as Wildfires Increase in Fragile Boreal Forest," *New York Times*, May 10, 2016, www.nytimes.com/2016/05/11/science/global-warming-cited-as-wildfires-increase-in-fragile-boreal-forest.html.
2. See Environment and Climate Change Canada's *National Inventory Report 1990–2016: Greenhouse Gas Sources and Sinks in Canada*, www.canada.ca/en/environment-climate-change/services/climate-change/greenhouse-gas-emissions/inventory.html.
3. See OECD Environmental Performance reviews 2017: Canada 2017, http://www.oecd.org/canada/oecd-environmental-performance-reviews-canada-2017-9789264279612-en.htm.

Chapter 1

1. James Hansen quoted in the *Guardian*, June 23, 2008. See also Eric Berger, "James Hansen Wants to Send Energy CEO Deniers to Jail?" *Houston Chronicle*, June 23, 2008, https://blog.chron.com/sciguy/2008/06/james-hansen-wants-to-send-energy-ceo-deniers-to-jail.
2. While tsunamis are not directly caused by climate change but usually by earthquakes, they can be directly affected and exacerbated by the death of coral reefs and deforestation.
3. See interviews with various scientists in Dahr Jamail, "The Coming 'Instant Planetary Emergency,'" *Nation*, December 17, 2013, www.thenation.com/article/coming-instant-planetary-emergency/.
4. In fact, the period may go back as far as between 650,000 and 800,000 years ago. See for example: Dieter Lüthi et al., "High-Resolution Carbon Dioxide Concentration Record 650,000–800,000 Years before Present," *Nature*, 453, no. 7193 (2008): 379–382.
5. See the interview with Guy McPherson, professor emeritus of evolutionary biology, natural resources and ecology at the University of Arizona, "The Coming 'Instant Planetary Emergency'" by Dahr Jamail in The Nation. For the permanent passing of the 400 parts per million threshold in 2016, see www.climatecentral.org/news/world-passes-400-ppm-threshold-permanently-20738.
6. Bill Hare and Malte Meinshausen, *How Much Warming Are We Committed To and How Much Can Be Avoided*, PIK Report 93 (Potsdam, Germany: Potsdam Institute for Climate Impact Research, 2004), 24.
7. For a summary of these predictions and fluctuations, see Jamail, "The Coming 'Instant Planetary Emergency.'"
8. See the calculations tabled prior to the Paris Climate Conference at United Nations Climate Change, *Synthesis Report on the Aggregate Effect of the Intended Nationally Determined Contributions* (October 30, 2015), https://unfccc.int/resource/docs/2015/cop21/eng/07.pdf.
9. See for example Mark Hertsgaard, "The Most Ambitious Pledges on the Table in Paris Would Still Result in Catastrophic Warming," *Nation*, November 30, 2015, www.thenation.com/article/the-most-ambitious-emissions-pledges-on-the-table-in-paris-would-still-result-in-catastrophic-warming/.

10. We live in a world of divisions on numerous fronts, including methods for doing measurements. Here, you will notice, measuring greenhouse gas emissions is done in at least two ways: giga*tons* (Imperial units) and giga*tonnes* (metric units). Although they may sound similar, the difference can be considerable when dealing with high volumes. For example, 56 giga*tonnes* = 62 giga*tons*.

11. Calculations here are based on data and analysis found in United Nations Environment Programme, *The Emissions Gap Report 2014*, issued November 19, 2014.

12. Pablo Solon's calculations here, (former Bolivian ambassador to the United Nations), were initially made in "How Did Leaders Respond to the People's Climate March?" *Focus on the Global South*, September 26, 2015, https://focusweb.org/content/how-did-leaders-respond-people-s-climate-march.

13. Ibid.

14. Bill McKibben, *Do the Math*, https://math.350.org. See also Bill McKibben's article, "Global Warming's Terrifying New Math," *Rolling Stone*, July 19, 2012, https://www.rollingstone.com/politics/politics-news/global-warmings-terrifying-new-math-188550/.

15. Global Carbon Project, *Global Carbon Budget*, www.globalcarbonproject.org/carbonbudget/index.htm.

16. For a discussion of the Global Carbon Budget and the research behind it, see Gabriel Levy, "The Paris Climate Talks and the Failure of States," *Bullet*, March 4, 2015.

17. One of the gaping holes in the Paris text is that the emissions from international shipping and air travel are left out of the review and transparency of the intended nationally determined contributions. In effect, this means that one of the fastest growing emitters of greenhouse gases in the global economy (according to the *Wall Street Journal*) gets a free pass.

18. International Maritime Organization, *Third IMO GHG Study 2014*, www.imo.org/en/OurWork/Environment/PollutionPrevention/AirPollution/Pages/Greenhouse-Gas-Studies-2014.aspx; Jad Mouawad and Coral Davenport, "E.P.A. Takes Step to Cut Emissions from Planes," *New York Times*, June 10, 2015, www.nytimes.com/2015/06/11/business/energy-environment/epa-says-it-will-set-rules-for-airplane-emissions.html; International Civil Aviation Organization, *ICAO Environmental Report 2013: Aviation and Climate Change*, https://cfapp.icao.int/Environmental-Report-2013/#3/z; Emily Gosden, "Paris Climate Change Deal 'Meaningless' without Plan for Deeper Emissions Cuts," *Telegraph* (London), December 10, 2015, www.telegraph.co.uk/news/earth/paris-climate-change-conference/12045071/Paris-climate-talks-Concern-as-new-deal-ignores-flight-and-shipping-emissions.html.

19. See Kevin Anderson (deputy director of the Tyndall Centre for Climate Change Research, U.K.), "Talks in the City of Light Generate More Heat," *Nature*, 528 (December 24/31 2015), 437.

20. Ibid.

21. Tom Baldwin, "COP21: Paris Deal Far Too Weak to Prevent Devastating Climate Change, Academics Warn," *Independent* (London), January 8, 2016.

22. International Energy Agency, *World Energy Investment Outlook* (Paris: Author, 2014), www.iea.org/publications/freepublications/publication/WEIO2014.pdf.

23. However, it appears the Oxfam report was overly optimistic. According to a report by Wikipedia, the *United Nations Framework Convention on Climate Change* has had serious fundraising problems when it comes to the Green Climate Fund. The initial goal had been to raise $100 billion but, as of May 2017, only $10.3 billion had actually been pledged. For more information and analysis see: https://en.wikipedia.org/wiki/Green_Climate_Fund.

24. See United Nations Climate Change, *Synthesis Report*.

25. Bill McKibben, "Global Warming's Terrifying New Chemistry," *Nation*, March 23, 2016, www.thenation.com/article/global-warming-terrifying-new-chemistry.

26. Cited in Jamail, "The Coming 'Instant Planetary Emergency,'" www.truthdig.com/articles/a-little-closer-t.

27. See "What These Climate Scientists Said about the Earth's Future will Terrify You," *Mother Jones*, December 2013, www.motherjones.com/environment/2013/12/climate-scientist-environment-apocalypse-human-extinction/. Interviews and discussion between scientists and journalist Dahr Jamail about the prospects of a methane meltdown in the Arctic seabed.

28. In March 2013, the prestigious journal, *Nature Geo-Science,* published a scientific study that concluded methane hydrates to be the prime cause of the Great Permian Extinction some 250 million years ago, which annihilated 90 percent of all living species on this planet. The study was called *Methane Hydrate: Killer Cause of Earth's Greatest Mass Extinction.* While the study received little media attention at the time, follow-up initiatives were organized, making connections between the study and current research on the possible 50 gigaton "burp" that could result in the release of methane hydrates, due to the rapid melting of the Arctic permafrost beneath the East Siberian Sea. For more insight into this follow-up connection, see Dahr Jamail, "Release of Arctic Methane 'May be Apocalyptic', Study Warns," *Truthout,* March 23, 2017, https://truthout.org/articles/release-of-arctic-methane-may-be-apocalyptic-study-warns/.

29. Ibid.

30. Cited in Mark Hathaway and Leonardo Boff, *The Tao of Liberation: Exploring the Ecology of Transformation* (Maryknoll, NY: Orbis Books, 2009), 5.

31. Alanna Mitchell, *Sea Sick: The Global Ocean in Crisis* (Toronto: McClelland & Stewart, 2009).

32. Ibid.

33. For a global perspective on the emerging worldwide water crisis, see Maude Barlow and Tony Clarke, *Blue Gold: The Battle Against the Corporate Theft of the World's Water* (Toronto: Stoddart, 2002).

34. Most of Kravčik's work is in Slovak. However, a summary of his work was published in English under the title *New Theory of Global Warming* in 2001. A shorter summary is also found in Barlow and Clarke, *Blue Gold,* 10–12.

35. Cited in Hathaway and Boff, *The Tao of Liberation,* 19.

36. Yvo de Boer's comment was cited in Alex Morales, "Kyoto Veterans Say Global Warming Goal Slipping Away," *Bloomberg,* November 4, 2013. See also Naomi Klein's discussion of these themes in *This Changes Everything: Capitalism vs Climate* (New York: Penguin Random House, 2014), 86–89.

37. See Kevin Anderson, "Climate Change Going Beyond Dangerous — Brutal Numbers and Tenuous Hope," *Development Dialogue,* no. 61 (September 2012), 16–40. Also, Kevin Anderson and Alice Bows, "Beyond 'Dangerous' Climate Change: Emission Scenarios for a New World," *Philosophical Transactions of the Royal Society A,* 369, no.1934 (2011), 20–44, www.doi.org/10.1098/rsta.2010.0290.

38. Anderson, "Climate Change Going Beyond Dangerous." See also Klein, *This Changes Everything,* 86–89.

39. See Oil Change International, *The Sky's Limit: Why the Paris Climate Goals Require a Managed Decline in Fossil Fuel Production* (September 2016), www.priceofoil.org/content/uploads/2016/09/OCI_the_skys_limit_2016_FINAL_2.pdf.

40. See Environment Canada, *National Inventory Report 1990–2016: Greenhouse Gas Sources and Sinks in Canada* (April 17, 2018), www.canada.ca/en/environment-climate-change/services/climate-change/greenhouse-gas-emissions/sources-sinks-executive-summary-2018.html.

41. See Jason Fekete, "Oilsands' Share of GHG Emissions to Double by 2030," *Ottawa Citizen,* January 29, 2016, https://ottawacitizen.com/news/politics/oilsands-share-of-national-

emissions-set-to-double-between-2010-and-2030; Pembina Institute, *BC LNG Proposals and GHG Emissions* (July 2013), www.northwestinstitute.ca/images/uploads/Pembina-LNG-GHG-July2013.pdf.

42. Klein, *This Changes Everything*, 21.

Chapter 2

1. Donella H. Meadows, Dennis L. Meadows, Jørgen Randers and William W. Behrens III, *The Limits to Growth: A Report for the Club of Rome's Project on the Predicament of Mankind* (New York: Universe, 1972).

2. Although the Trilateral Commission has played a pivotal role in the process of economic globalization over the past four decades, surprisingly little has been written about it. A good source, however, is M. Patricia Marchak, *The Integrated Circus: The New Right and the Restructuring of Global Markets* (Montreal and Kingston: McGill-Queen's University Press, 1993). For a summary and application, see also Tony Clarke, *Silent Coup: Confronting the Big Business Takeover of Canada* (Toronto: James Lorimer & Co. / Ottawa: Canadian Centre for Policy Alternatives, 1997), Chapter 2, "The Global Managers."

3. Clarke, *Silent Coup*, 43ff.

4. For a useful backgrounder on the rise of the WTO, see Maude Barlow and Tony Clarke, *Global Showdown: How the New Activists are Fighting Global Corporate Rule* (Toronto: Stoddart, 2001), 72–89. For a more detailed analysis of the WTO, see Lori Wallach and Patrick Woodall, *Whose Trade Organization?* (New York: New Press / Washington: Public Citizen, 2004).

5. This is the most often quoted range for direct government subsidies to the fossil fuel industry worldwide on an annual basis. See International Energy Agency, *World Energy Investment Outlook* (Paris: Author, 2014), www.iea.org/publications/freepublications/publication/WEIO2014.pdf; David Coady, Ian Parry, Louis Sears and Baoping Shang, *How Large are Global Energy Subsidies?*, IMF Working Paper WP/15/05 (Washington: International Monetary Fund, 2015).

6. Coady, Parry, Sears and Shang, *How Large are Global Energy Subsidies?*

7. Sir Nicholas Stern, *The Economics of Climate Change: The Stern Review* (Cambridge, England: Cambridge University Press, 2006).

8. Coady, Parry, Sears and Shang, *How Large are Global Energy Subsidies?*

9. Naomi Klein, *This Changes Everything: Capitalism vs Climate* (New York: Penguin Random House, 2014), 25. Also see 152–60.

10. Between 1960 and the 1990s, annual greenhouse gas emissions growth slowed down from 4.5 percent to around 1 percent a year. See Klein, *This Changes Everything*, 80.

11. Ibid.

12. Ibid., 78. For an analysis of the flaws in the global greenhouse gas emissions accounting process, see 79ff.

13. Ibid., 79. Moreover, global shipping emissions are expected to double and even triple by mid-century.

14. Andreas Malm, "China as Chimney of the World: The Fossil Capital Hypothesis," *Organization & Environment*, 25 (2012), 146, 165, cited in Klein, *This Changes Everything*.

15. For a more detailed analysis of the *Green Energy Act* in Ontario, see Scott Sinclair, *Saving the Green Economy: Ontario's Green Energy Act and the WTO* (Ottawa: Canadian Centre for Policy Alternatives, 2013), https://www.policyalternatives.ca/sites/default/files/uploads/publications/National%20Office,%20Ontario%20Office/2013/11/Saving_the_Green_Economy.pdf.

16. For a commentary on the Ontario government's response to the WTO ruling, see Scott Sinclair and Stuart Trew, "Keeping Green Energy Local and Public," *Hamilton Spectator*,

December 18, 2013, www.thespec.com/opinion-story/4276197-keeping-green-energy-local-and-public.

17. See Canadian Press, "Ontario to Change Green Energy Law After WTO Ruling," *Globe and Mail*, May 29, 2013, www.theglobeandmail.com/report-on-business/industry-news/energy-and-resources/ontario-to-change-green-energy-law-after-wto-ruling/article12236781/.

18. See Danish Energy Agency, "Facts about Wind Power: Facts and Numbers," www.ens.dk; see also Danish Energy Agency, "Renewables Now Cover More Than 40% of Electricity Consumption," press release, September 24, 2012.

19. After the withdrawal of the United States, the agreement comprises Australia, Brunei, Canada, Chile, Japan, Malaysia, Mexico, New Zealand, Peru, Singapore and Vietnam. Thailand, the Philippines and South Korea have also expressed interest in joining.

20. For a more in-depth analysis of the TPP, see Scott Sinclair, "Untangling the Myths and False Promises of the Trans-Pacific Partnership," Canadian Centre for Policy Alternatives *Monitor*, November/December 2016, 12–14, www.policyalternatives.ca/publications/monitor/web-deceit.

21. Ben Lilliston, *The Climate Cost of Free Trade: How the TPP and Trade Deals Undermine the Paris Climate Agreement* (Minneapolis, MN: Institute for Agriculture and Trade Policy, 2016), www.iatp.org/files/2016_09_06_ClimateCostFreeTrade.pdf.

22. On the rise and role of the BCNI and CCCE in Canada, see Clarke, *Silent Coup*, Chapter 1, "Corporate Canada"; Tony Clarke, "Corporate Canada: Washington's Empire Loyalists," in Ricardo Grinspun and Yasmine Shamsie, *Whose Canada? Continental Integration, Fortress North America and the Corporate Agenda* (Ottawa: Canadian Centre for Policy Alternatives / Montreal and Kingston: McGill-Queen's University Press, 2007), 74–104.

23. For an analysis and discussion of the MAI and the story of its defeat, see Tony Clarke and Maude Barlow, *MAI: The Multilateral Agreement on Investment and the Threat to Canadian Sovereignty* (Toronto: Stoddart, 1997) and *MAI Round 2* (Toronto: Stoddart, 1998).

24. See Suzanne Goldenberg, "Just 90 Companies Caused Two-Thirds of Man-Made Global Warming Emissions," *Guardian*, November 20, 2013, www.theguardian.com/environment/2013/nov/20/90-companies-man-made-global-warming-emissions-climate-change.

25. Rodrigo Estrada Patiño, "Seventeen Attorneys General Joint Climate Announcement," *greenpeace.org*, March 30, 2016, www.greenpeace.org/seasia/ph/News/greenpeace-philippine-blog/seventeen-attorneys-general-joint-climate-announcement/blog/56016/.

26. "350.org on Trump Selecting ExxonMobil CEO to be his Secretary of State," *350.org*, December 10, 2016, https://350.org/press-release/350-org-on-trump-selecting-exxonmobil-ceo-to-be-his-secretary-of-state/.

27. These cases include *Occidental v. Ecuador, Pacific Rim Mining Corp v. El Salvador, Vattenfall v. Germany* and *Renco v. Peru*, to name a few.

28. See Osgoode law professor and international trade law expert Gus Van Harten's proposal for an "investor-state carve-out" pertaining to climate change and other environmental policies.

29. See the actual document, *The Future We Want*, which came out of the Rio+20 Earth Summit in 2012, at www.rio20.net/wp-content/uploads/2012/06/N1238164.pdf.

30. For a more detailed examination of geoengineering strategies, see ETC Group, *Geopiracy: The Case Against Geoengineering* (Ottawa: Author, 2010), www.etcgroup.org/sites/www.etcgroup.org/files/publication/pdf_file/ETC_geopiracy_4web.pdf, and related documents.

31. See ETC Group, "The ABC's of Ensuring Precaution on Geoengineering," a briefing for delegates to the Convention on Biological Diversity, October 5, 2012.

32. See Emily Gilbert, "Climate Change and the Military," *Canadian Dimension*, November/December 2014, 30–33.

33. Ibid., 31.

34. Gilbert goes on to outline at least five major problems concerning the militarization of the Arctic. See "Climate Change and the Military," 33.

35. Robin Andrews, " Trump Picks Climate Denialist Currently Suing The EPA To Head The EPA," *IFLScience*, December 8, 2016, www.iflscience.com/environment/trump-picks-climate-denialist-currently-suing-the-epa-to-head-the-epa/.

26. Article 28, subparagraph 3 of the *United Nations Framework Convention on Climate Change* stipulates that if a country decides to opt out of the UNFCCC, it also automatically opts out of international climate agreements such as the Paris Agreement at the same time.

37. According to environmental law expert Michael Wara of Stanford University, President Trump would be able to make this move without consultation with the U.S. Congress, just as his predecessors, Jimmy Carter and George W. Bush, were able to withdraw the United States from various military treaties. Cited in Maxime Combes and Edouard Morena, "The End of the Paris Prophecy: Donald Trump's Election Win is Bad News for the Paris Agreement and Very Bad News for the Climate," *Jacobin* magazine, November 28, 2016, www.jacobinmag.com/2016/11/trump-climate-change-paris-agreement.

38. Cited in Ibid., 3.

39. Ibid.

Chapter 3

1. For an in-depth look at Indigenous cultures and societies before the colonial period, see Charles C. Mann, *1491: New Revelations of the Americas before Columbus* (New York: Vintage Books, 2006).

2. For an overview and more detailed analysis of these themes, see Tony Clarke, Diana Gibson, Brendan Haley and Jim Stanford, *The Bitumen Cliff: Lessons and Challenges of Bitumen Mega-Developments for Canada's Economy in an Age of Climate Change* (Ottawa: Canadian Centre for Policy Alternatives / Polaris Institute, 2013), especially 24–28.

3. For an overview of Harold Innis's career, see the profile of his work at https://en.wikipedia.org/wiki/Harold_Innis.

4. For a summary of this analysis of the "staples trap," see Clarke et al., *The Bitumen Cliff*, 21–24.

5. W.T. Easterbrook and M.H. Watkins, eds., *Approaches to Canadian Economic History* (1967; repr., Ottawa: Carleton University Press, 1984), Part One, "The Staple Approach," 1–98.

6. Author's summary and interpretation. See also Clarke et al., *The Bitumen Cliff*, 21–24.

7. Brendan Haley, "From Staples Trap to Carbon Trap: Canada's Peculiar Form of Carbon Lock-In," *Studies in Political Economy*, 88 (2011), 97–132.

8. Klein, *This Changes Everything*, 169. See also chapter 5, 'Beyond Extractivism', as a whole.

9. Terry Lynn Karl, *The Paradox of Plenty: Oil Booms and Petro States* (Berkeley: University of California Press, 1997). Drawing on the work of Harold Innis and other analysts, Karl observed the political economies of various oil-producing countries and concluded that petro-states differ from other states because "their dependence on oil profits breaks the necessary link between taxation and representation." Instead of state funds being extracted from citizens, "wealth magically comes from the ground." This makes governments unaccountable: it means that people don't demand to see how money is spent. "In turn," she says, "oil governments . . . tend to treat their citizens like subjects," to the point where "oil and highly centralized rule go together." In other words, "oil wealth permits governments to dismantle accountability mechanisms, weaken bureaucracies and undermine the rule of law," as evidenced in countries such as Saudi Arabia, Venezuela and Iran.

10. Other key events included the federal government's research on in situ technology from 1919 onward, which made it possible to extract bitumen from beneath the sedimentary

rock basis for crude oil production, and the transfer of power over subsoil mineral rights from Ottawa to the Alberta government in 1931.

11. Larry Pratt, *The Tar Sands: Syncrude and the Politics of Oil* (Edmonton: Hurtig, 1976). A more up-to-date rendition is found in Tony Clarke, *Tar Sands Showdown: Canada and the New Politics of Oil in an Age of Climate Change* (Toronto: James Lorimer & Co., 2008), Chapter 1, "Crude Awakening," especially 25ff.

12. For more details, see Clarke et al., *The Bitumen Cliff*, 65–67.

13. Terry Glavin, "The Real Foreign Interests in the Oil Sands," *Ottawa Citizen*, January 13, 2012.

14. The analysis that follows here is largely based on the report by Richard Girard and Daniel Cayley Daoust, *Big Oil's Oily Grasp: The Making of a Petro State and How Oil Money is Corrupting Canadian Politics* (Ottawa: Polaris Institute, 2012). It uses data provided by the Office of the Commissioner of Lobbying and Registry of Lobbying in Canada.

15. For more on this revolving door syndrome, see Clarke, *Tar Sands Showdown*, 107–109.

16. See the section on "Lobby Firms and Consultant Lobbyists" in Girard and Daoust, *Big Oil's Oily Grasp*, 7–9.

17. National Energy Board, *Canada's Energy Future 2016: Energy Supply and Demand Projections to 2040* (Ottawa: Author, 2016), 11, www.neb-one.gc.ca/nrg/ntgrtd/ftr/2016/2016nrgftr-eng.pdf.

18. Ibid., 7. The National Energy Board's 2016 projections assume that energy-related greenhouse gas emissions will continue to rise over the period of the 2020s.

19. See Keith Stewart's blog entry, "The National Energy Board's Pro-Oil Bias on Display," October 26, 2016, www.greenpeace.org/canada/en/blog/Blogentry/the-national-energy-boards-pro-oil-bias-on-di/blog/57844.

20. For a more detailed treatment of NAFTA challenges and implications, see Gordon Laxer and John Dillon, *Over a Barrel: Exiting from NAFTA's Proportionality Clause* (Ottawa: Canadian Centre for Policy Alternatives / Parkland Institute, 2008).

21. Scott Sinclair, *NAFTA Chapter 11 Investor-State Disputes (to January 1, 2005)*, www.policyalternatives.ca/sites/default/files/uploads/publications/National_Office_Pubs/2005/chapter11_january2005.pdf, and *NAFTA Chapter 11 Investor-State Disputes to January 1, 2015* and *Democracy Under Challenge: Canada and Two Decades of NAFTA's Investor-State Dispute Mechanism*, www.policyalternatives.ca/sites/default/files/uploads/publications/National%20Office/2015/01/NAFTA_Chapter11_Investor_State_Disputes_2015.pdf (Ottawa: Canadian Centre for Policy Alternatives).

22. See Jim Stanford, "Building a Diversified, Value Added, Productive Economy," Submission of the Canadian Auto Workers (now UNIFOR) to the Competition Policy Review Panel, Government of Canada, January 2008. For a more updated and comprehensive treatment of these themes, see Jim Stanford, *Economics for Everyone (Second Edition): A Short Guide to the Economics of Capitalism* (London, England: Pluto Press, 2015).

23. For an informative overview of Canada's extractivist heritage, see Ricardo Grinspun and Jennifer Mills, "Canada, Extractivism and Hemispheric Relations," in Kate Ervine and Gavin Fridell, eds., *Beyond Free Trade: Alternative Approaches to Trade, Politics and Power* (Basingstoke, England: Palgrave MacMillan, 2015).

24. For a discussion of Stephen Harper's speech (in London UK before attending his first G-8 meeting as prime minister) on the tar sands development as the launching pad for Canada becoming the world's next energy superpower, see Clarke, *Tar Sands Showdown*, Chapter 3.

25. See, for example, Clarke et al., *The Bitumen Cliff*, 51–54.

26. Author's chart summarizing Clarke et al., *The Bitumen Cliff*, Part II, "The Economic Impacts of the Bitumen Boom," 41–65, including Jim Stanford's research on the economic distortions of the bitumen boom.

27. On the issue of why building oil pipelines to transport landlocked bitumen to markets will not work, see Andrew Nikiforuk, "Four Harsh Truths for Canada's Lovestruck Pipeline Politicians: A Reality Check for Our Bitumen-Besotted Leaders," *Tyee*, October 21, 2016, https://thetyee.ca/Opinion/2016/10/21/Canadian-Pipeline-Harsh-Truths/. See also Jeff Rubin, "New Pipelines? The Oil Sands May Have Trouble Filling the Ones It Has," *Globe and Mail*, November 21, 2016, www.theglobeandmail.com/report-on-business/rob-commentary/new-pipelines-the-oil-sands-mayhave-trouble-filling-the-ones-it-has/article32601876.
28. For more details, see Girard and Daoust, *Big Oil's Oily Grasp*.
29. Ibid., 6, Tables 4 and 5.
30. Corporate Mapping Project, Canadian Centre for Policy Alternatives, Interviews with Shannon Daub and William Carroll co-directors. Check out Reports and Studies on Political Influence at http//www.corporatemapping.ca/category/resources/reports_and_studies/.
31. Rubin, "New Pipelines?"
32. Ibid.
33. Ibid.
34. Ibid.
35. Author's summary of main points in Haley, "From Staples Trap to Carbon Trap," plus more recent updates on greenhouse gas emission projections regarding the tar sands industry.
36. See Fekete, "Oilsands' Share of GHG Emissions to Double by 2030."
37. For an insightful analysis and breakdown of the greenhouse gas impacts of these projects totaling 90 million tonnes annually, see the report for the Green Economy Network by Marny Girard, *Assessing the Federal Government's Action on Climate Change*, 2017, www.greeneconomynet.ca/wp-content/uploads/sites/43/2017/02/Assessing-Fed-Actions-on-Climate-Change-2017-final-b.pdf.
38. See World Resources Institute, *Upstream Emissions as a Percentage of Overall Lifecycle Emissions* (2005), http://www.wri.org/resources/data-visualizations/upstream-emissions-percentage-overall-lifecycle-emissions.
39. See Camille Bains, "'Betrayed' Canadians Could Launch Unprecedented Protests over TransMountain Pipeline, Activist Warns," *Financial Post*, May 30, 2018, https://business.financialpost.com/commodities/energy/betrayed-canadians-could-launch-unprecedented-protests-over-pipeline-activist.
40. David Hughes, *Can Canada Expand Oil and Gas Production, Build Pipelines and Keep its Climate Commitments* (Edmonton: Parkland Institute, 2016), www.parklandinstitute.ca/can_canada_expand.

Chapter 4

1. See Andy Isaacson, "Extreme Research Shows How Arctic Ice is Dwindling," *National Geographic*, January 2016, www.ngm.nationalgeographic.com/2016/01/arctic-ice-environment.
2. The outlier in the Conservative leadership race was Michael Chong, who advocated putting a tax on carbon.
3. The NDP leadership candidates opposed to pipeline expansion and calling for new clean energy policies included Charlie Angus, Niki Ashton, Guy Caron and Jagmeet Singh, all advocating various approaches and strategies. However, Niki Ashton's platform seemed to go the furthest in outlining strategies for systemic change that are needed to address the climate challenge effectively.

4. For a summary of the environment commissioner's report and Environment and Climate Change Canada's response, see Karl Nerenberg, "Environment Commissioner Tells Trudeau to get Cracking on Climate Change," *rabble.ca*, October 5, 2017, www. rabble.ca/news/2017/10/environment-commissioner-tells-trudeau-get-cracking-climate-change; Elizabeth McSheffrey, "Environment Canada Touts 'Good Progress' on Climate after Scathing Audit," *National Observer*, December 11, 2017, www.nationalobserver. com/2017/12/11/news/environment-canada-touts-good-progress-climate-after-scathing-audit.

5. See, for example, the joint analysis prepared for Mission 2020 entitled *2020: The Climate Turning Point*, www.mission2020.global/wp-content/uploads/2020-The-Climate-Turning-Point.pdf.

6. Carl Myers, "Trudeau Government Delays Climate Action after Oil Patch Lobbying," *National Observer*, April 21, 2017, www.nationalobserver.com/2017/04/21/news/trudeau-government-delays-climate-action-after-oil-patch-lobbying.

7. See D.C. Fraser, "Carbon Capture Wrong Technology, Says New Report," *Regina Leader-Post*, July 6, 2017, www.leaderpost.com/news/politics/carbon-capture-wrong-technology-says-new-report.

8. For the IMF's updated global report on energy subsidies, see www.imf.org/external/pubs/ft/survey/so/2015/NEW070215A.htm.

9. For a summary of the 2015 IMF report on implications for Canada of the global update report on energy subsidies, see Mitchell Anderson, "Psst, Trudeau: IMF Now Pegs Our Fossil Fuel Subsidies at 46 Billion," *Tyee*, February 1, 2016, www.thetyee.ca/Opinion/2016/02/01/IMF-Fossil-Fuel-Subsidies.

10. See, for example, Margo McDiarmid, "Climate Change Survey Reveals that Canadians Fear for Future Generations," *CBC News*, November 28, 2014, www.cbc.ca/news/politics/climate-change-survey-reveals-canadians-fears-for-future-generations-1.2852605.

11. See Bob Berwyn, "Germany Reasserts Climate Leadership, Outlines Path to Carbon-Neutral Economy by 2050," *Inside Climate News*, November 17, 2016, retrieved from insideclimatenews.org/news/17112016/germany-climate-change-carbon-neutral-economy-cop22-paris-agreement.

12. See Megan Darby, "Sweden Passes Climate Law to Become Carbon Neutral by 2045," *Climate Home News*, June 15, 2017, www.climatechangenews.com/2017/06/15/sweden-passes-climate-law-become-carbon-neutral-2045.

13. See Arthur Nelsen, "Norway Pledges to Become Climate Neutral by 2030," *Guardian*, June 15, 2017, www.theguardian.com/environment/2016/jun/15/norway-pledges-to-become-climate-neutral-by-2030.

14. See the link to Environment and Climate Change Canada's latest *National Inventory Report* (2018): www.canada.ca/en/environment-climate-change/services/climate-change/greenhouse-gas-emissions/inventory.html.

15. Data found in Environment and Climate Change Canada, *National Inventory Report*, 2018.

16. See Christiana Figueres, Hans Joachim Schellnhuber, Gail Whiteman, Johan Rockström, Anthony Hobley and Stefan Rahmstorf, "Three Years to Save Our Planet," *Nature*, 546, no. 7660 (June 29, 2017), 593–95, www.nature.com/news/three-years-to-safeguard-our-climate-1.22201.

17. Ibid.

18. See Mission 2020, *2020: The Climate Turning Point*.

19. Because overall global temperature rise depends on cumulative global carbon dioxide emissions, the Paris temperature range can be translated, with some uncertainty, into a budget of carbon dioxide emissions that are still permissible. This is the overall budget for the century, and it lies within the range of 150 to 1,050 gigatonnes of carbon dioxide,

based on updated numbers from the Intergovernmental Panel on Climate Change. At the current global emission level of 39 gigatonnes of carbon dioxide per year, the lower limit of this range would be crossed in less than four years, so staying within that limit is already unachievable without massive application of largely unproven and speculative carbon dioxide removal technologies. Even the carbon dioxide budget corresponding to the midpoint of this uncertainty range, 600 gigatonnes of carbon dioxide, is equivalent to only 15 years of current emissions. Three scenarios regarding this budget are illustrated in the Carbon Budget Crunch graph with different peaking years for global emissions. The graph makes clear that even if we peak in 2020, reducing emissions to zero within 20 years will be required. By assuming a more optimistic budget of 800 gigatonnes, this can be stretched to 30 years, but at a significant risk of exceeding 2 degrees Celsius warming. (Note: Based on the author's conversations with researcher Marny Girard at the Green Economy Network and later confirmed by conversations with other researchers.)

20. United Nations Environment Programme, *The Emissions Gap Report 2017: A UN Environment Synthesis Report* (Nairobi, Kenya: Author, 2017), https://wedocs.unep.org/bitstream/handle/20.500.11822/22070/EGR_2017.pdf?sequence=1&isAllowed=y.

Chapter 5

1. See Hadrian Mertins-Kirkwood, *Tracking Progress* (Canadian Centre for Policy Alternatives, May 24, 2017), https://policyalternatives.ca/publications/reports/tracking-progress.

2. David Hughes, *Can Canada Expand Oil and Gas Production, Build Pipelines and Keep its Climate Commitments* (Edmonton: Parkland Institute, 2016), www.parklandinstitute. ca/can_canada_expand. For another sample of Hughes's basic argument and concerns about the Trudeau/Notley position, see David Hughes, *Can Canada Expand Oil and Gas Production*, Corporate Mapping Project (Canadian Centre for Policy Alternatives, June 2016), https://www.scribd.com/document/333946587/Can-Canada-Expand-Oil-and-Gas-Production.

3. See Alberta, "Capping Oil Sands Emissions," in *Climate Leadership Plan*, retrieved from www.alberta.ca/climate-oilsands-emissions.aspx.

4. Marc Lee, "Looking under the Hood of Alberta's New Climate Plan," in Canadian Centre for Policy Alternatives, *Behind the Numbers*, November 24, 2015, www.behindthenumbers. ca/2015/11/24/looking-under-the-hood-at-albertas-new-climate-plan.

5. Claudia Cattaneo, "Writing on the Wall for Energy East, but Trudeau is Making Costly Gamble," *Financial Post*, August 24, 2017, https://business.financialpost.com/commodities/energy/the-writing-is-likely-on-the-wall-for-energy-east-but-trudeau-is-making-a-big-costly-gamble.

6. Ibid.

7. Articles 315 and 605.

8. Hannah McKinnon, "Reality Check: The End of Growth in the Tar Sands. So Now What?" *Oil Change International*, June 30, 2017, www.priceofoil.org/2017/06/29/reality-check-the-end-of-growth-in-the-tar-sands-so-now-what.

9. Quoted in "The End of Growth: Industry Data Show Tar Sands/Oil Sands Entering Managed Decline," *Energy Mix*, June 30, 2017, www.theenergymix.com/2017/06/30/the-end-of-growth-industry-data-show-tar-sandsoil-sands-entering-managed-decline.

10. Ibid.

11. Gordon Laxer, *After the Sands: Energy and Ecological Security for Canadians* (Madeira Park, B.C.: Douglas & McIntyre, 2015), 130.

12. Within a week of being sworn in as Ontario's new premier after the June 18, 2018, election Doug Ford announced that Ontario would be withdrawing from the cap-and-trade regime with Quebec and California.

13. Clean Energy Canada, *A Year for the Record Books: Tracking the Energy Revolution —* *Global 2016* (Vancouver: Author, 2016), 2, www.cleanenergycanada.org/wp-content/ uploads/2018/03/A-Year-for-the-Record-Books_April.pdf; see also Clean Energy Canada's weekly report, *Clean Energy Review*, www.cleanenergycanada.org/clean-energy-review.

14. Brad Tennant, "'Big Oil' Leads in Innovations and Renewable Energy," *Canada's Energy Citizens* (Canadian Association of Petroleum Producers), January 5, 2016, www. energycitizens.ca/_big_oil_leads_in_innovations_and_clean_energy.

15. Willow White, "How Traditional Energy Companies are Building a Viable Future for Renewables," *Alberta Oil*, July 18, 2016, www.albertaoilmagazine.com/2016/07/oil-gas-companies-moving-towards-viable-renewable-energy-future.

16. Tennant, "'Big Oil' Leads."

17. Clean Energy Canada, *A Year for the Record Books*, 5.

18. For a critical discussion of the public ownership model and the need for a more "public interest" model of a Crown corporation, see Laxer, *After the Sands*, 150–58.

19. In Alberta, political economist David Thompson proposes the establishment of an Alberta Renewable Energy Corporation with a priority on manufacturing renewable energy products. As Thompson puts it, the objectives of such a Crown agency would be "to accelerate the development of renewable energy manufacturing capacity in Alberta." "Using a crown company," says Laxer, " to spark a green energy industry in Alberta" may seem, at first glance, to be a bit radical, but it falls in the tradition of Alberta's government-owned banks. It could help ignite and broaden a deeper diversification of the Albertan economy, adds Laxer, "in biotechnology, financial services, medical research and development, and environmental technologies" (*After the Sands*, 132–33; see also 150–52).

20. Iron & Earth, which organizes workers from resource industries advocating the shift from fossil fuels to renewable energy development, is an active proponent of these "incubator programs." See Iron & Earth's *Workers' Climate Plan Report: A Blueprint for Sustainable Jobs and Energy*, 83ff, https://docs.google.com/document/ d/1Ii7TCX9urxrLrgyEGtPVYhLUHB_issQcAk0IH1VGqu4/edit.

21. See the discussion of public interest ownership models and strategies, as distinct from more conventional public ownership enterprises, in Laxer, *After the Sands*, 150–58.

22. The call to *rethink*, from an ecological standpoint, the functions and operations of the basic economic model of our society (such as production and consumption) in relation to the climate change challenge was underscored by Canadian youth activists in their mission statement as the Canadian Youth Climate Coalition.

23. The most recently available official emissions trends data are for 2013, when Canada's total greenhouse gas emissions were estimated to be 726 million tonnes. Three sectors of the Canadian economy — energy, buildings and transport — were responsible for 81 percent or 588 million tonnes in 2013. Environment Canada, *National Inventory Report 1990–2013* (2015), Section ES2. Later, Environment Canada reconfigured its data to more closely follow the UNFCCC methodology and categories — hence the confusion caused by differences between earlier and later reports on greenhouse gas emissions in 2015.

24. According to Canada's 2015 *National Inventory Report*, electricity production accounted for 11 percent and heavy industry 10 percent of greenhouse gas emissions. See the "Greenhouse Gas Emissions by Canadian Economic Sector" pie chart in Chapter 4.

25. See Steering Committee of the Green Economy Network, *Making the Shift to a Green Economy: A Common Platform for the Green Economy Network* (2016), www.greeneconomynet.ca/ wp-content/uploads/sites/43/2014/07/GEN-Common-Platform-2016-EN1.pdf; for related education tools, visit the Green Economy Network's website at www.greeneconomynet.ca.

26. To date, most public policy platforms put forward by governments concerning climate change talk about the amount of public expenditure being committed but only refer to

either greenhouse gas reductions and/or job creation in generalities. By contrast, the Green Economy Network platform focuses on targeted public investments, specific job creation numbers (and even categories) plus measurable greenhouse gas emission reductions, with an emphasis on their strategic relationship and impact.

27. Steering Committee of the Green Economy Network, *Making the Shift*.

28. See Ibid., 6 (GEN pillar 1, A Renewable Energy Development Strategy).

29. See Ibid., 5–9.

30. Ibid., 7–8.

31. Ibid., 8.

32. Information cited in Ibid., 10.

33. Information based on conversations and interviews with Shaun Loney and others associated with the organizing of Aki Energy in Manitoba. For more information on Aki Energy, see http://www.gov.mb.ca/inr/major-initiatives/pubs/social%20enterprise%20and%20the %20solutions%20economy%20(email).pdf; see also Shaun Loney with Will Braun, *An Army of Problem Solvers: Reconciliation and the Solutions Economy* (Winnipeg, 2016).

34. For more details on the Green Economy Network homes and green buildings retrofit strategy, see pillar #2 of the network's platform in Steering Committee of the Green Economy Network, *Making the Shift*, 11–17.

35. For more information on the U.S. and U.K. "green buildings" programs, see Ibid., endnotes xix and xx.

36. There are also huge energy and financial savings to be gained by retrofitting Canada's buildings and improving building standards given this country's extreme cold and heat patterns. See McGraw Hill Construction, *Canada Green Building Trends: Benefits Driving the New and Retrofit Market* (Ottawa: Canada Green Building Council, 2014), www.cagbc. org/cagbcdocs/resources/CaGBC McGraw Hill Cdn Market Study.pdf.

37. Pay-as-you-save financing for building retrofits has been used in Manitoba as follows: "On-Bill Repayments with Manitoba Hydro's Power Smart Residential Loan provides financing of a minimum of $500 up to $7500 for energy efficiency improvements with no down payment required. The on-bill repayment system allows residents to pay instalments on their hydro bill for a maximum loan period of 5 years and starts at just $15/month" (Steering Committee of the Green Economy Network, *Making the Shift*, box on pay-as you-save financing, 13).

38. Ibid.

39. An example is Manitoba Retrofit, part of a social enterprise called BUILD in Manitoba, which puts a priority on hiring and training unemployed workers who have been in prison to do building retrofits. See Josh Brandon and Molly McCracken, *Creating Pride through Decent Work: Social Enterprises in Manitoba* (Winnipeg: Canadian Centre for Policy Alternatives, Manitoba Office, 2016), www.policyalternatives.ca/sites/default/files/uploads/ publications/Manitoba%20Office/2016/05/Social%20Enterprises%20Final.pdf.

40. See Environment Canada, *National Inventory Report 1990–2013* (2015), Section ES.3

41. For details, see pillar #3 of the GEN platform on a National Public Transportation Strategy in Steering Committee of the Green Economy Network, *Making the Shift*, 18–23.

42. Canadian Urban Transit Association, *Canadian Historical Government Funding Table 1980-2014* (Toronto: Author, 2015).

43. For details, see pillar #3 of the GEN platform on a national public transportation strategy in Steering Committee of the Green Economy Network, *Making the Shift*, 21ff.

44. HDR Decision Economics, *The Optimal Supply and Demand for Urban Transit in Canada* (Omaha, NE: Author, 2008).

45. Metropolitan Knowledge International, McCormack Rankin Corporation and Jeff Casello, *The Economic Impact of Transit Investment: A National Survey* (Toronto: Canadian Urban Transit Association, 2010), 3.

46. Ibid., 3, 28.

47. For details on job creation, see pillar #3 of the GEN platform on a national public transportation strategy in Steering Committee of the Green Economy Network, *Making the Shift*, 21–22.

48. Mitchell Anderson, "IMF Pegs Canada's Fossil Fuel Subsidies at $34 Billion," *Tyee*, May 15, 2014, www.thetyee.ca/Opinion/2014/05/15/Canadas-34-Billion-Fossil-Fuel-Subsidies.

49. To stimulate more investment in renewable energy development, the Ontario government, through its former Feed-In-Tariff (FIT) program, initially subsidized domestic and foreign corporations by paying higher prices for electricity generated from solar, wind and other clean energy sources. As a result, South Korea's Samsung, among other global corporations, has bought up large tracts of farmland in eastern Ontario to build its mega–solar farm called the Samsung Renewable Energy Project.

50. Oliver Geden, "The World Should Go for Zero Emissions, Not Two Degrees," *Energy Post*, December 22, 2017, www.energypost.eu/the-world-should-go-for-zero-emissions-not-for-two-degrees.

51. For details, see Mitchell Anderson, "Psst, Trudeau."

Chapter 6

1.   Mychaylo Prystupa, "At COP21, Oil Sands Worker Urges Smooth Transition Off Fossil Fuels," *Canada's National Observer*, December 8, 2015, www.nationalobserver.com/2015/12/08/news/cop21-oil-sands-worker-urges-smooth-transition-fossil-fuels.

2.   See Worldwatch Institute, *Green Jobs: Towards Decent Work in a Sustainable, Low-Carbon World* (Nairobi, Kenya: United Nations Environment Programme, 2008), www.ilo.org/global/topics/green-jobs/publications/WCMS_158727/lang--en/index.htm.

3.   The Canadian Labour Congress' call for a 'just transition' for workers when industries close down their operations dates back to the year 2000 when the term was then coined during union discussions at the International Trade Union Congress meetings. But there was little follow-up work done on this until recently. See the CLC's website for example: http://canadianlabour.ca/issues-research/issues/climate-change.

4.   Dale Marshall, *Making Kyoto Work: A Transition Strategy for Canadian Energy Workers* (Vancouver: Canadian Centre for Policy Alternatives, BC Office, 2002), www.policyalternatives.ca/sites/default/files/uploads/publications/BC_Office_Pubs/making_kyoto_work.pdf.

5.   See Karen Cooling, Marc Lee, Shannon Daub and Jessie Singer, *Just Transition: Creating a Green Social Contract for BC's Resource Workers* (Vancouver: Canadian Centre for Policy Alternatives, BC Office, 2015), www.policyalternatives.ca/publications/reports/just-transition.

6.   See Hadrian Mertins-Kirkwood, *Making Decarbonization Work for Workers: Policies for a Just Transition to a Zero-Carbon Economy in Canada* (Ottawa: Canadian Centre for Policy Alternatives, 2018), 9–10, www.policyalternatives.ca/sites/default/files/uploads/publications/National Office/2018/01/Making Decarbonization Work.pdf.

7.   Ibid., 24.

8.   Ibid., 26.

9.   To this end, researchers at the Canadian Labour Congress and the Green Economy Network plan to collaborate on a forecasting futures report on the oil and gas sector. It will be a four-part report as follows: (1) projections of the oil and gas industry (e.g., review of recent reports by Oil Change International and the National Energy Board); (2) an overview of labour market history of occupations in oil and gas; (3) an analysis of "sunset" and "sunrise" industries with a view to identifying which skills are transferable and what kinds of upskilling will be required for those that are not transferable; (4) profiles of those unions that are already undertaking training and upskilling programs for their members to transfer to new green economy jobs.

10. Mertins-Kirkwood, *Making Decarbonization Work*, 19–20.

11. For a summary of highlights of the commission's report, see Library of Parliament, Parliamentary Information and Research Service, *The Report of the Royal Commission on Aboriginal Peoples* (1999), https://lop.parl.ca/content/lop/researchpublications/prb9924-e.htm.

12. For a backgrounder on the declaration, see Asia Pacific Forum of National Human Rights Institutions and Office of the United Nations High Commissioner for Human Rights, *The United Nations Declaration on the Rights of Indigenous Peoples: A Manual for National Human Rights Institutions* (Sydney, Australia, and Geneva, Switzerland: Authors, 2013), www.ohchr.org/Documents/Issues/IPeoples/UNDRIPManualForNHRIs.pdf.

13. For highlights, conclusions and recommendations of the commission's report, see Truth and Reconciliation Commission of Canada, *Truth and Reconciliation Commission of Canada: Calls to Action* (Winnipeg: Author, 2015), www.trc.ca/websites/trcinstitution/File/2015/Findings/Calls_to_Action_English2.pdf.

14. Quoted phrases from John Ralston Saul, *The Comeback* (Toronto: Random House Canada, 2014).

15. The notion of Indigenous lands in Canada being viewed as "dead capital" is well described and documented by Donald Gutstein in his book *Harperism: How Stephen Harper and His Think Tank Colleagues Have Transformed Canada* (Toronto: James Lorimer & Co., 2014). See Chapter 4, "Liberate Dead Capital on First Nations' Reserves."

16. These and many related issues were on the agenda for meetings the Assembly of First Nations chiefs had with the Crown in the United Kingdom in January 2012. See, for example, Kazi Stastna, "First Nations to Raise 'Bread And Butter Issues' with Crown," *CBC News*, January 17, 2012, www.cbc.ca/news/canada/first-nations-to-raise-bread-and-butter-issues-with-crown-1.1157587.

17. For visuals and more information, see the Dehcho First Nation website at www.dehchofirstnations.com. For a further discussion of the Dehcho land use plan and concepts of land use, see Tony Clarke, *Tar Sands Showdown*, Chapter 8, "Dream Change."

18. For a more updated look at what's happening to the Dehcho plan, see Meagan Wohlberg, "This Northern First Nation is Teaching Canada How to Protect the land," *Canada's National Observer*, June 20, 2016, www.nationalobserver.com/2016/06/20/news/northern-first-nation-teaching-canada-how-protect-land.

19. Ibid.

20. For a platform of Indigenous resistance to pipelines in the US as well as Canada, see It Takes Roots to Weather the Storm, *We are Mother Earth's Red Line: Frontline Communities Lead the Climate Justice Fight beyond the Paris Agreement* (edited excerpt available at https://theleap.org/portfolio-items/we-are-mother-earths-red-line-frontline-communities-lead-the-climate-justice-fight-beyond-the-paris-agreement).

21. See Laurie Monsebraaten, "Jane-Finch Neighbourhood Wake-Up Call for Politicians," *Toronto Star*, November 14, 2015, www.the star.com/news/gta/2015/11/14/jane-finch-neighbourhood-wake-up-call-for-politicians.

22. Daniel Tencer, "Canada's Major Cities Turning into Islands of Wealth, Poverty as Middle Class Disappears," *Huffington Post*, February 6, 2018. See also Heather Scoffield, "Big Cities Attracting Poverty, StatsCan Data Shows," *Globe and Mail*, March 26, 2017, www.theglobeandmail.com/news/national/big-cities-attracting-poverty-statscan-data-show/article583854.

23. For background notes, see "Toronto's Largest Transit Project Continues Moving Forward," *Cision*, December 20, 2013, www.newswire.ca/news-releases/torontos-largest-transit-project-continues-moving-forward-513610811.html. See also the Eglinton Crosstown's official site regarding the community benefits agreement at www.thecrosstown.ca/community-benefits.

24. Definition here provided by Social Enterprise Toronto. Cited in Cheryl Teelucksingh and Laura Zeglen, *Building Toronto: Achieving Social Inclusion in Toronto's Emerging Green Economy* (Toronto: Metcaif Foundation, 2016), 37.

25. Cited in Ibid., 47–49.

26. See survey compiled by Lynne Fernandez, *How Government Support for Social Enterprise Can Reduce Poverty and Greenhouse Gases* (Winnipeg: Canadian Centre for Policy Alternatives, Manitoba Office, 2015).

27. For more background information, see Daphne Rodzinyak "Canada: Bill C-68 and Bill C-69: The Federal Government Releases Overhaul of Environmental Legislation," *Mondaq*, February 12, 2018, www.mondaq.com/canada/x/672562/Environmental+Law/Bill+C68+a nd+Bill+C69+The+Federal+Government+Releases+Overhaul+of+Environmental+Legis lation.

28. Brendan Haley, *A Green Entrepreneurial State as Solution to Climate Federalism* (Ottawa: Broadbent Institute, 2016), https://d3n8a8pro7vhmx.cloudfront.net/broadbent/ pages/4934/attachments/original/1456759450/A_Green_Entrepreneurial_State_as_ Solution_to_Climate_Federalism_Report.pdf?1456759450.

29. Mariana Mazzucato, *The Entrepreneurial State* (London, England: Anthem Press, 2013).

30. Actually, the Alberta government had been proactive in promoting the science and technology of oil sands development since the early twentieth century. See Larry Pratt, *The Tar Sands: Syncrude and the Politics of Oil* (Edmonton: Hurtig, 1976). For a summary of this early background to the present, see Clarke, *Tar Sands Showdown*, Chapter 1, "Crude Awakening," 14–47.

31. Haley, *Green Entrepreneurial State*, 5.

32. Ibid., 6–7.

33. Ibid., 4.

34. Ibid.

35. Ibid.

36. See, for example, John Dillon, *A Just Transition to a Life-Sustaining Economy* (Toronto: KAIROS, 2016).

37. Cited in J.L. Granatstein, *Arming the Nation: Canada's Industrial War Effort 1939–1945* (Ottawa: Canadian Council of Chief Executives, 2005), www.thebusinesscouncil.ca/wp-content/uploads/archives/Arming_the_Nation_A_Paper_Prepared_by_Dr_Granatstein_ May_2005.pdf.

Chapter 7

1. Bill McKibben, "The Question I Get Asked the Most," *EcoWatch*, October 14, 2016, www. ecowatch.com/bill-mckibben-climate-change-2041759425.html.

2. Ibid.

3. Most of the organizations listed here have their own websites. For example, Climate Action Network Canada is at climateactionnetwork.ca. Use your search engine to find out the web addresses of the organizations you may be interested in.

4. What follows here is mainly the author's own descriptive assessment of the climate justice movement-in-the-making in this country. To date, there have been few published works on the evolution of this movement. So what appears here is largely based on conversations with various players in the movement along with reflections of the author as one participant in this movement-building process over the past decade.

5. See the work of the Climate Action Network via its website at climateactionnetwork.ca.

6. See the work of Tar Sands Solutions via its website at transformingrelations.wordpress. com/2015/04/17/tar-sands-solutions-network.

7.   See the work of the Green Economy Network and the "one million climate jobs" challenge on its website at www.greeneconomynet.ca.

8.   Indigenous peoples through First Nations and other representative organizations became increasingly involved in campaigns against bitumen production in the Athabaska tar sands and various related pipeline projects in Canada from around 2005 onwards, often challenging environmental organizations to broaden and deepen their perspectives on the issues. The labour movement, through the Canadian Labour Congress, gradually developed public policy positions on climate change during this period, took action on some issues through affiliates such as the Communications, Energy and Paperworkers Union and was instrumental in organizing the Green Economy Network in 2009 and in the work done to build an ongoing campaign on climate jobs and a just transition for displaced workers.

9.   See *The Leap Manifesto* at www.leapmanifesto.org/en/the-leap-manifesto/#manifesto-content.

10.   For a sampling of signatories early on in the process, see www.leapmanifesto.org/en/whos-on-board.

11.   See the *United Nations Declaration on the Rights of Indigenous Peoples* (UNDRIP) at www.un.org/esa/socdev/unpfii/documents/DRIPS_en.pdf.

12.   For the final report and follow-up to the Truth and Reconciliation Commission, go to www.trc.ca/websites/trcinstitution/index.php?p=890.

13.   See RAVEN: Indigenous Peoples Legal Defence Funds to Protect Their Constitutional Rights at www.raventrust.com.

14.   See the Tar Sands Solutions Network website at www.transformingrelations.wordpress.com/2015/04/17/tar-sands-solutions-network.

15.   See Unifor's statements on energy projects, pipelines and green technology issues in its lobby sheet for Environment and Climate Change Canada at www.unifor.org/sites/default/files/attachments/unifor_lobby-sheet_environment_en.pdf.

16.   See Kiruthiha Kulendiren, "Economic Opportunity and Climate Change," *Labour Action*, Spring 2017, 12.

17.   See, for example, *Working for Green Jobs and Climate Justice — CUPE's 2015 Environment Highlights*, February 26, 2016, cupe.ca/working-green-jobs-and-climate-justice-cupes-2015-environment-highlights.

18.   Here is a sampling of websites for some of these organizations: Ecology Ottawa — ecologyottawa.ca/; Ecology Action Centre, Halifax — ecologyaction.ca/our-work; Council of Canadians, energy and climate justice campaigns — canadians.org/energy; KAIROS: Canadian Ecumenical Justice Initiatives — www.kairoscanada.org/; Canadian Centre for Policy Alternatives — www.policyalternatives.ca/offices.

19.   Kate Dubinski, "Energy Agreement is for 20 Years," *London Free Press*, April 5, 2015, www.lfpress.com/2015/04/05/energy-agreement-is-for-20-years.

20.   See Lauren Tyler, "BluEarth Bull Creek Wind Farm in Alberta," *North American Windpower*, January 15, 2016, nawindpower.com/bluearth-commissions-bull-creek-wind-farm-in-alberta; see also "Wind Catchers: How BluEarth, GE and Rural Schools in Alberta Are Bringing New Wind Power to the Province," *GEreports*, August 5, 2016, www.gereports.ca/wind-catchers-bluearth-ge-rural-schools-alberta-bringing-new-wind-power-province.

21.   See David Dodge and Dylan Thompson, "500 Alberta Schools Are Powered by the Wind," *Huffington Post*, August 2, 2017, www.huffingtonpost.ca/david-dodge/alberta-schools-wind-power_b_14638304.html.

22.   Sean McCarthy, "Push to End Energy Poverty in Indigenous Communities Underway," *Globe and Mail*, April 27, 2016, retrieved from www.theglobeandmail.com/news/national/the-push-to-end-energy-poverty-in-indigenous-communities/article33012480.

23.   Indigenous Climate Action was initially convened by Eriel Deranger of the Athabasca Chipewyan First Nation in July 2017. For the quotations here, see the document entitled

"Building Capacity for Indigenous Climate Action" and check out the ICA website at www. indigenousclimateaction.com.

24. Mardi Tindal, Moderator, United Church of Canada, open letter to Canadians, January 17, 2010, cited in "Climate Change a Crisis of Conscience for All Canadians," *Cision*, January 17, 2010, www.newswire.ca/fr/news-releases/climate-change-a-crisis-of-conscience-for-all-canadians-539228381.html.

25. See the Greening Sacred Spaces website at www.greeningsacredspaces.net.

26. For background information and analysis of social enterprises in Manitoba, see Lynne Fernandez, *How Government Support for Social Enterprise Can Reduce Poverty and Greenhouse Gases* (Winnipeg: Canadian Centre for Policy Alternatives, Manitoba Office, 2015), 5. In its first year, Aki Energy trained 30 Indigenous workers, who, in turn, installed 110 geothermal heating/cooling systems in two communities, the Peguis First Nation and the Fisher River Cree Nation.

27. Ibid.

28. For CUPW's response to the climate crisis, see its booklet *Delivering Community Power: How Canada Post can Be the Hub of the Next Economy*, www.deliveringcommunitypower.ca.

29. In recent years, there has been a boom in large-scale solar farms in rural areas of Ontario. See, for example, Richard Blackwell, "Solar Power Surging to the Forefront of Canadian Energy," *Globe and Mail*, July 26, 2014, www.theglobeandmail.com/reports-on-business/solar-power-surging-to-the-forefront-of Canadian-energy/article19787659.

30. There is also evidence that large-scale solar projects can reduce pressures on local farmland. See, for example, Sami Grover, "How Can Large-Scale Solar Power Reduce Pressure on Farm Land?" *Mother Nature Network*, May 2, 2014, www.mnn.com/earth-matters/energy/stories/how-can-large-scale-solar-power-reduce-pressure-on-farm-land.

31. See John Dillon's use of community benefit agreements as an example in his own *A Just Transition*.

32. The three waves of the fossil fuel divestment campaign were briefly yet well described by Wayne Wachell in an article entitled "Fossil Fuel Divestment Brings Us Closer to a Clean Energy Future," www.huffingtonpost.ca/wayne-wachell/fossil-fuel-divestment_b_16698578.html.

33. Ibid.

Chapter 8

1. See Steering Committee of the Green Economy Network, *Making the Shift to a Green Economy: A Common Platform for the Green Economy Network* (2016), 7, www.greeneconomynet.ca/wp-content/uploads/sites/43/2014/07/GEN-Common-Platform-2016-EN1.pdf. This is the basic platform that lies behind the Big Shift proposals that are outlined in this book.

2. See Peter Erickson, *Confronting Carbon Lock-in: Canada's Oil Sands* (Seattle: Stockholm Environment Institute, June 2018), www.sei.org/publications/confronting-carbon-lock-canadas-oil-sands/.

3. Ibid.

4. Ibid.

5. The Green Economy Network has decided to put a priority on developing and implementing a similar kind of bottom-up strategy to push for stronger commitments from provincial, territorial and municipal governments, as well as the federal government. Wherever possible, the Green Economy Network will offer assistance to local/regional groups in developing their transition plans, recognizing that it's important for all like-minded groups to join in this common effort.

6. Available for download at www.greeneconomynet.ca/campaign/one-million-climate-jobs and www.policyalternatives.ca/publications/reports/tracking-progress.

7. Graph prepared by Marny Girard, former research co-ordinator for the Green Economy Network, drawing upon data available as of May 2018.

8. See Jos G.J. Oliver et al., *Trends in Global CO$_2$ Emissions: 2016 Report* (The Hague: PBL Netherlands Environmental Assessment Agency and European Commission Joint Research Centre, 2016).

9. For a backgrounder, see Aaron, Beswick, "Ecology Action Centre: Nova Scotia Doing Well on Greenhouse Gas Emissions," *Chronicle Herald*, April 15, 2015, www.thechronicleherald. ca/novascotia/1280614-ecology-action-centre-nova-scotia-doing-well-on-greenhouse-gas-emissions.

10. See the first edition of *OilWire*, "The Big Picture," February 2018, at https://mailchi. mp/04f5f586549e/oilwire-the-fossil-fuel-era-is-ending-1461601?e=83a3aee873.

11. List of petroleum by-products put together by Marny Girard, former research co-ordinator for the Green Economy Network.

12. For the author, the term *eco-warriors* is based on the notion of "paradigm warriors," coined in the mid-1990s by Martin Khor, then an influential political economist and educator with the Third World Network. Khor used the term *paradigm warriors* several times in meetings of the International Forum on Globalization (IFG), advocating this as the role that the IFG (among other civil society organizations) needed to play, thereby enabling activists to better navigate the turbulent era of economic globalization.

13. See, for example, Christopher Landry's short film *Joanna Macy and The Great Turning* (2014), available at www.joannamacyfilm.org. Macy speaks about "the societal shift now underway from an industrial growth society to a more sustainable civilization." Her books include titles such as *Active Hope, Stories of the Great Turning* and *Coming Back to Life* (see www.joannamacy.net/books-dvds.html). After 30 years of studying Buddhism and deep ecology, Macy contends "that either humankind awakens to a new and deeper understanding of our interconnectedness with its planet or risks losing it."

14. See Paulo Freire's seminal work, *The Pedagogy of the Oppressed*, trans. Myra Ramos (New York: Herder and Herder, 1970). As an adult educator in Brazil, Freire revolutionized popular education with his pedagogy of the poor, the marginalized and the oppressed. Rooted in the tradition of Antonio Gramsci, he was considered one of the most influential thinkers about education in the latter part of the twentieth century. One of Freire's key concepts was the notion of *praxis*, which he described as "conscientization" through action and reflection. More specifically, it is "the process of acting and reflecting on concrete social realities (economic, cultural, political etc.) for the sake of transforming society."

15. A powerful and stimulating contribution to cultural turning concerning the current threats to the future of the planet is Pope Francis's encyclical *Laudato Si': On Care for Our Common Home,* issued in 2015. For a very useful guide to this encyclical, see Janet Somerville and William F. Ryan, SJ, with Anne O'Brien, GSIC, and Anne-Marie Jackson, *On Care for Our Common Home: A Dialogue Guide to* Laudato Si' (Ottawa: Canadian Conference of Catholic Bishops /Toronto: Jesuit Forum for Social Faith and Justice, 2016).

16. See John Dillon, *Indigenous Wisdom: Living in Harmony with Mother Earth* (Toronto: KAIROS, 2014). Dillon goes on to explain: "The original languages of Andean Indigenous peoples each have an expression that embodies this ancient wisdom: *suma qamaña* in Aymara; *sumac kawsay* in Quechua; *teko pora* in Guarani; and *kume mogen* in Mapuche. During an exchange with Indigenous peoples in Ecuador, facilitated by KAIROS, George Poitras, former chief at Fort Chipewyan in Northern Alberta, explained that the Cree term for the same concept is *miyo matsuwin*. These terms can be approximately translated into Spanish as *buen vivir* or *vivir bien* and into English as 'living well' or 'the good way of living.' A fuller translation might be, 'living appropriately so that others may also live.'"

17. Naomi Klein, "Why Unions Need to Join the Climate Fight," keynote address to the founding convention of Unifor, September 1, 2013, www.commondreams.org/views/2013/09/04/overcoming-overburden-climate-crisis-and-unified-left-agenda.

18. See Somerville and Ryan, *On Care for Our Common Home*, 8–15.

19. See Chris Turner, "The Oil Sands PR War: The Down-and-Dirty Fight to Brand Canada's Oil Patch," *Marketing*, July 30, 2012, www.marketingmag.ca/advertising/the-oil-sands-pr-war-582. For a useful commentary and tool regarding these ads, see "The Oil Sands and the PR War," *CBC News in Review*, December 2010, 19–30, media.curio.ca/filer_public/34/d9/34d91172-6e76-4e55-9b5f-db8c703d864b/dec10oilsands.pdf.

20. For a substantive discussion of these themes, see Joel Kovel, *The Enemy of Nature* (London, England: Zed Books / Halifax, NS: Fernwood Publishing, 2007), especially Part II on the "domination of nature."

21. Many commentators have pointed out the limitations of the GDP (Gross Domestic Product) as the prevailing measurement for economic growth and the need for a viable alternative. The GDP, for instance, views many life-destroying activities as having a positive value while keeping life-enhancing activities mainly invisible. From a GDP perspective, cutting down a rainforest is valued for generating monetary wealth, but the ecological costs of doing so in terms of the lost wealth of creatures, air, soil and water once sustained by the ecosystem are not calculated. In effect, the GDP measures the production of "artificial wealth," which, in turn, hides the "real wealth" of the planet and its destruction. As economist Herman Daly once put it: "There is something fundamentally wrong in treating the Earth as if it were a business liquidation."

    As an alternative to the GDP, some commentators are advocating the GPI (Genuine Progress Indicator), which differentiates between genuinely productive activities that are life enhancing and those that are life destroying. The former are classified as being productive, whereas the latter are calculated as costs. Here real economic progress is defined as "qualitative development" rather than "quantitative growth." Under the GPI, quantitative measures such as profits, efficiencies and productivity are questioned and redefined. To be sure, "growth" is needed, but not "cancerous growth" or growth in "superfluous consumption." Instead, there is a need for growth in knowledge and wisdom, access to basic necessities, nurturing the health of ecosystems, fostering beauty or preserving the diversity of life.

    For a more comprehensive discussion of the GDP versus GPI and related matters noted above, see Mark Hathaway and Leonardo Boff, *The Tao of Liberation* (Orbis Books, New York, 2009), especially Chapter 2, "Unmasking a Pathological System."

22. See Nathan VanderKlippe, "Power Shift: Solar's New Dawn," *Globe and Mail*, Report on Business, February 28, 2017, 8, www.theglobeandmail.com/report-on-business/industry-news/energy-and-resources/the-price-on-solar-is-so-low-it-could-compete-on-global-markets/article34133049.

23. Ibid.

24. See the discussion of the U.S.-Chinese trade relationship in Marty Hart-Landsberg, "Trump's Economic Policies are No Answer to Our Problems," *Bullet*, February 20, 2017, www.socialistproject.ca/2017/02/b1371.

25. Ibid. See the subsection "The US-Mexican Trade Relationship," 3–5, including an analysis by Washington, DC–based economist Mark Weisbrot.

26. See Barrie McKenna, "We will Pay a Price for Being Out of Step with Trump Policy," *Globe and Mail*, March 4, 2017.

27. Relevant research and analysis on the economic impacts of the Trump agenda is going on in some university departments and civil society organizations. For example, the Trade and Investment Research Project of the Canadian Centre for Policy Alternatives has done some extensive work on the trade and investment impacts of the Trump agenda that Eco-warriors should be aware of and engaged in.

28. For a capsule summary of the flaws of NAFTA from a Canadian standpoint, see Gordon Laxer, "Should Canada Give Up on NAFTA? Yes," Opinion Piece, *Toronto Star*, June 19, 2018. However, it is not at all clear that the Trump strategy would lead to a "win-win" for the United States given the extent to which some key sectors of the U.S. and Canadian economies have become so integrated via NAFTA over the past 24 years. For another perspective, see Knowledge @ Wharton, "NAFTA's Impact on the US Economy," knowledge.wharton.upenn.edu/article/naftas-impact-u-s-economy-facts.

29. See Mia Rabson, "Ontario Cancelling Cap and Trade Plan akin to pulling out of Climate Framework: Catherine McKenna." Available online at www.cbc.ca/news/politics/ontario-federal-government-cap-trade-1.4734182.

Index